Autism in your Classroom

A GENERAL EDUCATOR'S GUIDE
TO STUDENTS WITH
AUTISM SPECTRUM DISORDERS

TOPICS IN AUTISM

Autism in Your Classroom

A GENERAL EDUCATOR'S GUIDE TO STUDENTS WITH AUTISM SPECTRUM DISORDERS

DEBORAH FEIN, PH.D. &
MICHELLE A. DUNN, PH.D.

Sandra L. Harris, Ph.D., series editor

Woodbine House ◆ 2007

Cover photo by Nancy Bea Miller

All rights reserved. Published by Woodbine House, Inc., 6510 Bells Mill Road, Bethesda, MD 20817. 800-843-7323. www.woodbinehouse.com

Library of Congress Cataloging-in-Publication Data

Fein, Deborah.
 Autism in your classroom : a general educator's guide to students with autism spectrum disorders / by Deborah Fein and Michelle A. Dunn. — 1st ed.
    p. cm. — (Topics in autism)
 Includes bibliographical references and index.
 ISBN 978-1-890627-61-4
 1. Autistic children—Education. 2. Autism. I. Dunn, Michelle A., 1959- II. Title.
 LC4717.F45 2007
 371.94—dc22

                                                                2007029332

Manufactured in the United States of America

First Edition

10   9   8   7   6   5   4   3   2

To my patient, loving, and supportive family,
Joe, Liz, and Emily.
D. F.

To my husband, Steve, and my girls, Emily and Julia,
for supporting this and all my endeavors.
M.D.

And to the children and families
who teach us so much.
D.F. & M.D.

Table of Contents

Introduction

Who Can Use This Book?

You've just learned that you will have a new student with an autism spectrum disorder (ASD) in your classroom this year and you're feeling excited but anxious, too. Or maybe you've been struggling to teach a student with ASD because you weren't sure how to adequately meet his or her needs. Perhaps you're a motivated parent eager to help your child with ASD make a successful transition into an inclusive classroom. Or you're simply interested in understanding all types of children, even if you don't encounter them directly in your professional life. This book is mainly addressed to teachers of general education classes who may not have any specific training in special education. However, parents, special education teachers, and other professionals will also find useful information in it. Most of the information is geared to the elementary age child (5-12), but much of it also applies to teens with ASD.

Having mixed reactions to the placement of a child with ASD in your general education classroom is certainly understandable, especially if this is a new experience for you. Common reactions are feeling nervous, unprepared, helpless, even resentful. But knowing what to expect, knowing how you can best teach the child and help him develop as a person, and knowing how to make the situation a growth experience for all the children in the class will help you transform these feelings into positive ones of challenge and interest.

How We Got Here: History and the Law

Thirty-five years ago, teachers like you would have had no need for a guide like this. Regrettably, before 1975, education for children with ASD was haphazard when it existed at all. The public education system had no obligation to educate children with disabilities. Private special education schools were few and far between and used primarily permissive approaches that were ineffective. Some children were educated at home and some were placed in long-term residential treatment facilities even when their disability was relatively mild, a placement that sometimes guaranteed no chance for success in the wider world.

As much as educational practice has changed for typical children in the last few decades (and continues to change), thankfully it has changed much, much more for children with disabilities, and particularly so for children with ASD. In 1975, the U.S. Congress passed Public Law 94-142 (The Education for All Handicapped Children Act), which revolutionized education for children with disabilities. It mandated "Free and Appropriate Public Education" for all children, regardless of their special needs, thus putting the rights of children with disabilities to a public education on an equal footing with that of other children. (Of course, what constitutes an "appropriate" education for a given child can be the subject of vigorous disagreement.)

The law also mandated the creation of an "Individualized Education Program" (IEP) for each child in special education (see Chapter 6), and legislated that the child must be placed in the "Least Restrictive Environment" in which he could receive an appropriate education. Being placed in the "Least Restrictive Environment" (LRE) means that the child must be educated with typically developing peers to the maximum extent that will enable him to reach the educational goals in his IEP. This law has been amended several times since its creation, and in 1990 it was renamed the Individuals with Disabilities Education Act (IDEA), the name it currently goes by. The most recent amendments to the law were in 2004, so you may hear the law referred to as IDEA 2004.

In recent years, the requirement that children be educated in the LRE has been used to justify increasing "inclusion" of students with disabilities in regular classrooms. Sometimes students are "fully included" if they are able to meet all of their educational goals in the regular education classroom. At other times, students may be included for part of the school day but leave the regular education classroom to receive therapy or academic instruction from special education professionals.

More about disability and the law will be discussed in Chapter 6.

Why Is There a Need for this Book?

Given the mandated public education and the principle of "Least Restrictive Environment," the number of children with ASD in regular education classrooms has increased, particularly since 1990. However, as you probably know better than we do, teacher training has not kept up. You may be told that a child with ASD or another disability will be in your classroom, with or without an aide (sometimes just days before the year begins!), but be given little specific information about the child, or general information about the disability. Sometimes, the primary classroom teacher is given background information on the child, but is not permitted to share this information with an assistant teacher or with other teachers who may encounter the child.

Although teachers are part of the IEP team, and thus should have access to the child's evaluations, sometimes this happens too late to be of much use in planning, and information about the child's previous classroom experiences may or may not be accessible. This puts a terrible burden on the teacher, who may have to plan some of her teaching by sheer guesswork. In addition, you may be given no time or resources for professional development to educate yourself about ASD and educational issues. If you are given professional development opportunities, you may still lack the necessary time to implement what you've learned, and the resources provided may not be specific enough to be helpful. Although this book will not specify anything about your particular student (and children with ASD can vary tremendously), we hope it can give you a sense of how they are likely to differ from other children, and what some of their needs and characteristics will be.

Inclusion can be very successful for many children with ASD. Research and clinical experience have amply shown that being educated with typically developing children can improve the functioning of children with ASD, in particular, their social functioning. Children with ASD who are educated in inclusive classrooms, compared to those in self-contained special education classes, often engage in more social interactions and have more friends. In addition, their IEP goals tend to be more ambitious.

There are two crucial ingredients for a meaningful and successful inclusion experience. One is the child's own characteristics. We believe that inclusion is not appropriate for all children, and that certain child characteristics make inclusion much less likely to succeed (discussed in Chapter 7). You have no control over these factors. What you do have some control over is the second set of ingredients: teachers and other school personnel who are committed to inclusion, feel positively about it and think it can work well, and have the knowledge to implement an appropriate program for the individual child with ASD.

Researchers have argued that inclusion, done properly, is not a cost cutting measure. To be done right, inclusion needs as much of the school's resources as would be invested in a special education class. You will need (and should request) help from the school's specialists and consultants—psychologists, special education teachers, speech and language therapists, occupational therapists, behavior specialists. The child with ASD in your class may need a one-on-one aide to make inclusion really work. Again, as a teacher, you may have little power to put these things in place. What you do have control over—your understanding of ASD and your attitude about the challenge ahead of you—will make a big difference in your ability to make it the best experience possible for all concerned. This is what we hope to help you with.

What Will This Book Teach Me?

The first part of this book will provide you with an overview of up-to-date, research-based information about ASD. Based on current research and our own experience as psychologists, consultants, and teachers, this book will prime you on the issues you'll probably encounter teaching children with ASD in the regular classroom. Chapter 1 explains what defines autism and the other disorders on the autism spectrum, such as Asperger's disorder. Chapter 2 gives more details about how the children behave, what some of their difficulties often involve, and what you can expect their cognitive strengths and weaknesses to be. This chapter also discusses other syndromes that overlap with autism, and other disorders that the child with autism may be at risk for. Additionally, we discuss how common ASD is, and what we can expect for the children as they grow up. Chapter 3 presents information on what is known about the causes of autism. Chapter 4 discusses its impact on other family members. This part of the book finishes with a chapter (5) on the most common treatments for autism.

Part 2 focuses on the child in your classroom. Chapter 6 describes the possible educational placements for children with ASD and how the special education processes work, including appropriate teaching tools and strategies. Chapter 7 addresses issues that will get you started—setting up the classroom, what you can expect in the beginning of the year, how the child can be best prepared for an inclusion experience, and some of the best general principles for teaching children with ASD. Beginning with Chapter 8, we present specific aspects of learning, including attention, memory, organization, and motor skills (Chapter 8); language (Chapter 9); reading, math, and homework (Chapter 10); social skills (Chapter 11); problem behaviors (Chapter 12); and balancing the needs of general and special education students (Chapter 13).

Some issues we'll discuss are not problems per se, but merely ways in which children with ASD are different from most other children you teach. Understanding these differences can help you avoid problems before they arise. For example, children with ASD are often very visual learners and may have trouble focusing on language-based lessons unsupported by visual material. If you are aware of this, you may be able to provide pictures, charts, or graphics to help a child understand a lesson or keep himself organized. Without these aids, the child may become inattentive or disruptive.

Part 2 concludes with two stories of children we know—one who did really well in an inclusion setting—a success story—and one who tried education in an inclusion setting with a less than happy result.

We've also included a chapter addressing common myths, misconceptions, statistics, and frequently asked questions about ASD and those affected by it. Many of these questions come directly from teachers whom we surveyed about information needs. We've also included discussions of some issues that may not bear directly on the classroom, such as treatments that are used outside the classroom that your student may have encountered, the impact of autism on families, and what's known about the neurobiology of autism.

The final section of the book lists resources you may find helpful—organizations, websites, and other books that provide information for parents, teachers, and other professionals on ASD in general and educational issues in particular.

What Won't This Book Teach Me?

The focus of this book is on helping teachers learn to understand and manage the learning and behavioral characteristics that are unique to students with autism spectrum disorders. For many children with ASD, learning is further complicated by the presence of mental retardation (intellectual disabilities). It is beyond the scope of this book to explain how to handle learning and behavioral characteristics of children with mental retardation in the classroom.

If you have a student who has mental retardation in addition to ASD, this book will still help you understand how to deal with the child's characteristics that are due to autism. However, you will also need to consult other resources specific to teaching children with mental retardation in addition to this one (we have listed some good ones in the Resources at the back of the book). You will also need to consult with a special education teacher, and perhaps other special education professionals, for help in adapting instruction and materials for your student's needs, as discussed in Chapters 8 and 10.

Who Are We?

We are both pediatric neuropsychologists specializing in autism, with (between us) about 50 years of experience. We both do clinical work with children with ASD and their families, performing assessments, providing recommendations to parents about educational and other services, and tracking progress. Both of us also do research in this area. We supervise graduate students who are being trained in neuropsychology and in autism. In addition, one of us (MD) is certified as a general and special education teacher, and has taught typical fourth graders, and special education students from ages 4 to 21. We provide consultation to schools and make educational recommendations for the children we evaluate.

We have both seen classrooms where a single teacher is expected to teach 30 or more children and integrate a child with ASD into the classroom, as well. Sometimes the teacher gets the needed extra personnel to help; sometimes she doesn't. There's absolutely no substitute for adequate personnel, but whether you have the needed assistance or not, the more you know about the child with ASD in your class, the more able you'll be to set up the classroom and the curriculum to the best advantage of all the children in your class. And the more you'll be able to evaluate what you can expect of yourself and the child with ASD, and what you shouldn't expect. We are both very happy to have the chance to share our knowledge and experience with you.

Why Did We Write This Book?

Two years ago, one of us (DF) was having lunch with a close friend, a general education teacher, and talking about a book for parents that I was planning. "There are plenty of books for parents!" Jen exclaimed. "Why don't you write one for us, the teachers?" I immediately realized that she was right. Teachers are responsible for so much of the children's lives, but are often given little or no preparation for having a child with ASD in their classroom. What are children with ASD like? What do I need to do for them in order to help them learn the most? What are they capable of learning and what might they have difficulty with? What sorts of social problems will they have? How will the other children react to them? How can I minimize any behavior problems they might have? What is a child with "Asperger's" like? How is this different from autism, and how are the needs of a child with Asperger's different from a child with autism?

These are crucial questions that teachers need some answers to—not all the answers, of course, but enough to feel prepared, to get started. We have both chosen to work with children with ASD as our primary careers. We find these children endlessly fascinating, delightful, mystifying, and inspiring. We hope that the material in this book will communicate some of this fascination to you, so you can look forward, feeling prepared, to the prospect of teaching a child with ASD.

Part 1

What You Need to Know about Autism Spectrum Disorders

1 | What Is Autism?

This chapter is designed to give you an in-depth understanding of the autism spectrum disorders (ASD). We'll first describe the "official" set of defining features for these disorders and how each can translate into real behavior. Then we'll discuss how each disorder on the spectrum differs from the others.

The Defining Features of Autism Spectrum Disorders

Why are these called autism spectrum disorders? It is because all of the autism spectrum disorders (ASDs) share some features with classic autism, but they differ in the specific behaviors the children show and the degree to which they are affected by them. All ASD disorders share a set of defining features. These are grouped into three areas:

A. social impairment,
B. impairments in language, communication, and play, and
C. repetitive and restricted behaviors.

The A group, social impairment, includes four possible symptoms:
1. impaired nonverbal communication, including eye contact and gestures,
2. poor peer relationships,
3. absent or reduced "joint attention" (bringing things to show you, pointing things out, following your gaze or your point), and

4. impaired emotional reciprocity (tuning in to others' emotions, sharing happy emotions, noticing and helping when others are distressed).

The B group, language, communication, and play, also has four possible symptoms:
1. delays in learning to speak,
2. for those with enough language, impairments in the ability to hold a conversation,
3. a tendency to say the exact same thing again and again, or talk about the same topic too much, or repeat what someone else says instead of answering them, and
4. pretend play that is either absent altogether, or delayed for the child's age, or repetitive.

The C group, repetitive and restricted behaviors, also has four symptoms:
1. preoccupations with certain topics or activities,
2. strongly held routines or rituals, or resistance to change in the environment,
3. repetitive motor behaviors such as rocking, hand flapping, or walking on tiptoe, and
4. preoccupations with parts of objects, such as wheels on toy cars instead of the cars themselves.

Social Impairment

In the A group (social symptoms), which one of the four symptoms do you think is the most characteristic of autism? Surprisingly, the most central of the social symptoms is "joint attention." Think of joint attention as a triangle—the child, an interactive partner (parent, teacher, other child), and an object. Joint attention refers to the child's desire to coordinate his attention with that of his partner, so they're both attending to the same object. Children typically accomplish this by getting their partner to attend to what they are attending to ("look, Mama!"), or by noticing what their partner is looking at and transferring their attention to that, too.

Joint Attention

When they are little, children with ASD almost never point things out to their parents. (They may sometimes point things out that they want and can't reach, like a cookie package on a shelf, but not just to say, "Look at that—isn't that interesting!") And they are rarely interested in seeing what their parent is looking at. When they get older, especially if they are highly verbal and getting more social, they may point things out, but often when we press parents for *how* the child points things out, it turns out to be purely verbal. ("He would say, 'Look at the fire truck,' but I don't think he would point with his finger" is a typical answer). Similarly, if you ask parents whether the child brings objects to show them, they reply in the affirmative, but it often turns out that they are objects the child needs help with ("Read me this book"; "Open this jar"). They rarely bring objects just to show ("Look what I made"; "Look at this pretty flower").

Eye Contact

Difficulties with nonverbal communication are also very, very common in children with ASD. Eye contact is usually poor; you often will have to teach and remind the child to look at people and even then the eye contact tends to have an unnatural feel about it. Children with ASD typically do not use eye contact to guide turn-taking in conversation or to initiate interactions. Instead, they may follow "rules" they have learned about using eye contact. For example, a character with a type of ASD known as Asperger's disorder on *Law and Order: Criminal Intent* had memorized the following rule: "If I look at people less than one third of the time, I look evasive, and if I look at people more than two thirds of the time, I look aggressive." Naturally, this results in eye contact that is better than total avoidance but does not have a fluid, natural feeling to it.

For many children with ASD, eye contact actually feels unpleasant and they actively avoid it. Even children who are more motivated to be social and who less actively avoid eye contact may forget to look at people and need to be reminded. A minority of children with ASD may have eye contact that is *too* good. They may stare too fixedly at people when talking to them, and need to be reminded to look away occasionally and to keep the proper physical distance. Some children have been taught to make good eye contact, but they may still have serious difficulties with socialization, communication, and repetitive behaviors. No one behavior is required for the diagnosis of an autism spectrum disorder, and even if a child has relatively good eye contact, he may still have ASD.

Gestures

In addition, children on the autism spectrum do not compensate for their lack of conversational language by using gesture and body language. One of the ways to differentiate children with ASD from children with language disorders (at least in theory; in practice, this can be pretty hard) is that children with language disorders are more distressed by their lack of ability to communicate and try to use alternative means such as pointing and other gestures. (For example, they put a finger on their lips, make a beckoning gesture, and nod and shake the head for "yes" and "no".) Children with ASD, on the other hand, seem more impaired in their basic desire to communicate. Although they can learn gestures, the gestures seem less natural and more stilted, and they use them less often than do typically developing children or children with language disorders.

Peer Relationships

Peer relationships can be deficient in many ways. At the mildest end of the spectrum, there are children who want friends, who like to be around children, and who try to interact with others, but they interact like much younger children, using simplified versions of the social rules children go by. These children, who often have a diagnosis of Asperger's disorder, may think that any child who talks to them is automatically their friend. In later childhood and adolescence, when typical children are less tolerant and accepting of children who are different, the child with Asperger's disorder may be mercilessly excluded, bullied, teased, and tricked. At the severe end, there are children with ASD who will relate to adults to get their needs met but really have no interest in other children at all.

Emotional Reciprocity

Emotional reciprocity (reacting appropriately to others' emotions), surprisingly, is sometimes relatively good. As long as the other person's emotional display is obvious (people smiling, laughing, clapping, saying "yay" enthusiastically), the child with ASD may notice and imitate. Similarly, if the other person's distress is obvious, and it's someone the child cares about, he may try in a clumsy way to make the situation better. On the other hand, many children with ASD are oblivious to others' distress. One of us was once testing a high functioning young man with autism, hitched her chair into the table, and smashed her knee against an iron table leg, exclaiming with pain. She looked over at the young man, who had noticed nothing whatsoever, although he was less than two feet away.

We then went on to study this seeming lack of empathy systematically in a group of children with ASD, simulating a painful accident and losing a valued object. The children with ASD who were functioning in the mentally retarded range of cognitive ability tended not to notice either event. The "higher functioning" children were divided: some appeared not to notice, while about half clearly noticed but did not know how to respond until they were given instructions ("Could you help me look for it?"), at which time the vast majority tried to help. So, you may find that the children with ASD in your classroom are not unfeeling, and may want to help others, but need to be specifically instructed in how to do it. They may also miss emotional displays by others unless they are very obvious, and may need to have their attention called to more subtle displays. ("Bobby is sitting in the corner. How do you think he feels?")

Language, Communication, and Play

Delayed Language

In the B group of symptoms (language, communication, play), one of the most common symptoms among children on the autism spectrum is delayed language. This is defined as no spoken words by age two and no phrases by three, but this is not meant to be a rigid definition. Language is often considered to be delayed if, as is often the case, the child uses a small number of words before age two, but not very frequently or very communicatively, and his vocabulary does not grow by leaps and bounds as in normal development. Sometimes the child does develop a number of words (or, rarely, phrases) that he uses often, but then, during the second year, he stops using these words and does not replace them with others.

Impaired Conversation Skills

Impaired conversational ability is almost universal in ASD. If you think about what's needed for normal conversational ability, the essence of it is reciprocal social interaction. That means that a baby or toddler will babble, look at Mom, smile with delight, and wait for him to babble or talk back, as if he is having a real conversation. For a preschool child, conversation may be disjointed, but there's asking and answering questions, making comments (not just to give or seek information but to maintain social contact), looking frequently at the other child or adult, smiling. Sometimes the "best" conversations are in the course of pretend play, where children imitate adult conversations they have heard. For the older child, there's "real" conversation, with turn-taking, active listening as well as speaking, staying on topic, changing the style of vocabulary to suit the partner (they talk differently to their baby sister than to their friend), checking the partner's reactions, reacting to the emotions of the partner, etc. And the normal adolescent, of course, is a master of many subtle and complex rules of interaction.

Most of these skills and motivations are lacking or impaired in children with ASD. If they have enough language for conversation, they "talk at" you. The essence of their motivation is to get the information they need or indulge their pleasure in talking about their favorite topics. They do not usually check the reactions of their listeners or pick up on nonverbal cues, they avoid eye contact, they switch topics without warning with no regard for what their partner is expecting or thinking, they may use language that seems appropriate for a lecture rather than a conversation, they talk about topics that may be inappropriate for the situation, and they give endless detail rather than important points.

Repetitive Language

When a child with ASD does have a lot of language, you may notice that it is very repetitive. This occurs at several levels. The child may actually use the same words or phrases again and again. These are usually phrases that he has heard before, from adults or on TV programs or movies. One little boy one of us worked with started saying "Super job, Peter!" (his name) in exactly the same chirpy tone of voice, with the same rising inflection, each time, and we realized that he was imitating the way we spoke to him! Or the child may not use the same actual sentences, but the topic may be the same. He may choose to talk about nothing but Pokemon or more socially unacceptable topics such as brands of bathroom tissue.

Pretend Play

Pretend play suffers from the same repetitiveness. Children with ASD may reenact scenes from videos, movies, or TV programs (which they often like to watch repetitively as well). These scenes are usually reenacted with great exactness, and woe betide the play partner who is unwilling to stick to the script! If they're not yet doing pretend play, their more sensory-motor or functional play (playing with cause-and-effect toys, rolling cars but not really pretending they're real cars) is also repetitive, with the same toys and the same actions preferred again and again.

The presence of pretend play is a positive sign in a child with ASD. A recent study by one of our honors students at the University of Connecticut (UConn) indicated that the presence of pretend play in the preschool years is a good predictor that the child will have adaptive skills such as self-help skills and social and communication skills at school age. In fact, she found that this is a better predictor than IQ scores. But remember that this is not a perfect correlation; there are some very bright children with ASD who have little or no interest in pretend play. One of us recalls one very illuminating episode with a bright child of seven who was (and still is) quite autistic. I was playing with a dollhouse. He was insisting on lining up the kitchen equipment and I was doggedly trying to get him to join me in making a family scene. After ten minutes, he gave me a really irritated look, put the baby doll in the crib, covered her, stuck a bottle in her mouth, said "night-night," and went back to lining up his objects. The message was very clear: "I know what you want me to do and I can do it, but I see no reason why anyone would want to. Now leave me alone!"

Repetitive and Restricted Behavior

In the C group of symptoms (repetitive and restricted behavior), behaviors vary, depending on the children's ages and ability levels. The very young and those with significant intellectual disabilities do not have preoccupations with topics, for the simple reason that they are not intellectually ready for understanding topics. Similarly, resistance to change or insistence on routines is rare in this group (except that young children with ASD may have some favorite routines such as bedtime routines, just the way typically developing children do). We see a lot of young children (below age 5) with ASD these days and find that resistance to change and rituals are the exception rather than the rule for these children.

Visual Self-Stimulation

What you do see in the young and the more intellectually impaired is preoccupations with parts of objects, which is more often called "visual self-stimulation." These types of behaviors may include:

- staring at lights,
- staring at ceiling fans,
- staring at water,
- staring at straight lines, often from different perspectives,
- staring at shifting shadows through leaves,
- moving the fingers in the peripheral visual field in order to make strobe-like patterns,
- squinting,
- looking at things out of the corner of the eye.

Repetitive Movements

Repetitive movements are also common. These can be whole body movements (jumping, bouncing, rocking, pacing) or movements of limbs (arm flapping) or fingers (finger twiddling). Finger twiddling can be considered a repetitive motor behavior but also a visual "stim" if the child stares at his fingers while he is twiddling them. One child we know would probably spend every waking moment, if allowed, in making thin strings of Play Doh and staring at them as they fall.

Resistance to Change and Preferred Topics

Older children and children with higher intellectual ability show real resistance to change in routines and in the physical environment, as well as preoccupation with specific preferred topics. *The Siege* by Clara Park (see Suggested Reading) gives the most evocative description of how the author's daughter with autism would dissolve in distress if the pattern of lights in the college library at night was not as it was supposed to be. Changing the furniture, or even moving books in a bookshelf, can be very disturbing to the child. Their routines, such as insisting upon a specific order of events at bedtime, can seem normal except for the intensity of the distress which greets any change. Or they can seem like the routines or compulsions of a person with obsessive compulsive disorder (OCD); for example, having to touch certain objects in the bedroom in a certain order a certain number of times, before leaving in the morning. In contrast to people with OCD, however, we've noticed that many children with ASD like to talk about strangely neutral topics—constellations, train schedules, calendars, *National Geographic* magazine, toilet paper brands—whereas OCD obsessions are often highly emotional—death, dirt, blood, germs.

How Common Is Autism?

You may be surprised at how variable the prevalence figures are for autism spectrum disorders. Some authorities cite a figure as high as 1 in 150, while others cite 1 in 1000. The figures vary because different studies have produced different results, probably because of the year in which the study was done and the different ways the definition was applied. While everyone in the U.S. agrees on the DSM-IV criteria for autism, this agreement is not as solid as you might imagine. What is meant by "poor peer relationships"? Does the child have to be uninterested in peers? What about a child who wants friends but is socially immature and clumsy, or bossy and aggressive? Does he meet the definition? While no one knows for sure whether autism itself is on the rise (see page 286 for more on this issue), it does seem certain that more children genuinely in need of autism educational services have been identified in recent years.

Disorders on the Autism Spectrum

What we've given in this chapter so far is a description of autism in general. However, there are several different disorders on the autism spectrum that differ in how severely affected the child is, and, to some extent, in the specific behaviors the child shows. In the next section, we will describe the different disorders that fall on the autism spectrum.

Autism

The core disorder of the spectrum is officially called "**autistic disorder**," but is often just called **autism.** It was first identified in 1943 by Leo Kanner, in a paper in which he described eleven children with this syndrome. Kanner's clinical description has held up remarkably well over the years and still forms the basis for the "official" diagnosis of autism in the *Diagnostic and Statistical Manual of Mental Disorders* (DSM-IV). The DSM, which is published by the American Psychiatric Association, lists the diagnostic criteria used by mental health professionals in the United States when deciding what disorder best fits the person they are diagnosing. (Much of the rest of the world uses the *International Classification of Diseases* (ICD), which is in its 10th edition. The diagnostic criteria for autism spectrum disorders in ICD-10 are not identical to those in the DSM-IV, but are very similar.) Only a few aspects of what Kanner described have turned out not to be correct, such as that the children's "intelligent physiognomy" (meaning that their faces didn't look like those of children with mental retardation) suggested that they all had average IQs.

Autism is diagnosed when a child has at least 6 of the 12 features listed above in the section of defining features. In addition, 2 must come from the A (social) group of symptoms, and at least 1 from the B group (language, communication, play) and 1 from the C group (repetitive behaviors). The symptoms must appear before the age of 3 and must be severe enough to cause impairment in the child's daily life.

Autism is the syndrome from which autism spectrum disorder gets its name. It is the typical ASD disorder, with all of the major symptom areas represented. The other disorders on the ASD spectrum are considered variations on the theme of autism.

Children with autism are a very, very heterogeneous group. At the "high functioning" end, they will look like children with Asperger's (see below). At the lowest end, they may have severe mental retardation, with virtually no social relationships, few self-help skills, and no meaningful way to communicate. Here are two children, to illustrate the extreme variability in children with a diagnosis of autism:

Henry received excellent early treatment starting at age two and a half, and was functioning cognitively in the normal or superior range on most skills. He was included in a regular education classroom in second grade, and did not have any difficulty with the academics, since he was already reading well and doing simple math. However, he was very distraught at the size of the classroom and the movement and noise in the room, and had little interest in being with the other children. He would cry inconsolably when he felt overwhelmed. Pulling Henry out for long periods in the resource room allowed him to calm down and move ahead in his academics, but did not make reintegration into the classroom any easier.

Henry's parents tried hard to find children with whom he could play, but his extreme rigidity made it impossible. He always had a schedule of activities he wanted to do with the other child, each in a specific way, and he would break down when the other child tried to vary the plan or even respond in a way not exactly as Henry expected. His "conversations" with other children or adults consisted of him asking repetitive questions or lecturing them on preferred topics. Henry's parents put him in a regular summer camp for a few weeks, with an aide. When asked how he had liked it, he replied that it would have been good if there had been no other children there.

Ray was born several weeks late and probably had compromised blood circulation to his brain. At the age of eight, he had the mental ability of approximately a one-year-old. He had virtually no comprehension of any language except "NO." Self-help skills were limited to feeding himself with fingers, removing his socks, and pulling his pants up from halfway up. He was attached to his mother, but paid no attention to any other human being, appearing not to notice when people talked to him or tried to hug him, except to pull away. Why was he diagnosed with autism and not just severe mental retardation? Because his social connectedness was even more impaired than his other abilities (a six-month-old baby is interested in other people and smiles at adults, but Ray did not), and because his preferred activities were completely repetitive (staring at lights and rocking back and forth with his mother).

Henry and Ray represent two extremes of autistic disorder. Most likely, you will not have a child like Ray in your regular education classroom, but you are likely to come across a Henry. We will come back to Henry at the end of the book, and describe what happened to his schooling, and speculate about what could have been done differently.

For fascinating descriptions of individuals with autism who found their paths in life, we recommend especially Clara Park's two books about her daughter and Temple Grandin's autobiographical works (see Suggested Reading).

Asperger's Disorder (Asperger Syndrome)

Gerry was diagnosed with Asperger's disorder in third grade and came to us for evaluation in fifth grade. His parents wanted a confirmation of the diagnosis and also wanted to know how to help him with his social skills, which were getting more problematic as the social environment at school became more complex. He was involved in looking at magazines in the waiting room and his mother had to prompt him to look at us and greet us. He wanted to know if we had any National Geographic magazines because he was missing a few issues in his collection. When allowed, he would talk almost exclusively about this collection and about the magazine—its editorial staff, the topics it covered in each issue, how many pictures there were in each issue, etc.—but he seemed quite incurious about the actual content of the pictures and articles.

Gerry's vocabulary and grammar were excellent for his age, but his voice was loud, and his prosody (the melody of his speech) sounded odd and didn't fit with what he was saying. He avoided eye contact except when he was asking a direct question. He was very hard to deflect from the topic of National Geographic magazines. The examiner had to finally use an opportunity of talking about National Geographics as a reward for talking about school, and for completing some testing tasks.

Gerry's testing revealed a very high IQ in the verbal sphere, with good abstract ability, and average ability in the visual, nonverbal sphere (he could be seen talking his way through the visual tasks). In school, his performance was very uneven, with good math, science, and vocabulary skills, but reading comprehension that suffered when material was abstract, social, or inferential. His writing suffered at all levels, from handwriting to organizing material in a way that made sense. He never seemed to be able to keep the "big picture" in mind, but focused in linear fashion on detail after detail.

Gerry wanted friends and had preferences among the other children, but gravitated to the quiet children who would listen to him talk. The other children were becoming more intolerant of his oddness and wanted little to do with him. His social standing suffered even more from the difficulties he had with sports and physical games due to his gross motor clumsiness.

Like Gerry, most children with Asperger syndrome have intelligence that tests in the average or superior range. The child has one or more favorite topics and preoccupations, and little sensitivity to the fact that others may not be interested in hearing about it. He is not really interested in others' reactions and is usually insensitive to their body language. (Another child might be backing out the door but Gerry wouldn't notice unless the other child said directly, "I don't want to talk about this any more.") They often do well with academics in the early grades, since reading and basic math sometimes (but not always) come easily, but often start suffering by third or fourth grade, with increasing demands for organization, making connections, and inferential thinking.

Socially, these children tend to be rather clueless. They are uninterested in playground games, games involving role-playing, and the social structure of the classroom. If they are fortunate, they may find some like-minded children to whom they can relate around shared interests. It is beneficial if their preoccupation is one that is reasonably socially acceptable (Pokemon, Yu-gi-oh, and Japanese anime have been a great boon to children with Asperger's!), rather than something like electric blanket controls.

Asperger's disorder is named for Hans Asperger. In 1944, as a medical student in Austria, Asperger described four boys with severe social impairment, preoccupations with special interests, and motor clumsiness. He was unaware of the paper published by Leo Kanner one year earlier that described a similar syndrome, although, coincidentally, both used the term "autism" for the self-absorption they observed, taken from the earlier psychiatric literature on schizophrenia. Probably because the paper was published in Germany during WWII, it was ignored by English-speaking psychiatrists until Lorna Wing, an English psychiatrist, brought it to the attention of English and American professionals in 1981. The original paper was translated by Uta Frith in 1991 and the syndrome has received a great deal of attention since then.

The diagnostic criteria for Asperger's disorder in the DSM IV are:
1. social disability (with the same criteria as those for autism);
2. preoccupations and resistance to change (with the same criteria as those for autism).

In other words, the individual must meet the social and preoccupation criteria for autism, but not the language and play criteria. In fact, early language development must be normal (using words by 2 years, phrases by 3 years), as must adaptive skills and curiosity about the environment. But children with Asperger's disorder can still have symptoms in the language and communication domain, even though they're not necessary for a diagnosis, such as impaired ability to have conversations or tell a story, and repetitive pretend play.

In practice, individuals diagnosed with Asperger's disorder tend to look a lot like high functioning individuals with autism (see below). They tend to have IQs in the average to above average range, and be less impaired overall than individuals with autism. Still, there are many children and adolescents who could easily be diagnosed with autism by one expert and Asperger's by another. According to DSM-IV, a diagnosis of autism takes precedence. In other words, if the child meets the criteria for autism (autistic disorder), a diagnosis of Asperger's is not considered. In practice, this rule is often ignored, since many professionals consider a diagnosis of Asperger's to be less severe or stigmatizing than a diagnosis of autism.

Is There Really a Difference between Asperger's and High-Functioning Autism?

"High-functioning autism" refers to children who meet the criteria for autistic disorder *and* have either verbal or nonverbal IQs in the average range (over 80 or 85). Opinion is quite divided on this question of whether Asperger's is really different from high-functioning autism. Many researchers and clinicians believe that a real distinction between Asperger's and high-functioning autism has yet to be demonstrated. They believe they should see different cognitive profiles, different effective treatments, different outcomes, different family patterns, different brain abnormalities, different genes implicated, etc., in order to be convinced that these are not really just variations on the same clinical picture. These differences have not been definitely shown.

Many other researchers do believe that Asperger's is different enough from autism to be considered a separate syndrome, as it is in DSM-IV. See, for example, the 2001 article by Drs. Fred Volkmar and Ami Klin in the Bibliography for a discussion of this issue in detail. Here are the major differences cited by these and other authorities (do remember that there are many individual exceptions to these generalizations):

- *Children with autism have many language problems, while children with Asperger's have generally good language but use it in socially inappropriate ways.* This means that learning verbal rules for behavior or relying on language-based learning strategies may work better for children with Asperger's than for children with autism.

■ *Children with autism are often good at visual-spatial and visual-motor skills such as manipulating small objects dexterously and doing puzzles, while children with Asperger's have relative deficiencies in this area.* This means that using visual organizers or visual cues for learning or behavior may work better for children with autism than for children with Asperger's. However, there are many exceptions to this. Children with Asperger's *may* do fine with visual-spatial material. Visual-spatial problems are not a requirement for the diagnosis. Therefore, the graphic organizers discussed in Chapter 9 often work very well for children with Asperger's disorder.

■ *Children with autism often prefer to be alone and do the minimum they can get away with socially, while children with Asperger's want to have friends and are motivated to learn social behaviors (although appropriate social behavior may be very difficult for them to learn).* This means that if you have a student with autism, you may not be able to rely on a desire to have friends and you may have to provide other reinforcers for good social behavior, while the child with Asperger's may respond to the idea that good social behavior will get others to like him.

■ *Children with autism are likely to have more severe and more pervasive cognitive deficits. Since delayed onset of language can't be present in Asperger's disorder, children with Asperger's are much more likely to have a good outcome.* That is, they are more likely to complete regular high school or even college, hold a job, have meaningful social relationships, and even marry and have children.

■ *Children with autism are more likely to show their repetitive behaviors in motor patterns (rocking, toe-walking, jumping, flapping) and visual "stims," while those with Asperger's will show preoccupations with topics (train schedules, dinosaurs, magazines, constellations, etc.).* However, this may be largely a function of the fact that children with autism are more likely to have IQs in the mentally retarded range.

Some Problems with the Asperger's Diagnosis

As we alluded to above, it can be very difficult to differentiate between autism and Asperger's. If a psychologist is evaluating a ten-year-old, he or she may have to rely on the parents' memory of early language development to make the differentiation, and (as you know if you have your own children) it can be difficult to remember what children were like last year, let alone seven or eight years ago!

The diagnosis of Asperger's is, unfortunately, now in fashion. (Psychiatric diagnosis definitely goes through fads and fashions, just the way education does.) This means that more children, and different kinds of children, are being given the diagnosis. We have had children referred to us for evaluation who had been given diagnoses of Asperger's by a professional with good credentials. Some of these children (it seemed to us) had pure attention–deficit/hyperactivity disorder, some had unusual personality disorders, some were oppositional and had potentially serious behavior disorders, and many clearly met criteria for autism. Frequently, we could understand the diagnosis of Asperger's, because two of the social criteria were met (typically *poor peer relationships* and *poor emotional reciprocity*—children who want friends but either fumble around not understanding other children's emotions or how to relate to them or are aggressive, impulsive, and insensitive). However, the feeling one gets in trying to have a conversation with these children is quite different from the feeling one gets talking to the "little professor" types who are clearly on the ASD spectrum.

One reason for the increase in diagnoses of Asperger's (as well as all ASD diagnoses) is the services that come with this diagnosis. That is, typically more educational (and sometimes medical) services are available for children with diagnoses on the autism spectrum. We consulted to one mother whose child had received diagnoses of Asperger's, AD/HD, and depression from various professionals, and we had to advise her that the AD/HD and depression diagnoses would not likely increase her child's educational services, but the Asperger's diagnosis would.

What, therefore, does this over-diagnosis of Asperger's mean for teachers? You can start with the assumption that a child diagnosed with Asperger's will have a mild form of autism, with cognitive ability in or near the normal range, but with social disability and repetitive behaviors similar to those in autism. However, keeping in mind that the

"Asperger's" label may be applied to many different kinds of children, you should also watch for other problems, such as anxiety, depression, attention problems, or aggressive behaviors that may go beyond what is implied by "Asperger's disorder." Although no one expects you to question a diagnosis, it would be helpful for you pass along observations to parents or school psychologists which might suggest that the child needs help in these other areas.

Are Children with Asperger's Violent?

This is a question that teachers sometimes ask us. There have been a very few reports in the literature suggesting that individuals with Asperger's are given to rages and can even be violent against property and against other people. There is too little research to draw any definite conclusion about this, but our clinical experience (and that of Volkmar and Klin, see their 2001 paper cited in Resources and Bibliography) does not bear this out. Drs. Volkmar and Klin conclude that children and adolescents with Asperger's are more likely to be victims than victimizers, and that accords with what we've observed. Many children on the ASD spectrum may have a day when they're stressed out by sensory overload, academic and social demands, illness, fatigue, etc., and they may be less able to control their irritability than other children of the same age, so may, perhaps, have a full-blown tantrum. But aggression designed to injure others is rare.

One reason for the observations in the literature may be misdiagnosis. As noted above, the diagnosis is becoming more common and we've seen a few children who have the capacity to be dangerous adolescents and adults who (we believe mistakenly) were given an Asperger's diagnosis. By the way, the character with Asperger's on *Law and Order: Criminal Intent* whom we mentioned earlier turns out to be a serial killer. The portrayal was generally excellent, but given the severity of this character's social disability, which was beautifully acted, the ideas that a) he was married with two children, and b) that he could and would cold bloodedly murder several people for gain were unrealistic.

Rett's Disorder

Rett's disorder (also known as Rett syndrome) is a relatively rare disorder listed in the section on autism spectrum disorders in the DSM-IV. You are very unlikely to encounter any children with Rett's disorder in a regular education classroom. These children have a specific genetic disorder that results in significant mental retardation. The disorder affects girls almost exclusively, and a gene responsible for many cases has recently been identified.

Rett's disorder follows a characteristic early course, with normal physical and mental development for a few months, followed by a plateau or regression in skills, and then the appearance of "hand wringing" or "hand washing" movements along with a loss of purposeful hand movements. Although the child eventually starts moving ahead again in her development after several months or sometimes years, her intellectual ability usually tests in the severe or moderate range of mental retardation, and she often needs a wheelchair for mobility. Many feel that Rett's disorder does not belong on the ASD spectrum; it is there, at least for the present, because social withdrawal and language impairment is part of the early regression in skills.

Childhood Disintegrative Disorder (CDD)

This is another disorder on the autism spectrum you are unlikely to encounter in a regular education setting. This is partly because it is quite rare, and partly because the outcome is likely to include significant mental retardation. The disorder is characterized by typical development for at least two years, followed by a dramatic deterioration in language, social, cognitive, and/or motor skills, that appears to be neurological. It used to be called "infantile dementia" or "Heller's syndrome." The symptoms can resemble autism, but it is differentiated from autism by the long period of normal development, and the severe regression that ensues. In addition, children with CDD usually do not make as much progress in social, language, and cognitive skills as children with autism.

Pervasive Developmental Disorder – Not Otherwise Specified (PDD-NOS)

PDD-NOS is a "remainder" term. It is used for children who are on the autism spectrum, but don't meet criteria for any of the specific diagnoses (Autistic Disorder, Asperger's disorder, Rett's disorder, CDD). To receive a diagnosis of PDD-NOS, children must have at least one symptom in the social realm, *and* one in either the language/communication/play realm *or* one in the repetitive behavior realm. So, this diagnosis is intended to be used for children with a partial syndrome; that is, some symptoms of ASD but not a complete set.

In practice, PDD-NOS is often used for this purpose, but is used in four other situations as well:

1. for children with mild autism,
2. for children with high-functioning autism,
3. for children with autism who were evaluated by a diagnostician who does not want to use the word "autism," and
4. for children who used to meet criteria for classic autism, but who are improving to the point where they no longer do.

Ten years ago, PDD-NOS was a very common diagnosis and it still is, but "Asperger's" has replaced it for many children who have good cognitive ability and relatively mild symptoms. In almost all research studies that have contrasted children with PDD-NOS with children with autism, the findings are the same: children with autism have the most severe symptoms or lowest ability level, followed by children with PDD-NOS, followed by children in the "normal" comparison group.

What, therefore, does a diagnosis of PDD-NOS mean for the teacher of the student? As with Asperger's disorder, a wide variety of children might have this diagnosis. You can generally expect a child whose cognitive functioning is higher and whose social disability is milder than in classic autism, although in some cases this will not be true.

The best rule of thumb is not to place too much emphasis on the specific diagnosis. Although children with "autistic disorder," "Asperger's," and "PDD-NOS" are supposed to have different characteristics, this may not apply in all cases. The similarities among children with these different ASD diagnoses will be greater than the differences, and the information given in this book might well apply to children with any of these labels. The most important thing is to find out the particular child's strengths and weaknesses. The diagnostic label is only a starting point. A diagnosis of Asperger's disorder might lead you to expect that verbal strategies would work better than visual ones, but discussion with parents, the school psychologist, or previous teachers, and your own beginning experiences with the child, might rapidly reveal that this is not the case.

In the next chapter, we will describe other characteristics of children with ASD that will be helpful for you to understand but that aren't necessarily listed in the official DSM criteria.

2 | More about Autism Spectrum Disorders

This chapter will tell you more about what children with autism spectrum disorders are really like. We will go into more detail on some of the key behaviors that you'll observe in school, how autistic symptoms develop, cognitive strengths and weaknesses, possible overlap with other disorders you may be familiar with, the incidence of autism, and the possible outcomes for children on the autism spectrum.

Frequently Associated Features

There are many symptoms and behaviors that are common in ASD but are not part of the defining characteristics listed in the DSM. Among the most important are **behavior problems, issues with eating and sleeping, and sensory abnormalities.**

Challenging Behavior

Problem behaviors will be discussed in more detail in Chapter 12. In brief, however, children with autism spectrum disorders often seem to march to the beat of their own drummer. What motivates them, pleases them, and interests them can be different from other children. Pleasing the teacher, defying the teacher, impressing other children, mastering new skills, pleasing their parents—these fundamental motivations are not necessarily lacking but may be less pressing in children with ASD. Instead, other motivations may be more pressing, such as being allowed to do their preferred repetitive activities, talking about their favorite subject, or avoiding unpleasant sensory stimulation.

Furthermore, you must always remember that the child with ASD often has to work extra hard to do what may come easily to the other children. Anything involving complex language is likely to require additional concentration and mental effort in a child who already may be challenged in the area of sustained attention. Is it any wonder, given all these factors, that they may sometimes become noncompliant, irritable, or shut down and withdrawn?

Sleep

Sleep can be a real problem for children with ASD. This is most true in early childhood, but sleep problems can persist into the school years. Some children, perhaps because of the stresses of getting through the day, are very keyed up at night, and it can be very difficult for them to relax enough to get to sleep. Sometimes, a rather lengthy and predictable bedtime routine, including relaxing activities such as back rubs, quiet music, and being read to, can help. Some children wake more frequently during the night than is usual, and may be up for quite a while.

In your initial and ongoing discussions with parents, it would be worthwhile for you to check with the parents about whether sleep is difficult for their child. If so, you might want to suggest that they let you know when the child is having a particularly hard time sleeping, so you can be on the lookout for irritability or fatigue and perhaps adjust your demands on the child accordingly. Being sensitive to this issue will help parents understand that you care about their child as a person and understand that the hours outside of the school day will affect her performance at school.

Eating

Eating can also be an area of challenge for children with ASD and may be related to sensory issues (see the next section). Some children cannot tolerate extremes of temperature in their food, while others only like food hot or cold and not at room temperature. Some like only soft foods, while others can't tolerate soft foods and like crunchy, salty food. Most of the children with ASD we've seen don't show these extreme sensory intolerances (and when they do, it tends to be when they're in preschool). Nevertheless, children with ASD still can be pickier than their peers. Some children with ASD will only eat their favorite five or six foods and absolutely refuse to try anything new, although these five or six favorites tend to be the usual childhood favorites—chicken fingers, macaroni and cheese, peanut butter and jelly sandwiches, pizza.

Picky eating is mostly a problem when a major food group is missing (e.g., some children refuse all fruits and vegetables). Of course, it is up to the parents, in consultation with their pediatrician or a nutritionist, to figure out whether the child is getting adequate nutrition, but providing parents information about what the child will eat in school (snack or cafeteria food) may be helpful, especially since some children will try new things in one setting, such as school, which they refuse at home.

Another eating issue concerns *special diets* that the child may be on. There are various reasons for these diets. Some children, of course, have allergies that have been diagnosed by a doctor and it can be dangerous for them to eat certain foods. Other allergies are more hypothetical. That is, some parents on their own or in consultation with "alternative" medicine professionals have decided that their child's behavioral or other problems are associated with eating certain foods, and feel that the child has a "cerebral allergy"—an allergy that shows itself not with a rash or other usual allergic reactions, but with a change in behavior.

Rarely, a child is placed on a special diet because of medication or to help control seizures. The "ketogenic diet" to control seizures is a really difficult diet to follow, in which every calorie must be strictly counted and only very specific foods are allowed, but it has been shown to be effective in helping control certain types of seizures.

Finally, many parents of children with ASD (as we go to press) believe that keeping their child's diet free of gluten (a protein found in wheat, barley, and other foods) and casein (found in dairy products) helps their development and behavior. To date, there is no scientific evidence for this theory, although there are several ongoing studies that might find such evidence. However, many parents firmly believe that they can see changes in behavior with even the smallest violation of this diet.

In our experience, some parents rely on anecdotal evidence to support their beliefs in diets or other alternative treatments. Other parents want to use a more objective method to investigate the usefulness of such treatments. In these cases, teachers can be extremely helpful by agreeing to be kept in the dark about what the child is eating at home, and keeping a daily log of the child's mood, attention, and behavior.

This can give parents and doctors an unbiased look at whether the child is indeed influenced by diet or medication.

With all of these types of food restriction, of course, school staff must abide scrupulously by parents' directives. This can be a real problem when other children bring in birthday cupcakes or there's a pizza party. If a student has any dietary restrictions, it is really important for teachers to try to notify her parents about classroom treats ahead of time, so that they can send in a special, allowable treat. Although these treats are seldom as desirable (just try a gluten-free cake!), at least they will help child feel a little less isolated. Children generally understand allergies, so if classmates want to know why Jenny can't eat the pizza, you can ask if any children have allergies and have foods that are not good for them, and explain that this is the same for Jenny.

Sensory Abnormalities

Sensory abnormalities are seen very often in children with autism spectrum disorders. Although they may take different forms, they are very common at all levels of cognitive functioning, so you are very likely to encounter these sensitivities in children with ASD in your class.

There are several ways to break these sensitivities down into different catgegories. One useful way is by the type of behavior that occurs in response to a sensation: *under-reactivity, over-reactivity, and "sensory seeking"* behaviors.

Under-reactivity

You will often see children with ASD *under-react* to sensory events—ignoring sounds or conversation, or looking through people as if they weren't there. Although this can be seen at any cognitive level, it tends to be more common in children with mental retardation. In dramatic cases, they may ignore stimuli that should be painful. One father we know put his child with ASD in a car seat in the rear of their car, unwittingly closed the car door on the child's fingers, and walked around to the driver's door. After he had started the car, he became aware of a faint whimper. Knowing the boy, he stopped the car and went to investigate, and discovered the situation. If you have a student who has some sensory under-responsiveness, it might be worth checking with parents to make sure the child's response to pain is normal. You don't want to miss a skinned knee or worse because the child doesn't complain!

Over-reactivity

Over-reactivity is common in children with ASD at all intellectual levels. Such children can be exquisitely sensitive to sensory stimuli. They may be unable to tolerate bright lights, loud noises including music, loud talking, machines (such as drills or vacuum cleaners) or airplanes, certain tastes and smells, and certain kinds of touch. Fire drill alarms can be excruciating for children with ASD. They may cover their ears to block out loud noises, and appear to be bothered by noises that most of us can hardly hear (such as the hum of fluorescent lights).

Some children with ASD may over-react to a sound at one time but appear oblivious to it at another time. For example, at the first school assembly of the year, a child covered her ears, complaining that the sound of the other kids talking before the assembly hurt her ears. However, at the next assembly she did not react to the sound of the crowd at all. When a child over-reacts to a sound it may help to give her a routine that she can practice with you ahead of time and then use when a sound such as a fire alarm goes off (e.g., put her fingers in her ears, take a very deep, slow breath, count to 10, while walking to her assigned place) and then give her a reinforcer (reward) for coping with the sound successfully. See Chapter 12 for more on using reinforcers.

Within the tactile realm, children with ASD may like or even crave deep pressure, such as a firm neck or back rub or piling heavy pillows on top of themselves. At the same time, they may pull away from light touch (this is called tactile defensiveness). They may hate certain kinds of fabric next to their skin, and you may notice that all their clothing tags have been cut out, that they only wear soft cottons to school, or that they always wear short sleeves, even in winter. Although not usually bothered by smells, they may be extremely sensitive to smells, such as perfumes.

Sensory-seeking Behaviors

Sensory seeking behaviors are ones the child uses to provide herself with certain repetitive sensations, such as twiddling her fingers in front of her eyes or in front of lights, or rocking back and forth. These are discussed more in the chapter on handling behavior (Chapter 12). In brief, there are several ways to handle them. If they are not disturbing the child or anyone else, they can be ignored. However, if they are making the child look very odd to her peers, or if they are distracting the child and preventing her from learning, you should try to minimize them.

One simple technique is distraction: if the child is twiddling her fingers, give her some other activity to do with her hands, such as drawing a picture, or even a more socially acceptable alternative such as a fiddle toy. These behaviors are habits, like habits that non-autistic individuals have. If you can distract a child from doing them often enough, she may learn not to do these behaviors in your classroom, although they may still be present in other settings. There are other techniques for working on reducing this behavior, including behavioral plans, and even (for older and cognitively normal children) discussing with the child that the behaviors are disturbing to other children. These should be done with the help of the school's psychologist or behavioral consultant.

Classifying Behaviors by Sensory Modality

Another way to classify behaviors related to sensory processing difficulties is by the sensory modality in which they appear: visual, auditory, tactile. A recent study by Miriam Liss and Celine Saulnier at the University of Connecticut suggested that the first classification (under-reactivity, over-reactivity, and sensory seeking) is the more valid, and that a child who is over-reactive in one modality tends to be over-reactive in other modalities as well. The most common sensory behaviors are:

- *over-reactivity to tactile and auditory stimulation* (intolerance for certain noises, and intolerance of being touched),
- *under-reactivity to visual and auditory stimulation* (not noticing visual stimuli or people talking to them), and
- *sensory seeking behavior involving visual stimuli and repetitive motor behaviors* (such as twiddling the fingers near the eyes).

More about Social Behavior

Lorna Wing, eminent British psychiatrist and author of several excellent books on autism, proposed a classification of social behavior in children with ASD. At one end are the children who are socially aloof. This describes the child with "classic" autism, who basically wants to be left alone and only interacts with others to get his or her needs met.

The second type is the passive child. This child may respond to social overtures from others but rarely initiates unless it is to get needed information or objects. Third is the child who is "active, but odd." This child actively initiates interactions with other people, but gives an odd appearance. She may talk about unusual topics, stand too close to others, make unwavering intense eye contact, and be insensitive to others' reactions. In our experience, children who are most likely to be included in regular education classrooms are of the "active, but odd" type, although some may be passive as well.

Another way to think about social behavior that we have found helpful is to think about a hierarchy of interactions, crossed with a hierarchy of partners:

	mother	other adult	sibling	peer
is aware of				
responds to				
initiates interactions with				
sustains interactions with				

The hierarchy of interactions, from lowest to highest, is awareness, followed by response, then initiation, and, finally, sustained interactions. The hierarchy of partners, from easiest to hardest, varies from child to child, but will often be mother, other adults (such as teacher), sibling, peer. The easiest interaction, therefore, will be awareness of mother, and the hardest will be sustained interaction with a peer. It may help you (particularly with the younger or more cognitively impaired child) to think about each of these categories: Does she respond to a teacher's overtures? another child's overtures? Can she sustain an interaction with mother, father, sibling, and teacher, but not a peer? A child who does not even respond to another child will not have a sustained interaction—you must work first on responding, then on teaching the child to initiate, and then try to build sustained interactions. Other ways of thinking about social skills, and helping the child to build them, will be presented in Chapter 11.

In the next section, we will describe what is known about the usual patterns of cognitive strength and weakness in children with ASD.

Cognitive Strengths and Weaknesses

Language

As explained in Chapter 1, all children with autism spectrum disorders experience at least some difficulties in acquiring and using language. There is a rich history, more than 30 years worth, of research into language in children with ASD. For those who want a more detailed or technical summary of some of this literature, we suggest the works by Helen Tager-Flusberg listed in the References. More specific advice on helping children with language-related issues in the classroom is provided in Chapter 9.

Language can be divided into several functions that can be studied separately. We will summarize the general literature in each of these functions, but please remember that we are summarizing results for a group. For each of the functions, there will be individual children who are impaired and those who are strong; the possible exception to this is with semantics and pragmatics, where most children with ASD are impaired.

Phonology and Syntax

Phonology and syntax are the structural aspects of language. **Phonology** refers to the speech sounds of the language. Can the child discriminate among the sounds that others make when they are speaking, and can she produce the sounds consistently and understandably? In general, children with ASD who do not also have mental retardation function well in this area. They can generally understand and produce the sounds of their language with a skill that is consistent with their overall mental level, and sometimes this area is a real strength. However, a subset of children with ASD have significant and persistent problems with hearing and producing speech sounds.

Another area of language is **syntax** or **grammar.** There are two major components to grammar usage: 1) using and understanding word endings (e.g., the plural "s," the possessive "s," the past "—ed" verb ending, etc.) and 2) using and understanding correct word order (forming a sentence by putting the words in the correct order). With some exceptions, this is also an area of relative strength for many children with ASD. They learn word endings in roughly the same order as typically developing children, and often have highly grammatical speech. In fact, it can be too grammatical, lacking the variety and informality that usually characterizes children's speech.

Prosody

Prosody refers to the melody of our speech—the pitch, volume, and rate changes that carry meaning and emotional information. Imagine, for example, saying "YOU drove to the carnival?" which expresses surprise that it was you and not someone else, as opposed to "You DROVE to the carnival?" which expresses surprise at the mode of travel, as opposed to "You drove to the CARNIVAL?" which expresses surprise at where you went. Prosody can also indicate that a statement is a question, an exclamation, an affirmation, and that it carries surprise, sadness, anger, etc.

Prosody is almost universally impaired in children with ASD. They sometimes speak in a flat monotone, with no prosody to add subtlety and emotional richness to their speech. They may speak in an exaggerated sing-song manner, which conveys as little information as the flat monotone. Although there is little research in this area, indications are that children with ASD have as much difficulty understanding prosody as using it. This means that they will miss a lot of the nuances and emotional subtleties of your speech and the speech of other children, and need to have things made verbally explicit that other children will just "get." This doesn't generally apply, however, to obvious displays of negative emotion, like a raised, angry voice, to which they may be very sensitive. But don't expect them to get a sarcastic tone of voice. Your student may take you very literally if you say sarcastically, "Nice job cleaning up, Jenny!"

Semantics

Semantics refers to the meanings of words. Skills in semantics encompass understanding not only the formal definition of the word, the explicit thing it refers to, but the unspoken, implicit connotations that one picks up just by hearing the word used. These connotations are often poorly understood by children with ASD, so that they use a word which may be technically correct but which sounds odd in the context. Take, for example, the word "crispy" which has recently come into wide use in spoken English, especially in food commercials. No one ever explicitly told you what it means, yet you know that you can call chicken crispy but not a brisk fall day. This method of language learning—picking up the connotations and subtleties from hearing the word used—is a weakness for children with ASD.

Semantics also includes relationships among concepts. For example, does the child know that "dog" is a member of the class of "animals" and that "terrier" is a member of the class of "dogs," and, by implication, that everything she learns about animals applies to dogs, but not vice versa? In other words, can she reason about the concepts she has learned? Some recent data from UConn suggest that even very successful children with ASD can have subtle difficulties with this kind of reasoning. You would do well to check that conclusions that seem obvious to you (or other children) have actually been reached by the child (e.g., if a brown rabbit likes carrots, a white rabbit will too).

Research about the semantic abilities of children with ASD is mixed, probably more so than for any other area of language. Many studies, including some by Tager-Flusberg, by us, and by many others, have found that understanding and producing single words in isolation (for example, labeling objects or pictures) is a relative strength for most children with ASD. They are particularly good at looking at pictures and producing a label for the picture. They may be a bit less good at picking the right picture from an array that matches a word. Why would that be? Wouldn't understanding a word have to come before saying it? Strangely enough, some children with ASD learn to understand a word *after* they have learned to say it in the proper context, and sometimes the usual order of teaching (understanding then saying) has to be reversed.

It may be that children with ASD learn some of the features of meaning of a word—enough to assign the correct label to an object with those features—but not enough to demonstrate complete comprehension. For example, one four-year-old boy was easily able to pick out a box from a group of objects when it was made of cardboard but not if the box was made of plastic. He appeared to have not understood the features of a box that make it a box. Children with ASD may do more poorly on receptive vocabulary tests than expressive tests for other reasons as well. Tests of understanding words require the child to pick a picture from three or four choices. This requires the child to remember the word, scan the pictures systematically, and not make an impulsive choice, while the tests of expressive vocabulary are more stimulus-response—show the picture, ask "what is it?" It's always a good idea to pay attention to skills required by the test that are not what the test is trying to measure!

Other studies suggest that children with ASD have some deficiencies in understanding and producing single words. One of us (MD) found that when asked for examples of categories, children with ASD gave unusual, or less typical, examples more often than typically developing children ("aardvark" rather than "dog"). Children with ASD may be specifically impaired in the use of "mental state verbs"—verbs that reflect others' mental processes, such as "know," "think," "expect," "hope," "remember." The child in your class may show a subtle lack or misuse of these words and may benefit from some extra teaching in this area. If you notice difficulty with mental state verbs, this would a useful piece of information for you to pass on to the speech-language pathologist.

Discourse

Discourse generally refers to the ability to put together a higher level of connected speech, such as when telling a story. This is also an area of great difficulty for most children with ASD, even those with generally good language. If asked to tell a story, they will often give a set of descriptions of separate events, but without weaving them into a coherent narrative, or even seeming to understand that there is supposed to be a causal chain of events, with each event leading to the next. For some children, this probably reflects some general impairment in the ability to sequence a long string. For others, it may primarily reflect a tendency not to think in causal terms.

Many children with ASD learn their basic "Wh-" questions much later than would be expected from their level of vocabulary. They may do all right with the concrete and visual "what," "who," and "where," but have much difficulty with the more abstract "when," "why," and "how." You may notice that when you ask a "why" question, you get an answer that starts with "because"—they've learned that much—but then the answer that follows does not really answer the "why" question but gives you some irrelevant fact about the topic.

Children with ASD also have trouble when learning to put sentences together. When they are young, they often learn language in a "formula" way. That is, they learn sentences as whole chunks, rather than by putting together new sentences with new words to mean new things. You may find as you get to know the child that even though she can put together good sentences, she uses sentences as a single chunk, and she may not really understand the meaning of the sentence as a typical child would. Similarly, even though she may say a particular sentence, you may find that if you say it to her, she doesn't really understand what you mean. The only way to tell is to check her comprehension. This often applies to children diagnosed with Asperger's disorder as well.

Pragmatics

Pragmatics refers to the social use of language. Here we find a universal impairment in children with ASD. Pragmatics includes analysis of speech acts or functions, including things like greeting, commenting, asking questions, answering questions, agreeing, requesting, protesting. In general, although this is less true for higher functioning children, children with ASD use their language more to regulate their environment than to be social. Especially when young, they regularly make requests and protests but do less commenting, greeting, and asking questions (unless they need to know the answer or the question is a favorite repetitive topic).

The area of pragmatics also includes conversational skills such as staying on topic, acknowledging the other person's statements, and expanding on and adding to what the other says, as well as maintaining an appropriate degree of eye contact and physical distance. Children with ASD are challenged in all of these areas.

Written Language

Written language is often a strong point for children with ASD. Children with ASD who are in the average or near-average IQ range often do well in the decoding aspects of reading, and may spell well. Where they suffer is in the higher level conceptual and content areas—in understanding what they read, especially if it requires making inferences rather than just literal understanding, and in having well-organized and sensible things to write.

In addition, many children with ASD have fine motor problems that make writing difficult, and sometimes they have difficulty in grasping that words are separated by spaces. Of course, difficulty with the mechanics of writing leads to more difficulty in writing what you want to say! Many children with ASD benefit from the use of keyboards or computers, to get around the handwriting problem. This is discussed in more detail in Chapter 8.

Idiosyncratic Features of Language

In addition to these language areas, some idiosyncratic features of language in ASD have been noted since Leo Kanner first wrote about children with autism in 1943. Foremost is **echola-**

Can Language Impairments be "Cured?"

A University of Connecticut graduate student, Beth Kelley (now at Queens University in Canada), recently completed an important study that sheds light on what kinds of language abilities you may find in students with ASD in the regular classroom (Kelley, E., Fein, D., Naigles, L., 2006). She identified fourteen elementary-school-aged children who had been diagnosed with ASD in early childhood and had been so successfully treated that they were now totally included with minimal or no support, functioning successfully in regular classrooms. She gave them a battery of language tests to see if they were really functioning at a normal level in all areas. What she found was very revealing.

First of all, the children all functioned within the average range on all standardized tests of language, including grammar and vocabulary. But there were remaining difficulties in specific areas that showed up on more sensitive testing. First, they still had trouble reasoning about mental state verbs— understanding, for example, that "know" was more certain than "guess." They didn't always reason correctly about categories despite having average IQs— knowing, for example, that behavior that was true of "white rabbits" was true of "brown rabbits."

In addition, the children's story-telling was quite impaired. They described specific events, and gave a lot of sound effects, but did not tell a connected, cause and effect, chain of events. One wonders whether, despite their remarkable successes, speech and language or other special help had been discontinued prematurely and whether these subtle deficits would give them academic or social trouble in later grades. What is obvious to other children about making up a story may be far from obvious to your student with ASD. She may need help by getting more structure for the task than you would usually provide- -for example, an outline or rubric that gives the necessary story elements such as beginning, conflict, resolution (even if each is only one sentence), plus attention to what characters are thinking and feeling and what their motivations are.

lia—a tendency to imitate what others say to an unusual degree. Immediate echolalia, repeating what someone else says right after he or she says it, is found more in younger and more intellectually limited children, but you may still encounter a great deal of delayed echolalia in school-aged children. Delayed echolalia is repeating words—which may be as short as a phrase, or as long as an entire movie script—that have been heard at a previous time. Sometimes this seems to serve a "self-stimulatory" function—it just pleases the child to do it. Sometimes it seems more social and even appropriate to the situation (e.g., you ask a question about movies she likes and you get a recitation of dialogue).

Related to echolalia is **scripted language.** Often parents tell us that the child has learned certain scripts to run in certain situations and that if you didn't know the child well, you would think the language was appropriate and natural, but if you do know the child, you know that this is the "script" she has memorized to use in certain situations. This is not necessarily a bad thing. It can be a very useful tool to help the child be more socially acceptable to peers, and language often becomes less scripted as the child gets more adept at understanding social situations and at producing complex language.

So, to summarize this complex information: some children with ASD have persistent problems with structural aspects of language (phonology, syntax), but many children with high-functioning autism as well as Asperger's do not. Most children with autism, even those with high-functioning autism, as well as many children with Asperger's, have persistent and significant problems with semantics, pragmatics, and prosody. The children do well with concrete language but have increasing difficulty as the language becomes more complex, hierarchically organized, abstract, or inferential.

Memory

Memory is an understudied area in autism spectrum disorders. However, certain generalizations can be made from the existing published research:

- Visual memory is generally an area of strength; in fact, it can be extraordinary. High functioning children with ASD sometimes have remarkable memories for routes and locations of objects.

- Memory for music is sometimes a real talent in children with ASD.
- Memory for verbal material, on the other hand, can be quite difficult (except in children with a diagnosis of Asperger's disorder, who tend to have strong verbal memories).

One interesting finding in a study we were both involved in was that making the material more organized and meaningful did not help the children with ASD remember it, as it did for non-autistic children with language impairment. The children with ASD did better than the language-impaired children on remembering a string of meaningless numbers (no meaning), did equally well on remembering a sentence (some meaning), but did worse on remembering a story (highest level of meaning). The children with ASD did not use the framework of the story to help them remember details. They remembered details in the story as if they were unrelated bits of information. Your student with ASD may operate this way. For example, she may not automatically extract the most important elements of a story or paragraph unless you help her to do so.

Sometimes children with ASD show extraordinary memories for certain types of material. In particular, they may remember events and facts in great detail. For example, if you ask a student with ASD if she's ever been to the zoo, she may reply, "We went to the Bronx Zoo on Sept. 14, 2004. It was raining. I wore my blue jacket and grey pants and my brother wore his red jacket and blue jeans. We had tuna fish sandwiches and ice cream pops for lunch." And yet, there can be an impersonal quality to these memories, as though the child is remembering facts and not recollecting a personal event. And the same child can have trouble remembering something you thought she had learned yesterday! No one has come up with a good explanation for these feats of memory or the inconsistencies within memory. Probably, it has something to do with attention, with what the child considers important, interesting, or easy to remember. As with other splinter skills (see below) the challenge is in finding a way to make the unusual ability useful in the real world.

Attention and Executive Functions

Attention and executive functions in ASD have been fairly well studied, although theoretical debate about the role of both attention and executive functions in ASD still rages.

Attention

Attention is very problematic in people with ASD. Many children with ASD show frank symptoms of an attention deficit disorder (see below). Most children with ASD do not have a real impairment in the ability to sustain attention but have a striking disconnection between their ability to attend to preferred topics and activities (where attention span can be unusually long) and their ability (or desire) to attend to nonpreferred activities. This is very often a problem.

A psychologist and colleague, Helen Garretson, did an interesting experiment on the attention of children with ASD. She gave them a rather boring task in which they had to sustain their attention for a period of time. Under normal conditions (intermittent praise for correct responding) these children appeared extremely impaired. Their attention waned quickly and they started making mistakes. However, when she gave them preferred tangible reinforcers (snacks, coins) their attention was every bit as good as that of the typical children matched for mental age. This suggests that motivation is crucial in helping students with ASD optimize their attention when performing tasks they may not intrinsically enjoy. Make the material as interesting as possible, keep the requirements for sustained attention to a reasonable level, and use external reinforcers as necessary (not necessarily candy, but checks, stickers, opportunities to earn a preferred object or activity).

We explore motivation in more detail in Chapter 12, and you can also find an excellent discussion in *Incentives for Change: Motivating People with Autism Spectrum Disorders to Learn and Gain Independence* by Lara Delmolino and Sandra Harris.

You will also find that attention varies with the material even more than it does with most children. A child's attention to a language-based lesson may be adequate when the subject matter is highly motivating (e.g., bugs), but her attention may wane completely and suddenly when she loses interest. You may help her focus her attention by

- using hands-on activities,
- relating the material to subjects of interest to the child,
- giving intermittent brief gross motor breaks (running an errand, erasing the board), and
- anticipating a simple quiz with opportunities to earn powerful reinforcers for good performance.

Executive Functions

"Executive functions" refers to cognitive and decision-making activities that are similar to what the head of an organization does for the group—hence the name. These include such processes as:

- organizing parts of a job into the proper sequence and relationships,
- suppressing inappropriate or irrelevant responses,
- keeping attention to the task at hand,
- putting forth mental effort or concentration on a task over a sustained time,
- initiating problem solving activities,
- holding one thread of information in mind while working on another so the two can be put together at the end,
- calling to mind previously learned information without any cues or prompts, and
- working for a reward that is in the future instead of doing what brings immediate gratification.

The role of executive functions in ASD has received a lot of attention over the past twenty years but is still hotly debated. Some theorists believe that executive function problems are not only universal in ASD but are the actual central cause of these disorders. Others believe that executive functions are not as central as the social problems but are frequently present and cause the children a lot of difficulty. In either case, you will probably observe your student with ASD to have trouble with one or more of these aspects of behavior. Most of these functions have been found to depend heavily on the frontal lobes of the brain. Depending on the age and intellectual capacity of your student, your job may be to, in effect, serve as the child's frontal lobes (helping her to organize, plan, and inhibit by setting up external structure) or to help her develop strategies to do these things for herself.

If you think about which academic subjects tend to place the most demands on executive functions, it may help you anticipate difficulties your student is likely to have. For one, writing calls heavily on executive functions. There is the blank piece of paper (or computer screen)—we've all known the sinking feeling it can produce. It gives you no structure, no guidance, no help in calling forth the relevant information and suppressing the irrelevant, or in organizing the information once you have obtained it, no assistance in maintaining your attention and concentration or internally manipulating the pieces of information or perceiving connections among them. Some children with ASD can write nice stories, because their imaginations don't have to be constrained by facts and because they use the structure of stories they've heard before. Yet, when it comes to reports or papers that require planning and organization of material, difficulties can become very apparent.

Math is another subject requiring planning, organization, and concentration. Some children with ASD are talented at math, but for those who are not, the executive demands can make it very difficult. Be alert also to visual-spatial problems (see below) that can affect math skills. Children with weaknesses in visual processing can have difficulty with number lines, estimating, grasping place values, and keeping columns of numbers and carried numbers properly aligned. They may need paper with vertical lines to assist them with columns.

Just as for children with AD/HD, the executive function problems in children with ASD can make homework agonizing for the child and the family. You can help by:

- keeping in steady communication with parents,
- giving very manageable chunks of homework (probably better to give three short assignments than one long one),
- giving ample rewards for completed work, and
- encouraging parents to assist by providing reinforcers and structured routines for homework time.

One mother we knew sat with her child during homework time providing a neck massage as long as the child was actively working on homework. Whatever works! Parents can also help greatly with the organizational components of homework without doing any of the actual work—for example, by helping the child organize facts on index cards into the proper order for a report. When writing is particularly difficult, parents can type while the child dictates, and perhaps have the child copy it into her handwriting when it's finished, thus disassembling the overwhelming job into manageable elements.

Visual-spatial Skills

Visual-spatial (or visuo-spatial) skills are skills that require you to perceive basic visual elements (shapes, colors, movements) as well as the relationships among them. Visual-motor skills depend on visual-spatial skills, but also add the motor component (e.g., cutting out shapes, copying words or designs, quickly moving pegs from one hole to another, completing puzzles, hitting a ball). Visual-spatial skills are often an area of strength for children with ASD; less often, visual-motor skills can be a strength.

Some children with autism or PDD-NOS are very capable when it comes to visuo-spatial tasks such as drawing or cutting; visual cues or visual organizers can help them grasp and remember academic material (see Chapter 10 for more specifics). They may, however, have difficulty with very complex visual material because of the necessity for understanding its complex organization.

Others, particularly those with a diagnosis of Asperger's syndrome, find visual-spatial skills to be difficult. They do better with detail than with the overall picture and may have trouble seeing visual relationships. For these children, putting things into words that they can use to cue themselves may work better than making visual images or pictures. For each child, this is something you'll need to find out by trial and error. If using visual imagery or graphic organizers doesn't seem to help much, try giving the child specific verbal rules or scripts to help her organize and control her behavior and to remember academic material. *It should be the case that the children with diagnoses of PDD-NOS or autism will do better with visual strategies, while those with diagnoses of Asperger's will do better with verbal strategies.* In real life, however, the diagnoses are used so interchangeably that it would be unwise to make these assumptions. Try various strategies and see what works and what the child likes.

Social Cognition

Social cognition refers to understanding the social world—the child's ability to grasp what others are feeling, understand why they feel and behave as they do, and understand what is expected of her. There are multiple components of social cognition, and ASD children may have trouble with all of them.

Processing Faces

First of all, there is visual processing of others' faces. From earliest infancy, we all focus heavily on others' faces. They are of intrinsic interest to most people and by the preschool years, we are experts at recognizing and understanding others' faces. We automatically pick a familiar face out of a crowd and we react instinctively to another person's expression of happiness, fear, sadness, or anger. Not necessarily so for the ASD child. She may use a particular feature, perhaps a nose or a haircut, to recognize another person. Consequently, she will take a long time to learn to reliably recognize you or her classmates, and she may recognize only exaggerated expressions of emotion.

Ami Klin at Yale and others have investigated how children with ASD watch others interacting. They have found that individuals with ASD focus on unusual aspects of the picture, such as the characters' hairline or mouth, or an object in the background, rather than scanning the characters' eyes for clues to their emotions and reactions.

Empathy

If the child does understand someone else's emotions, she may not respond automatically with the "correct" response—for example, she may find the crying of a baby merely irritating or amusing. You may need to help her recognize emotional expressions of other children or characters in a story, and discuss the proper response to each situation. You might need to help her recognize and label her own emotions, as well.

This, of course, relates to the child's capacity for empathy—feeling with or feeling for another person. Many children with ASD surprise us by having a lot of empathy for other children, especially younger ones. They perceive their distress and want to do what they can to help, although their efforts may be immature or ineffective. This should be applauded and encouraged, and the child taught more effective means of helping. Other children with ASD seem to have a reduced fundamental "resonance" with others' emotions and must be explicitly taught to notice when others are happy or upset, and how to respond appropriately.

Interestingly, some children with ASD have particular empathy with animals. One child we knew who largely ignored other children and their emotions was exquisitely tuned in to the family pets and was the only one to notice a very slight limp in their dog. Temple Grandin, in her books listed in the Bibliography, described the simple and straightforward animal emotions that roused tremendous empathy in her, and led her into her present career in animal husbandry.

Theory of Mind

Another aspect of social cognition that has received a lot of attention in the ASD literature is called "theory of mind." This refers to the understanding we have of others' minds—the fact that what others think, see, know, remember, and feel is not necessarily what we think, see, know, remember, or feel.

The classic test of theory of mind is to present the child with a scenario in which a treat is hidden in front of two dolls. One doll leaves, the other doll moves the treat, then the first doll returns. The child is asked where the returning doll will look for the treat. Evidence of theory of mind is shown if the child knows that the doll will look for the treat where it was originally hidden, because that doll doesn't know about the new location. Absence of theory of mind is shown when the child says that the returning doll will look in the new location, where the child herself knows the treat to be. The child doesn't understand that just because she herself knows where the treat is, the returning doll doesn't know that too.

Many younger children with ASD or those who have mental retardation have difficulty with even simple theory of mind tasks such as this one. Older or more cognitively able children with ASD may pass these simple tests, but have difficulty with more complex or higher order theory of mind tests, such as knowing what Bobby thinks Gerry knows about Carla. It is always a good idea to check with your student explicitly about what she understands about what others think, know, and feel; things that are obvious to other children may not be obvious to her.

Friendship
Children with ASD often have immature and oversimplified notions of "friendship." They may think that anyone they know or have played with once is a friend, not understanding that true friends prefer each other because of common interests, feel positive emotions when interacting, and share special bonds of confidence and trust. Other children may not notice this naiveté in the preschool years and the earliest school grades, but in the older elementary grades, will view it as odd.

The best way to help a child form a mutual friendship is for parents and teachers to cooperate in picking out some likely children who share specific interests with the child with ASD. (Pokemon and Digimon was a major blessing to many children with ASD!) Seeking friendships with other children who share specific interests remains the best way to establish peer relationships into adolescence (music, computer games, rock climbing, science). Children can be encouraged to find other children with common interests in after school clubs. You can play a very important role here in helping the child (or her parents) to identify one or more other children with whom she might develop a friendship. It can also help to identify children whose personalities seem to fit with that of the child with ASD (quiet, rowdy, motherly). In addition, it may help to encourage friendships with children whose families are already friends, or where siblings are friends with one another.

Play dates must be arranged and facilitated by an adult, either a parent or therapist, especially initially. The child with ASD should be given specific rules for interacting, such as turn-taking, offering to share games and toys, and asking the other child for his or her preferences about what to do. The adult may need to start out by staying in the room to assist, and may be able after some time or after a certain number of play dates to hover nearby, ready to intervene when necessary. One mother made a point of passing the room every few minutes. Whenever she overheard her child being rigidly focused on a certain activity being done in a certain way, she would walk through the room, raise an eyebrow at her child (a prearranged signal), and he would then say to the other child "OK, now what do *you* want to do?"

Many children with ASD pass the social milestones of having one strongly preferred friend or even a mutual best friend, but encounter difficulty when they are interacting in a group. Group games on the playground or in the neighborhood require children to constantly shift attention and understand subtle rules of interaction (who's talking to whom, when it is OK to talk or to direct the play, who's the de facto leader), understanding the rules (explicit or implicit) of the game, and processing fleeting and subtle social signals rapidly. Children with ASD may need specific teaching in understanding the rules of the game, controlling impulses to play differently, and tolerating losing. They often also need special coaching in group interaction (even in a group of three), and the speech-language therapist or school psychologist in your school may be able to help with this.

Motor Skills

Motor skills vary a lot from child to child. Some children with ASD, especially those with Asperger's disorder and those with mental retardation, have lots of motor problems. They may be clumsy and uncoordinated in gross motor activities, with poor balance. They may have trouble with fine motor dexterity, resulting in poor handwriting, poor coloring and drawing, and trouble manipulating objects in hands-on lessons. On the other hand, high functioning children with autism may appear remarkably graceful and well coordinated, and occasionally do well in organized sports and games. In our clinical experience, however, this is the exception rather than the rule. They may be very dexterous in performing highly preferred activities (one child we knew could make a tiny trash can with handles and lid out of paper in about fifteen seconds) but usually have less than stellar writing and gross motor coordination.

Writing and sports are perhaps the two activities most affected by motor difficulties. We will address these in more detail later in the book, but be aware that the child may need lots of sensitive help in getting over his or her dislike of writing activities, and in minimizing the social handicap represented by not doing well in sports and playground games.

Splinter Skills

Splinter skills are areas of ability that are above what the child can do in other areas. Strictly speaking, the skill should be in the normal or even unusually superior range compared to other children, but sometimes the term is used to describe skills that are just high points for that particular child. Most of you will have seen the movie *Rain Man* (if not, we highly recommend it!). The Dustin Hoffman character, based on several real-life autistic "savants" (the term sometimes used to describe individuals with striking splinter skills), is a good illustration of someone with the most frequently encountered skills—in this case, numeric calculation ability, calendar calculation (knowing the day of the week for dates far into the past and future), photographic memory, and visual processing (as when he "sees" the number of spilled matches). Other splinter skills may include musical memory, balance and coordination, and memory for routes and locations of objects.

Most splinter skills, unfortunately, are not of much use to build on when you're trying to teach the child useful skills. One exception is reading. Some children with ASD display what researchers call "hyperlexia"—the ability to decode written language at a young age. Although comprehension of written material almost always lags far behind the striking ability to read aloud, some of these children do understand written language at a higher level than they can understand spoken language. No one really knows why—whether it's the fascination they have with written language, or because no social interaction is needed to read, or because written language sits still on the page and doesn't require rapid processing as does spoken language. For whatever reason, some children can use written words and sentences as a gateway for communication. One child our colleague, Doris Allen, told us about was fascinated by numbers. The first time he ever spoke to his mother, he said "Hi, 303" (303 is 'mom' turned on its side!). See Chapter 10 for more information about reading abilities.

What Is the Connection between ASD and AD/HD?

Many of the characteristics of ASD that we've been discussing, such as poor attention, social difficulties, and communication handicaps, also apply to children with attention-deficit/hyperactivity disorder (AD/HD). As you are probably aware, AD/HD is a disorder that includes pronounced symptoms of inattention, hyperactivity/impulsivity, or both, and also frequently causes difficulties with executive functions.

Whether there is a relationship between AD/HD and autism is a complex question that is receiving increasing attention in the professional literature. One recent study by Helen Tager-Flusberg and colleagues found that although most children with AD/HD would not meet criteria for autism, many children with autism would meet criteria for AD/HD.

According to the DSM-IV, a child with autism cannot also be given a diagnosis of AD/HD because the autism supposedly "explains" the attention problems. Many researchers and clinicians feel that this is misguided, and it may well change in the next edition of the diagnostic manual. A recent book by a parent (Kennedy et al., 2002) explored the relationship between autism and AD/HD, especially the overlap in symptoms, and teachers may find this book useful. A recent paper by one of us (Fein et al., 2005) reported on a series of children who were diagnosed in early childhood with classic autism or PDD-NOS, and by middle childhood appeared to have classic AD/HD instead. In addition, some of the same medications that help children with AD/HD may be helpful for children with ASD who have notable problems in attention. These facts raise very interesting speculations about the relationship between the two sets of disorders. Marcel Kinsbourne, an eminent pediatric neurologist, has suggested that autism and ADHD are on a continuum, and should be regarded as involving the same brain systems.

In any case, symptoms of AD/HD are common in autism and may need specific intervention. In fact, many of the same techniques recommended for students with AD/HD are useful for students with ASD who have AD/HD behaviors:

- ample use of rewards,
- modification of the classroom environment and curriculum to make them interesting (using high interest materials and hands-on activities),
- keeping tasks, especially relatively boring tasks, short,
- reducing distractions from other interesting activities in the vicinity.

Other Related Syndromes

Semantic Pragmatic Language Disorder

You may see a child with ASD who also has a diagnosis of "semantic pragmatic language disorder." This is a term usually used by speech-language pathologists (SLPs). It refers to a language syndrome in which words are used in unusual ways and in which the pragmatic (social) uses of language are a weak point. Although not 100 percent overlapping, semantic pragmatic disorder and autism have a lot in common, and many children qualify for both diagnoses. If you have a child with this label, be sure to consult with the SLP about how best to adapt written and spoken language for the child, and also keep your eye out for social problems related to communication difficulties.

Nonverbal Learning Disorder

Nonverbal Learning Disorder (NVLD or NLD) is another syndrome that shares many features with ASD. Although not an official diagnosis in the DSM-IV, it has received a great deal of research attention recently. Just as specific language disorders are thought to reflect relative weakness in the left hemisphere of the brain, NVLD refers to a constellation of behaviors thought to reflect a weakness in the efficiency of the right hemisphere. These include:

- difficulties in getting the big picture (as opposed to focusing on details)—they can't see the forest for the trees;
- trouble with complex, abstract, and inferential aspects of reading comprehension;
- motor coordination difficulties;
- problems with math (with the spatial aspects of math more impaired than the simply computational procedures);
- spatial processing difficulties (shapes, routes, locations, geography, geometry, diagrams); and
- impaired social skills.

Children with NVLD also often have difficulty sustaining attention.

NVLD shares features with both AD/HD and ASD. A group of researchers at Yale (Fred Volkmar, Ami Klin, Sara Sparrow) who specialize in autism collaborated with a neuropsychologist who specializes in NVLD (Byron Rourke) and concluded that many children, although not all, with a diagnoses of NVLD would qualify for a diagnosis of Asperger's, and vice versa. The major difference between the two diagnoses is that NVLD is defined by a cognitive profile, while Asperger's is defined by a set of behaviors, but many children would meet criteria for both.

There are several books that outline useful teaching strategies for children with NVLD and you may well find their suggestions helpful in teaching children with Asperger's or other ASDs (see Suggested Reading). Keep in mind also that a child does not have to have impaired social skills for a diagnosis of NVLD. Some children with NVLD have normal social skills, although they may tend toward depression.

What Other Disorders Are Children with ASD at Risk For?

Anxiety

Many children with ASD have significant anxiety, while many others do not. In fact, there is an enormous range of anxiety in this group of children. At one extreme, a small number of children actually seem to lack anxiety when it would be appropriate. They have no sense of danger, and although they may express frustration, anger, or aggression, anxiety seems not to be on their menu.

In the middle of the anxiety continuum, many children with ASD express anxiety in situations where it would be expected: when demands are placed that they cannot meet, when something unpleasant is looming on the horizon (e.g., a doctor's visit), when they are in a strange place and they don't understand what is happening, or when their firm expectations are being violated. Compared to other children, they may have many more situations in which these feelings are present, may experience them more intensely, and may have more difficulty modulating their reactions.

At the extreme, a small number of individuals are incapacitated by extreme anxiety. One young man came to see one of us for a neuropsychological evaluation. He was so devastated by anxiety that the softest, simplest question (which picture is a banana?), well within his capacity to answer, produced a bout of hyperventilation, jumping, hand-flapping, and moaning, which it took his father several minutes to calm. This had all the appearance of extreme anxiety, rather than behavior designed to escape the demands being placed on him.

When anxiety interferes significantly with a child's functioning, it must be addressed directly, by relaxation training, cognitive behavior therapy (if the individual has the cognitive ability to benefit from it), or medication. If you have a student who seems extremely anxious, consult the school psychologist about how to deal with this in class; the school psychologist may also feel it is appropriate to counsel the child individually.

Depression

Some children with ASD develop clear-cut depression, especially at puberty or during adolescence. This is especially common in children with ASD who have the cognitive ability and insight to notice and be bothered by differences between their typically developing classmates and themselves. Some signs of depression to watch for are:
- sad or irritable mood a lot of the time;
- loss of interest or pleasure in activities they used to enjoy;
- changes in sleep or eating habits;
- negative self-statements ("I'm stupid," "I should never have been born," "I'm ugly," "Nobody likes me");

- frequent expectations of failure;
- frequent bodily complaints (headache, stomachache), and, of course;
- talk of suicide or doing oneself harm.

In some children, depression takes the form of irritability—being on a short fuse or irritated easily—rather than actual sadness.

Suspicion of depression should never be ignored, for several reasons: it can lead to self-destructive behavior, it can get ingrained, it can lead to a downward spiral of self-fulfilling negative expectation and behavior, and it can be treated. If you're concerned about signs of depression, talk to the guidance counselor, principal, or the child's parents.

Bipolar Disorder

Some children appear to cycle through periods of "highs" and "lows." They may go through days, weeks, or months of showing signs of depression or irritability, as described above, while, at other times, seem especially silly or hyperactive, with problems sleeping. All children have mood swings, and children with ASD are especially vulnerable to having good days and bad days. Furthermore, bipolar disorder (formerly known as manic-depression) is not known to be common in children with ASD. However, bipolar disorder can occur. Symptoms may include:

- mood swings that are pronounced, whether they're long, as in adults (weeks to months) or even short, as sometimes happens in children (hours to days),
- changes in mood that appear unrelated to what's going on in the classroom or not related to any specific event

If you notice these types of problems, it's worth mentioning to the parents, principal, or guidance counselor. If you have a student who is known to have bipolar disorder, you should talk to the child's parents or the school psychologist about what to expect and ask if there's any way you can help, such as keeping track of the child's attention and mood in school.

Psychosis

Psychosis is a serious psychological condition in which the individual loses touch with reality, either believing things that are not true (delusions), seeing or hearing things that are not there (hallucinations), or having severely disorganized thinking or speech. There have been case reports in which children with autism or Asperger's disorder went on to develop clear-cut psychoses, in most cases schizophrenia, a severe form of psychosis.

Most modern authorities, however, do not consider children with ASD to be at high risk for developing a psychotic disorder. One reason for the early written reports that associated ASD with schizophrenia may be pure chance. If 1 percent of the general population develops schizophrenia, then one might expect 1 percent of children with ASD to do the same. These cases might come to professional attention and be written up in the literature, leading people to believe there is a causal connection. Another reason may be misdiagnosis of psychosis by professionals not very familiar with ASD. We've seen several cases where typical autistic preoccupations were (in our opinion) misdiagnosed as delusions and thought disorder, resulting in a diagnosis of schizophrenia. In fact, childhood schizophrenia is quite rare, especially before the teenage years. In the unlikely event that you suspect that a child in your class is seeing, hearing, or believing things that are bizarre or unreal, consult with the school psychologist.

Obsessive-Compulsive Disorder (OCD)

This is a disorder that is more common in adolescents and adults than in children, but that gets its start in childhood. It is characterized by obsessions (unwanted, intrusive, repetitive thoughts of an unpleasant nature) and compulsions (mental or physical acts that the individual is compelled to repeat), that are thought to be for the purpose of warding off the obsessive thoughts. Compulsion can include, for example, checking and rechecking the gas or the lights to make sure they are off, counting, over-cleaning, and arranging things in a super-orderly manner.

You can see that autism has some features in common with OCD. As discussed in Chapter 1, many children on the autism spectrum have topics of interest or habits that they seem to be obsessed with. And, in fact, there has been some speculation that the repetitive behavior part of autism represents a form of OCD. What would be important for you as the teacher to notice is:

- whether the child becomes more than a little upset or anxious when not allowed to carry out her repetitive behaviors, or

- whether these behaviors seem to take up so much of her attention, effort, and time that they form a significant obstacle to learning, or
- whether they are taking on a different character (e.g., focusing on emotional topics such as illness or death, or becoming obsessed with another child), or
- whether the behaviors are increasing in intensity.

If you do observe any of these features, you should let the parent, principal, school psychologist, or guidance counselor know. There are some psychological treatments that can help (cognitive behavior therapy), as well as effective medications that can be prescribed. Chapter 12 offers strategies for handling some autistic repetitive behaviors, but if the child has frank OCD, you will need help from the school psychologist or an outside therapist on how to handle this in the class. You might also want to read one or two books on childhood OCD, such as Aureen Wagner's *What To Do When Your Child Has Obsessive-Compulsive Disorder.*

Tourette's Disorder (Tourette Syndrome)

Tourette's disorder is a syndrome in which there are both vocal and motor tics over a period of time. Vocal tics are involuntary sounds (grunting, throat-clearing, coughing) or verbal exclamations, including, unfortunately, curses. Motor tics are involuntary body movements, such as shoulder shrugging or eye closing.

Although not frequent in autism, some studies have found that Tourette syndrome is more common in ASD than in the general population. Some psychiatrists believe that stimulant medication given to improve attention in children with ASD can elicit tics in children who are predisposed to them, although some recent studies cast doubt on this. With removal of the medication, the tics may abate. However, sometimes they persist and it is felt that the stimulant medication simply unmasked a predisposition for a tic disorder. If the medicine significantly improves the child's functioning, it will usually be continued. Tics can be reduced and sometimes eliminated with other medication, and for the higher functioning child, may be helped with behavioral therapy in which the child learns to partially control her own tics.

What Happens to the Child with ASD in Adolescence and Adulthood?

There is very little research on long-range outcomes for children with ASD who have been through public school programs. There is even less that breaks down outcomes by diagnosis (autism vs. PDD-NOS vs. Asperger's) or by intellectual level. Drs. Fred Volkmar and Ami Klin (2001) reviewed some of the research on outcomes and concluded that about two-thirds of even high-functioning individuals with autism continue to need supervision and support, while one-third achieve some degree of independence and self-sufficiency. Few achieve complete economic and social independence as adults, and even fewer marry and have families.

This picture may be changing, however. First of all, most adults with autism in the current outcome studies were educated ten or twenty years ago or more. Education today is generally much better for children with special needs, and so the outcome for today's children may be more positive. In addition, ASD diagnoses in the past were not applied to some individuals with high functioning autism or Asperger's disorder, who may have the best outcome. Even though they may continue to struggle with social, communication, or sensory handicaps, they may reach economic and social independence and develop meaningful and satisfying social relationships.

Finally, a significant number of young children with ASD who receive aggressive early intervention, especially behavioral teaching, may truly overcome their social disabilities and may participate in school, home, and community life with minimal supports. These children, although they may still have some relatively minor difficulties with attention, social subtleties, or specific academic difficulties, have an excellent prognosis and may be no more different from their typical peers than children with minor learning differences or somewhat unusual personalities.

3 | What Causes Autism Spectrum Disorders?

This chapter will review what is known about the causes of autism spectrum disorders. Although this information will not directly affect how you understand or deal with your students with ASD, many teachers have asked us for a summary of this information, so they can understand what is believed to cause ASD. It might affect how you deal with, or understand, the child's family, since outdated notions of the causes of ASD held that how the parents (especially the moms) treated the child was directly responsible for "autistic withdrawal." It is important to know that this is not true.

This is a very rapidly changing field, with many large-scale studies being conducted on genetics, brain chemistry, brain organization, and other aspects of biology, so the discussion may be a bit outdated before it's even published! All this research is an excellent thing for the field of autism, although so far it has not led to any highly effective treatments.

Introduction

Families and professionals have been wondering about the causes of these mysterious disorders since Leo Kanner first described "infantile autism" in 1943. Have we made progress? The short answer is that while we don't yet know the specific causes, we have been zeroing in on the areas in which the answers will be found. Those areas are genes, abnormalities in brain development, the chemistry of the brain, and possibly environmental factors. These are not mutually exclusive: a set of genes may be found that result in abnormal brain development and/or brain chemistry, and these may interact with environmental factors to cause autism.

There is a sad history in medical thinking about the causes of autism. Kanner's first intuition was that autism was an "innate defect"; that is, biological, but the times were against him. Freudian and other psychodynamic branches of psychiatry ruled, and for several decades, the prevalent view was that the parents' treatment of the child was somehow responsible for his withdrawing from reality and from human relationships.

Looking back, we wonder how something so implausible could have been accepted by so many. Parents who appeared perfectly normal and had three other normal children were thought to have done something to their child so subtle it couldn't be seen but so harmful that he sat mute in a corner rocking and twiddling his fingers! What started the turn toward the search for biological causes was the general movement of psychiatry toward biological thinking, but more specifically Bernard Rimland's 1964 book *Infantile Autism: The Syndrome and Its Implications for a Neural Theory of Behavior.* In this groundbreaking work, Rimland elegantly pointed out the farfetched nature of the psychological arguments, and put forth a plausible brain-based theory. Biological study of autism really got going in the 1970s and has accelerated greatly in the last ten years.

The Genetic Basis of Autism

As recently as the mid-1970s, autism was thought not to be inherited, but then Michael Rutter and Susan Folstein showed that it tended to run in families. Several types of genetic studies have been done since then, with most of the work done quite recently. First, family studies have examined:

1. the risk of having another child with autism once you've had one,
2. the risk of having a child with some autistic features such as language delay once you've had a child with autism,
3. what other disorders run in the same families, and
4. characteristics of family members, especially parents.

Research generally suggests that the risk of having a second child with autism is somewhere between 2 and 10 percent, but that the risk of having a child with other learning difficulties such as a delay in learning to speak may be as high as 30 percent. If one identical twin has autism, the chances are about 60 percent that the other twin will have autism and perhaps as high as 90 percent that the twin will have some form of learning disability. This strongly suggests a genetic link.

Some research suggests that autism may be linked to other psychiatric disorders in families, such as depression, but this is not firmly established. Other studies suggest that parents, especially fathers, may show some of their children's tendencies in mild form, such as social isolation, trouble communicating, feeling more comfortable with intellectual than social pursuits, preference for routines, and a tendency to obsessive interests. We hasten to point out, however, that while this may be true, it can be a very subtle effect, requiring sophisticated methodology to demonstrate it, and that most parents we deal with are sensible and dedicated, with the same range of personality issues as the rest of us.

Other studies are scanning the entire set of human genes, looking for particular forms of genes that are found in children with autism. The problem with these studies is not that they are failing to find links to specific genes, but that they are finding too many, and not the same ones in each study! Some experts estimate that there may be anywhere from 10 to 50 different genes interacting to produce autism, and that these may be somewhat different in different families. Thus, autism clearly has a genetic basis, but the genetics involved appear to be highly complicated, and research does not appear to be on the brink of a breakthrough that will identify *the* autism gene.

Brain Abnormalities

Brain abnormalities have been investigated by studying the brains of individuals with autism who have died and whose brains have been donated to researchers by their families in order to help our understanding of the disorder. Brain abnormalities have also been studied by looking at the brains of living patients with CAT scans and MRIs.

One consistent finding has been that people with autism tend to have larger brains than others of the same age. Very recently, Eric Courchesne, a San Diego researcher, reported that many children with autism are born with rather small heads, but that their heads grow too fast during the first year of life, and they wind up with overly big heads.

This discovery may lead to new theories about brain development in autism and may help identify the children very early. Other researchers, such as Margaret Bauman and Tom Kemper, Boston neurologists, report that children with autism have small, tightly packed, immature-looking cells in areas of the brain known to control emotion, learning, and motor coordination.

An important technological development, known as functional Magnetic Resonance Imaging (fMRI for short), allows researchers to actually watch different areas of the children's brains "light up" as they are activated while performing tasks. This research is just getting started, but the first studies suggest that children with ASD use different brain areas than typically developing children do (although generally the brain areas are close to each other) in understanding what other people are thinking, or in understanding others' facial expressions. Another recent study suggests that different brain areas that are supposed to be working closely together as the child does a task, such as understanding sentences, are not working together or communicating as they should be. These studies offer tantalizing clues about how the autistic brain may be working differently from typical brains, but this field is still in its infancy.

Possible Environmental Factors

Whenever such potentially devastating conditions strike, it is very natural to search the environment for potential causes or triggers, and autism is no exception. Witness the search for environmental toxins in cancer clusters. You may be able to think of times in your own life when you searched for an environmental cause of an illness or accident. (What did I eat? What could I have done differently? What could I have avoided?)

The search for environmental causes of autism has so far not been successful. Several instances of apparent clustering of cases—for example, in New Jersey and Massachusetts—have set parents and professionals looking for toxic dumps, chemical plants, and the like. So far, however, no definite link has been established between such sites and increased incidence of autism.

Another environmental suspect has been early childhood vaccination, specifically the MMR vaccine. Autism sometimes starts in the second year of life, around the time of the measles-mumps-rubella (MMR) vaccination, and some parents suspected that the vaccination (sometimes followed by a reaction including fever) triggered or caused their child's development of autistic symptoms. Some thought it was the combination of three vaccines in one that put too much stress on the immune system. Consequently, some parents now insist that the three inoculations be given to their children separately. Others thought it was specifically the measles component, on the theory that it injured the lining of the stomach and made it too permeable ("leaky gut"), while still others thought it might be the thimeresol (a form of mercury) included as a preservative in the vaccine.

Several studies recently completed strongly suggest that vaccination is unrelated to the onset of autism, including a study in Denmark of many thousands of children, which found there was no more autism in vaccinated than unvaccinated children. Furthermore, recent studies have pointed out that removing the thimeresol does not seem to have reduced the number of cases of autism. This issue is still hotly debated, however, with some parent groups lining up on one side and the medical establishment generally on the other side. The Centers for Disease Control in Atlanta has taken the position that current vaccinations are safe and unrelated to autism, and strongly stresses the dangers of not vaccinating children. In fact, measles may be on the upswing in some areas, especially in England, where some parents are refusing to let their children be vaccinated. This issue is far from settled, however, and as we go to press, a court case concerning autism-related injury from vaccines is making headlines.

Another popular theory is that certain foods can cause or worsen symptoms of autism in certain children. Foods containing wheat or dairy are particularly suspect, and many children have been tried on the "gluten-casein-free diet" (see Chapter 2). Many parents report improvements in behavior and in gastrointestinal functioning (in particular, less diarrhea). Large-scale controlled studies of this diet are just getting started, so we can only speak from our clinical observations. Many children with ASD, particularly those with more challenging behaviors, can vary in mood and behavior from day to day. It is easy to attribute a bad day to the sip of chocolate milk that the child took before he could be stopped. However, we have seen little consistent improvement in behavior or cognitive skills in children on "the diet."

Some nutritionists are concerned about the restricted diet that results from eliminating all casein- and gluten-containing foods, and worry that the child may be missing crucial nutrients. We also worry about the social isolation that can result when a child has to eat special food and can't accept pizza, ice cream, or birthday cake (unless, of course, a real allergy exists). However, we all must wait until the studies are completed to see if there are specific children who do better with these foods removed from their diets, and, of course, we must respect the parents' wishes and directives concerning what their children eat.

Does Family or Society Have Anything to Do with Causing Autism?

The simple answer is: not as far as we know.

Most families we've met are doing the best they can with difficult children. Some are well meaning but don't know how to control their children. Some mistakenly think that their job is to prevent the child from experiencing any distress, a distress the child may need to go through in order to start making serious progress. (But what parent hasn't felt that way?) As with any child, some parents will engage in child abuse, out of frustration, grief, rage, or despair. Some parents are superbly effective in loving and educating their child and helping him to reach his full potential.

So, parents can affect the outcome for their child with autism, by their parenting skills and by advocating effectively for the best education and other treatments, but they didn't cause the autism in the first place.

There are some extreme social-environmental conditions (such as in the worst orphanages in eastern Europe and Asia) where the children are so deprived of love, attention, language, opportunities to play, and even opportunities to move around, use their hands, and have adequate food, that physical and mental retardation can result. In some cases, these children will have symptoms that are reminiscent of some features of autism (such as hand flapping, aggression, failure to speak, or failure to emotionally attach normally). However, these children usually make rapid progress once placed in optimal environments and do not show the full autistic syndrome. Furthermore, they can be easily identified by their history.

Is There an Autism "Epidemic"?

There have been innumerable reports of autism on the increase. Some reports suggest that the incidence of autism has gone up as much as six-fold in the last twenty years. What could be causing this apparent increase?

First, there could indeed be a real increase in the incidence of autism. Perhaps parents who would have stopped having children in the past after having one child with autism are now seeing better outcomes and are therefore continuing to have children. Perhaps toxins accumulating in our environment or other factors such as exposure to radiation are causing the increase. There is, however, no scientific evidence for any such links.

Another factor could be society's increased sensitivity to the presence of autism. Ten or twenty years ago, some "lower functioning" children with ASD might have been diagnosed with mental retardation rather than autism, and "higher functioning" children with ASD might have been diagnosed with a different behavioral disorder such as AD/HD, or not diagnosed with anything.

A related possibility is that the application of the diagnostic criteria has gotten broader. Perhaps twenty years ago, a socially clumsy child who wanted friends would not have satisfied the diagnostic criterion of "poor peer relationships" but now he would.

An important factor is doubtless the increased awareness that if a child receives an ASD diagnosis, he can get ASD services. ASD services have greatly improved over the past twenty years, and can benefit children with classic autism as well as those who are less affected, such as those with PDD-NOS, Asperger's disorder, and even children with other diagnoses altogether. Previously, these less affected children might not have received a diagnosis on the autism spectrum because the professional wanted to spare the parents' feelings, or the parents did not want their child stigmatized by an autism diagnosis. Now, the child is likely to get the diagnosis, because, as special education services are cut for other disorders, they are generally increasing for children with ASD because of effective parent advocacy.

So, our conclusion on this subject is that the jury is still out. Autism could be on the increase, but rigorous studies that really control for different applications of diagnostic criteria and for more children being brought to professional attention have not yet been done.

4 | The Impact of Autism on the Family

The child with ASD in your classroom is part of a family. Whether it's a two-parent, traditional nuclear family, or some other configuration, the child's life is nested for most of the hours of the day in a family. Her mood, behavior, and communication skills will depend partly on her family's functioning. Your ability to form a working partnership with the family will be helped if you are sensitive to the possible stresses the family may be under and the overall impact of autism on all the members of the family.

Effects on Parents

Emotional effects on parents of having a child with an autism spectrum disorder can be profound. The early emotional effects include shock, denial, despair, grief. Parents often have to go through a process of mourning for the bright, sociable, "normal" child everyone expects to have. It is natural to seek the cause: Was it the fall I had when I was pregnant? Was it the one drink of alcohol I let myself have? Was it the doctor being late for the delivery? Was it the vaccination our child had shortly before the autism became apparent? Anger and blame can be turned inward on the self, outward on the doctor or the manufacturer of the vaccine, or on the marriage partner.

Most of these feelings will be resolved to some extent by the time the child is in grade school, but their effects linger. Until the child is well into adolescence (and sometimes not even then), some parents wonder about how much "recovery" is possible—how close to "normal" the child will be able to be. They must live with much more than the usual uncertainty we all face about our children's futures. Each new milestone may renew, although hopefully in muted form, their feelings of loss and grief. For example, all the other children in first grade have speaking parts in the school play, but Jasmine just stands with her aide on the stage in a costume. On the other hand, parents can learn to focus on small achievements and rejoice in small successes. So, the fact that Jasmine can understand that there *is* a play and that she is a part of it, and stand quietly for twenty minutes on the stage, may be a matter of celebration and gratitude.

Marital Stress

Coping with a disability affects marriages in many possible ways. When the marriage is strong to begin with, and especially when the parents share deeply held values rooted in religion or cultural values, or in beliefs about the solidity of their marriage, and when each has confidence in themselves and trust in the other, this stress can weather and strengthen a marriage. Parents learn that they can trust each other and that they can depend on one another to share burdens and provide emotional support. We have both seen many wonderful relationships endure and thrive with even the most difficult children.

One factor that plays an important role here, in our clinical observations, is the father's comfort with the child, and with children in general. The men who are "naturals" with children, the ones you can imagine happily fathering a brood of six children, often do very well in handling and adjusting to a child with a significant disability. The fathers who are more emotionally remote, or just uncomfortable with children, sometimes put up major barriers to good early intervention because they convince themselves that their child is "just a little late to talk, like I was." Mothers are sometimes put in the position of having to search for proper services for their child while their husband tells them they are overreacting or harming the child by labeling her with a disability. Of course, it can work the other way, but it usually doesn't!

If you're married and have nice, typically developing children, you may have sometimes allowed yourself a little smugness: "Look at the great kids our marriage produced—doesn't that prove we were meant to be together?" So, what does the child with a disability say to parents about their marriage? This possible loss of faith in the marriage can be counteracted by a firm belief in the rightness of the marriage, by the presence of typically developing children in the family, or by religious beliefs.

More mundane issues also place tremendous burdens on the marriage: Each parent is now under more emotional stress and in need of comfort and reassurance. The breadwinner is under more pressure to bring in the money the family may need more than ever. In a family where both parents work, the mother may feel torn between the need to work and the need to be home to look after and advocate for the child with ASD. The child with a disability may need inordinate amounts of time from the main caretaking parent, leaving the other parent to feel emotionally abandoned. Parents may disagree about the best way to handle the disability, medically or educationally, or about how to balance the time needed for other children.

Single Parents

Single parents shoulder extra burdens. Their time is stretched even thinner, handling the responsibilities of work, household, and children all by themselves. With no steady partner with whom to discuss problems and possible solutions, the single parent must rely on his or her own judgment. Two-parent families in our modern society often feel themselves on the brink of collapse, and feel that one more stressor—a serious illness, an aging grandparent needing more help, an extra financial burden—will topple the whole edifice. How much more does a single parent feel that way: there is truly no margin of error, no reserves to call upon.

The most important factor for single parents is the emotional and financial support of their extended family or other support system. Grandparents often come through with much-needed childcare help, and we've known many a single mom who was accompanied to evaluations by her own parents. For single mothers who are more socially isolated, or who have friends but no reliable help with childcare or decision making, raising a child with a disability can be extremely difficult.

If your student with ASD, therefore, has a single parent, keep in mind that this parent may be stretched quite thin in time and resources. He or she may have little flexibility when planning time to meet with you, and may not have the time or energy that others might have in helping with homework. Any assistance you can provide in flexible meeting times or specific assistance with homework suggestions is likely to be very helpful.

Social Pressure

One stress faced by many parents of children with a behavioral disability (rather than an obvious, physical one) is social pressure from the larger community. Imagine taking your four-year-old child with autism to the grocery store and trying to hold the line on giving her candy (or whatever her preferred treat is). When the disability is not immediately visible, many people will automatically assume you're just a bad parent who can't control your child. Parents will often be blamed, even by their own extended families, for aspects of their child's behavior or development that are beyond their immediate control, compounding their own sense of guilt, responsibility, and helplessness.

How Are Family Resources to Be Allocated?

This is another set of issues that is difficult for any family to resolve, but is more difficult for families who have a child with ASD. The family is moving to another state; do they move to the town with the best special education programs, even if it is not necessarily best for the other children? Do they go to Elizabeth's sixth grade school play or attend the monthly clinic about Charley? Emotional, financial, and time resources are stretched even thinner than in other families.

Many families, of course, cope beautifully. We are filled with admiration on a regular basis for families who are managing to stay psychologically healthy and keep a positive attitude, communicating openly with all family members, meeting the needs of other children, keeping their sense of humor, and appearing devoted to and respectful of each other's opinions. But we remind ourselves regularly of what kind of effort and strength it's taken them to achieve this state.

Effects on Siblings

What about the effects on siblings of having a sister or brother with ASD? This depends on the child's personality, the relative ages of the siblings, the family resources, how the parents treat the children, and how they explain the autism spectrum disorder. Effects can, of course, change with the children's development. The reactions of siblings run the gamut: we've heard many stories about siblings who adore their sisters or brothers with ASD, take care of them, play with them, become a miniature therapist for them, and let them tag along. We've also heard many stories about children who have tremendous resentment against the child with ASD or want nothing to do with him or her.

If you teach young children, you know that they can accept amazing things as long as they are presented in a matter-of-fact manner. (I'll never forget my kindergarten daughter telling me happily that Susie was back in school after several months, with a toy leg because the doctors cut her leg off!) Children in the early grades may tell you straightforwardly that their older or younger sibling has autism and needs special help to talk or to play. Very young children will adapt their play to suit the capacities of the sibling with ASD; instead of playing superhero or building a rocket ship with Legos, she may have to settle for chase and tickle games. However, things get more complex and confusing as the child gets older. She will begin to really question why Charley can only do certain very simple games with her, and express sadness or loneliness that she can't really talk to her older brother like her friends can talk to their siblings. She may worry (perhaps unconsciously) about whether she did something to cause her sibling's disability (just as parents do).

Having a sibling with ASD can cut into a child's social life. He or she may be embarrassed by the sibling's behavior and may be unwilling to have friends over to play. This has become less true over the last twenty years, as more and more of the general public understand something about autism or Asperger's syndrome. The child with ASD can still present a problem for siblings and their friends if the child destroys their property or insists on joining a game that is beyond her understanding. Parents are wise if they safeguard the other siblings' time with friends and make sure that they are not expected to include the child with ASD at least part of the time.

Resentment is common in later childhood and adolescence. One reason is that the child with ASD may intrude on the sibling's space, destroy his or her possessions, or even be physically aggressive. Sometimes, the child with ASD doesn't get punished for doing the same things the sibling gets punished for—how unfair does that seem to a child!

Even in families where the adolescent sibling feels a great responsibility for the child with ASD and tries to help out, he or she may resent the amount of family resources that have to go toward helping the child with ASD. Money for her summer camp, for example, may have to go instead for extra summer therapy hours for the child with ASD. Mom may be unable to go to her soccer game because she has to take the child with ASD to an OT session. Parents may be tired, emotionally exhausted, worried, financially strained, and pay less attention to any difficulties or successes the sibling has than they would under other circumstances.

One family we knew had three children, one with ASD. The family had been discussing a trip to Disney World, but the mother was afraid the child with ASD couldn't handle the plane ride or the park, and didn't feel it was fair to take the siblings on a trip the child with ASD couldn't enjoy. In the end, they found a nice solution by taking another adult along, so the child with ASD could splash in the motel pool while the siblings went on the rides.

Every child needs time alone with a parent—to confide successes, problems, and anxieties, or just to get undivided attention and affection. With a child with ASD in the family, it may be very difficult for the sibling to get that undivided attention on a regular basis, unless it's been built into the family routine. If a sibling of a child with ASD confides resentment or other negative feelings to you as her teacher, you should listen sympathetically, reassure her that these feelings are understandable, and encourage her to be direct with her parents about these feelings, if she can. If the feelings seem really negative, or you suspect the child is depressed, you should let the parents know (and don't make promises of confidentiality that you may not be able to keep).

Sometimes siblings of children with ASD, whether older or younger, take on a prematurely adult role in the family. They give up some or even all of their childhood pleasures and take on too much adult responsibility—a "pseudo adult" syndrome. Of course, some of this extra responsibility—such as babysitting—may be driven by the family's financial status and can't be helped, but it also occurs in families of ample financial means. Sometimes the child is being driven by a sense of guilt, a deep-seated anxiety over the parents' distress, or a strong desire to nurture the parents and ameliorate their distress.

Siblings of children with ASD are at a somewhat higher risk, not only of having a form of ASD, but also of having milder learning difficulties, such as language and reading problems or AD/HD. We've seen many families who had one child with ASD and one (or more) with AD/HD. The child with AD/HD may have the potential for great academic and social success, but may need extra parental help to achieve this. If the child with ASD demands a lot of the parents' time, they may forget, or be unable, to give extra assistance to the child with AD/HD. If Amanda needs constant supervision, it can be very difficult to help her brother Tommy with math homework, or call another mom to arrange a play date with Tommy's potential friend.

On the positive side, as with all disabilities, if siblings develop a sense of responsibility and a desire to help their parents, this can sometimes draw the family closer together, and the nondisabled sibling can benefit from this family solidarity. There are several excellent books for and about siblings of children with disabilities, some specific to autism, including *Siblings of Children with Autism* by Sandra Harris and Beth Glasberg, in the same series as this book. Dr. Harris's book explores the emotional reactions of siblings in detail, as well as how to discuss autism and related disorders with them.

Do Parents Usually Want Their Child Included in Regular Education?

Before addressing this question, it is important to understand two points:

1. Under the federal special education law known as the Individuals with Disabilities Education Act (IDEA), a child's educational placement is supposed to be based on where he or she can best achieve her goals and still have the maximum contact with typically developing peers. Put another way, students should be placed in the most inclusive setting where they can achieve their individualized goals.

2. The purpose of inclusion is *not* to enable a child to "keep up" with the regular curriculum and learn everything that her typically developing peers are learning. Instead, the purpose is to allow the child contact with typically developing peers and access to the regular education curriculum, provided she can meet her goals in that setting.

As you can see, the child's goals are supposed to be of paramount importance in determining how much (if any) inclusion is right for any given child. If the child has goals she can achieve in a general education classroom, she should be in a general education classroom. If the child has goals she cannot meet in a general education classroom, she should not be in a general education classroom.

Some children (especially at younger ages) may not be working on grade level, but may still have goals that can be achieved in a general education class. For example, a student with ASD might have a goal to learn to write a one-paragraph essay using a keyboard while her peers are learning to write a three-paragraph report in cursive, and that student's goal might be achievable in an inclusive classroom. Or a student whose academic skills are far below grade level might be placed in a regular classroom for at least part of the day because her primary goals are to learn to share, to make eye contact, and to use an augmentative communication device to communicate with typically developing students. Then again, there may be students who are working on grade level or above but who cannot achieve their goals in a regular classroom for one reason or another (e.g., the setting is too distracting for them).

So, ideally the educational placement that parents want for their child with ASD should be based on careful consideration of their educational goals for their child. And these goals should, in turn, be based on a realistic assessment of the child's learning strengths and challenges. (As you will read in Chapter 6, these goals are to be jointly decided upon by parents, teachers, and therapists, and written up in an official document called an Individualized Education Program, or IEP. Everyone who works together to develop the IEP is called collectively the IEP Team.) Together with teachers, therapists, and other members of the IEP team, everyone should determine how and where the child's goals can best be met.

In practice, the answer to the question as to whether parents want inclusion is:

1. Some parents **want** their child to be included, because either:
    a. they think that is where their child can best achieve her goals, or
    b. for other reasons (e.g., they want their child to go to the same school as a sibling or other reasons discussed below).

2. Some parents **do not want** their child to be included, because either:
   a. they think she would achieve her goals better in another setting, or
   b. for other reasons (e.g., worrying that other children would tease their child in a typical class or any of a myriad of reasons discussed below).

As you can see, some parents want their child to be included or not included for the "right" reasons under the law (1a and 2a) and some parents have other reasons for their preferences. If you are a member of an IEP meeting making a placement decision (see Chapter 6), you will have the opportunity to try to help guide parents and the team to making the "right" decision based on that child's individualized goals and your opinion of whether they can be met in a general education classroom. However, if a child is placed in your classroom, it is your responsibility to try to help her achieve her goals, whether or not you think your classroom is the best place to work on them.

To help you understand some of the reasoning that may lead to a student with ASD being placed in a general education class, we have divided parents into several groups below. Remember, though, that many parents do not fit neatly into one of these groups and may have entirely different reasons for thinking that their child does or does not belong in an inclusive classroom.

Parents Who Want Their Child Included

To Meet Academic Goals

Parents often want their child to be included when she has some or many cognitive abilities that are "normal" for her age, and can clearly learn at least a good part of the grade level material, perhaps with some extra help or modifications to the curriculum. Sometimes these children have developed this way without too much early intervention, and may fit into the category of Asperger's disorder. Or they may have been more severely autistic as a toddler and reached their current development only by heroic efforts by parents and teachers. These parents feel, rightly, that the child's social behavior will be most normalized by exposure to typical peers, and by interacting with these peers with some adult help. They are also hopeful that their child can learn some or most of the regular education curriculum.

Since IDEA mandates inclusion when possible, and because inclusion tends to be less expensive than some other options, these parents may not meet much resistance from the school system. But in some school systems, the prevailing belief is that children with autism should be in separate classes, both for their benefit and for that of the teachers and other children. Or, it may be less expensive for the school to put the child in an autism classroom than to provide the one-on-one aide that will make inclusion possible. In this case, the parents may have a dispute on their hands.

To Learn Other Skills

Sometimes when a child is more disabled by ASD and lacks basic skills such as a workable communication system or full toilet training, a parent might think she can learn these skills in an inclusive classroom. Other members of the IEP team might think that a better use of the child's time might be to learn a basic functional communication system, or improve her verbal communication, plus learn self-help skills such as toileting and dressing, and master simple academic concepts (shapes, colors, letters, etc.), or listen to stories.

Whether or not this child will be placed in an inclusive setting for all or part of the school day depends on a number of variables, including her age, the types of specialized settings available in the community, how forcibly the parents and their advocates argue for inclusion, the attitudes of the principal and special education team, etc. Even if this child is not placed in an inclusive setting in the beginning, it is possible that she may learn skills that enable her to be at least partially included at a later time.

An example of a child who in our opinion would be better served outside of an inclusive classroom is Davey:

Davey is seven years old. He has the communication skills of a 12- to 18-month-old child. He can say a few words, mostly requests for food items or preferred activities, and he understands some simple commands and words for objects. He shows no interest in other children. He is only partly toilet trained. He does not dress himself and does not help with any chores around the house.

What is to be gained by placing him in a regular first grade class on a full-time basis? Will he understand any part of the classroom activities or material? Or will he waste precious time that could be spent teaching him better communication and self-help skills, perhaps along with spending some limited time with the typically developing children during nonacademic time?

For Other Reasons

Just a few of the other reasons parents may have for wanting their child with ASD to be included are:

- They may think that placing their child in a separate educational program is a final admission that the child is, and always will be, different.
- They may think that their child will be able to copy the typical children's behavior and will thereby be able to catch up with social skills. Or they may not want their child to copy the inappropriate behavior of children in disability-specific classes.
- Even if they don't think their child can catch up, they don't want the child discriminated against and stigmatized by being kept separate.
- They may think that the alternative programs—whether for children with autism or disabilities in general—are not good ones, or are not appropriate for their child and therefore that the regular classroom is the best option. Perhaps they have gone to visit the noninclusive options in the community and have been horrified by the lack of materials, teachers' attitudes or lack of skills, behavior management methods, or other things they observed in those classrooms.
- They may have read studies finding that students in inclusive classrooms learn more than those in segregated classes.
- They may believe that their child has better cognitive skills than revealed by intelligence testing and that she is capable of learning some or all of the regular curriculum even though she cannot (yet) communicate her understanding.
- They may want their child with ASD to attend the same school as her siblings do.
- They may feel that the school will be less accountable for what and how much their child learns if she is not in a general education classroom—especially if the school

wishes to place the child in a program where an "alternative" test is administered to track progress instead of the one given to most other students.

- They may have tried a more segregated classroom for their child and concluded it didn't work.
- Other parents in the community with children with ASD may have convinced them their child will do best in an inclusive class.

Parents Who Do Not Want Their Child Included

What about parents who do not want their children in an inclusive classroom? In some cases, this will be because the child is like Davey, above. He or she has significant disabilities and the parents believe their child really would benefit more from a full-time specialized program (in our view, the parent is correct to resist including the child, in these instances). In some cases, where the child is really quite suited to inclusion, the parent may have read that specialized programs, especially ABA programs, are the child's best hope for a good outcome. The parent may not realize that their child has developed beyond the need for mainly one-on-one teaching and is ready to benefit from a typical classroom—a great milestone for a child with ASD.

Some other reasons parents may not want their child to be included:

- They are afraid their child will be bullied or teased by typically developing students.
- Although their child is making some progress in the regular classroom, they think she would make more progress in a smaller class with more specialized teaching—perhaps because she also has AD/HD or a nonverbal learning disability (NVLD).
- They think their child will be overstimulated or get lost in a crowded, noisy environment.
- They think she would benefit from social skills classes or organizational help available in a specialized program for students with Asperger syndrome.
- The public schools in your area (rightly or wrongly) do not have a good reputation among parents for including students with ASD effectively.

Parents Who Are Not Sure How They Feel about Inclusion

The best path for a parent who is not sure what the best educational option is may be to get an outside professional evaluation and ask the professional for his or her opinion about the best placement for the child at that time in her development. This evaluation should be performed by someone who is not involved directly in the child's education. The evaluator may have his or her own biases, but will not have a vested professional or financial interest in the placement.

What It's Like for Parents to Cope with the Special Education Maze

Some parents master the intricacies of the special education labyrinth more easily than others. You might think this would be a function of their education, social class, or occupational level, but we haven't generally found this to be the case. We've seen many working class parents without a higher education who are familiar with the main regulations governing their child's education, have a good sense of what their child needs, and are assertive but not hostile or adversarial in trying to get the best services for their child. We've also seen highly educated, sophisticated parents, some in health professions, who do not recognize that their child has a disability until it is pointed out to them, and who do not understand their child's educational rights until they are explained to them rather late in the game.

Some parents enter the school system when their child is three with a rather naïve trust that the school's only motivation is to provide their child with the best possible services. The dawning understanding that the school system may have other priorities and other needs, such as saving money on their child's program so that they can hire a desperately needed teacher for their overcrowded fourth grade, may result in a sudden disillusionment. As a result, they may find it difficult to trust their child's welfare to anyone in the public school.

IEP team meetings and evaluations can be overwhelming for parents. Everyone else on the team has done this a hundred times, knows the procedures, probably knows what the school is proposing for a program, and doesn't have a vested emotional interest. The parent, on the other hand, may be new to the procedures, may not understand the technical aspects of evaluations that are reported, may find the IEP extremely confusing, and may not know that they have the right to disagree with an IEP in whole or in part. They may also disagree with evaluations that show that the child is or is not progressing well, but have no idea how to contradict the experts' data and opinions.

We have attended team meetings where the team was sensitive to the parents' feelings and truly solicited their opinions about what was being said and what was being suggested. On the other hand, we have attended team meetings where the parents were ignored, denigrated, or even ridiculed, and where their obvious emotional distress was treated with coldness or with disdain. There is no excuse for such behavior on the part of education professionals.

If you ever feel tempted to entertain such reactions, try putting yourself in the parent's shoes. You will most likely only have the responsibility for this child for a few hours a day for nine or ten months. The parent has the responsibility for the child forever, in addition to the intense emotional attachment that makes the outcome so important. The parent may feel (to some extent correctly) that progress in each school year can affect the child's ultimate happiness and independence. How would you feel, and what would you do, under similar circumstances?

The Importance of Teacher-Parent Communication

What should you expect in dealing with the parents of your student with ASD? The answer to this may be obvious from the foregoing discussion. A lot will depend on the parents' previous experiences with teachers. Have they found teachers to be generally competent, caring, and sensitive? Or have they encountered some who were rigid, inexperienced, or indifferent? Have the teachers been good but the school administration unreachable?

You may pay the price, at least initially, for the behavior of past teachers or administrators. Parents may have expectations for the year that you will rapidly determine to be unrealistic. Parents' anxieties may make them seem demanding or needy. On the other hand, parents may treat you as an all-knowing savior, and not feel the need to communicate any specific information about their child.

The most important factor in determining how the year will go is whether you can develop a working relationship with the parents; in psychological jargon, a therapeutic alliance—a partnership between teacher and parent designed to help the child. If parents do not feel the need for communication above and beyond what you would have with parents of typical children, don't take the easy way out and accept this. Let them know that you will be better able to teach their child if you know how the child is doing at home, and set up some regular system of communication, either by phone, e-mail, note, or face-to-face meetings (if this has not already been specified in the child's IEP).

How often you communicate is up to you and your school. If you can get a half hour built into your schedule each week or every other week, this may suffice. For parents who make unrealistic demands on your time, suggest that you will set aside some specific time for them, to meet or talk on the phone, in addition to sending written notes (see below). If they know they will talk to you at 12:30 on Wednesday, they will be more likely to be able to hold what they have to say and they can always send notes about emergency situations.

The importance of communication between you and the child's parents would be hard to overestimate. In many places throughout the book, we suggest topics that may fruitfully be discussed between teachers and parents. Some of these concern questions you may want to ask parents about their child, to seek information that you feel will help you teach her most effectively from day to day. Some of them concern things you observe about the child, things you feel that parents should know—either general observations, or changes in behavior that are important for parents to know about. Sometimes you will have the child's successes to communicate, sometimes difficulties. This is not always easy. Parents may not want to hear about difficulties. They may resent questions. They may be difficult to get on the telephone or may not respond to notes or e-mail. But it is your professional responsibility to try your best.

Earning the Parents' Trust

As psychologists, we also encounter difficulties—for example, when we have to tell parents that an assessment suggests that their child is not doing as well as they thought. The key is trust. If we have spent enough time really listening to parents, so that they know we are concerned and will give them the most useful and honest information we can, communication is made much easier. The same can hold for teachers. You will form the basis for a good working relationship if you spend time talking to parents, and let them know that:

- You really want to form a partnership for the year the child will be in your classroom.
- The information you seek is in order to know what's best for the child.
- You will respect their privacy.
- They don't have to answer any questions that make them uncomfortable.

If that relationship is formed early in the year, it will be much easier to communicate about any difficulties that arise or concerns you have that you want them to know about, as the year goes on.

What to Communicate and How

Parents of children with autism spectrum disorders need more communication than parents of typically developing children do. Chances are, if the child is really ready for inclusion, the parents have invested a tremendous amount of time, effort, and emotional energy. They need to know what is going on in the classroom. They need to know in what ways the child is being successful and what areas need work, including perhaps things that can be worked on at home. Weekly or even daily notes that go home with vague comments that Stephanie had a good day, or that things are "going well" are not very helpful. Parents need specifics so they know what to work on, what things to tell any outside therapists the child has, what to tell the doctor or psychologist who sees the child. They need to have realistic information about just how much the curriculum needs to be modified for their child. Some also need feedback about how well medications are working for their child.

We understand that communicating specifics can be time-consuming. One shortcut is to work out a checklist with parents that includes any areas they're particularly concerned about (e.g., learning math concepts, attention in class, social behavior on the playground) or that you come to feel is important. Then you can make brief notes about each topic on a weekly basis. Any instances of negative behavior that necessitate the child being removed from the classroom or having privileges removed should be communicated to the family. Many children will be on a behavior plan (see Chapter 12 on troubleshooting behavior) to increase on-task or social behaviors and eliminate negative behaviors. If the child has a one-on-one aide, he or she may be taking data for this behavior plan, and this can form a shortcut summary that can be communicated to parents.

Communicating specifics can serve another purpose as well. It is unfortunately true that some teachers get squeezed between the family and the school administration. The family wants to know what's going on and the administration may put pressure on teachers or therapists to keep parents satisfied with current services, which may be an impetus for the "Stephanie is doing great" kind of communication. If you establish a habit early in the year of communicating specifics with parents on a weekly basis, you don't have to decide whether Stephanie had a great week or not; you simply tell parents that she had no tantrums this week, or that she had one meltdown during an unexpected fire drill, or that she had two tantrums every day!

This kind of communication will also encourage parents to let you know what's going on in the child's life outside of school. It may be helpful for you to know that Stephanie is irritable because the family is moving, or because she was ill over the weekend. If parents let you know what Stephanie did over the weekend, this will allow you to work on conversational skills. Conversely, if you send home a simple note in the lunchbox with one notable event from the school day, it will allow parents to help their child learn to discuss her experiences, a simple and crucial skill that is particularly difficult for children with ASD.

Between us, we've known literally thousands of parents of children with ASD. In general, they are extremely grateful to teachers who they feel genuinely care about their child, and who take the time to read up on autism and to develop an alliance with them. Once such a relationship is established, communicating about difficult subjects becomes much, much easier.

Building this alliance won't be possible with all parents—some will come with an adversarial or, worse, an indifferent attitude that you won't be able to bridge no matter what you try. Other professionals who deal with parents, such as therapists, doctors, and psychologists, face the same issues. It is up to all professionals who deal with families of children with autism spectrum disorders to adopt a caring, professional attitude, no matter how difficult a relationship with an individual parent may be. You won't always succeed, but you'll know you did your best.

5 | What Treatments Are Used for Children with Autism?

In this chapter, we will describe the main kinds of treatment programs that are used for children with autism spectrum disorders; in the next chapter, we will describe the most common educational placements. Some of the treatments we present are very widely accepted, while some are considered "alternative" treatments. This list is far from exhaustive. It can't be. New treatments are emerging all the time. Some blaze in the sky for a short time, not to be heard from again. Others are incorporated into the mainstream of treatments and become standard additions to frequently used treatments. Although the treatments described here will generally not occur in your classroom, they may significantly affect your student and his family, and the child and parents may benefit if you are somewhat familiar with how they work and what they are supposed to accomplish.

For each treatment approach, we will describe what it involves, the specific aims and theoretical basis, if any, and how and by whom the treatment is applied.

We will also describe what is known about each approach's effectiveness, based on existing research and clinical experience. However, data on the effectiveness of most of these treatments are sorely lacking. To really know whether a treatment is effective, you would have to randomly assign one group of children to the treatment in question and another group to a different treatment (or no treatment). You would have to get test results or behavioral observations done by parents and teachers who *do not know* which treatment the child was receiving, so their preconceived ideas about the treatment didn't influence their rating. A few such studies are under way to test specific social skills programs, early communication interventions, behavioral treatments, dietary interventions, and medications. However, the overwhelming majority of treatments for children with ASD have not been tested in this way. Therefore, to evaluate a treatment's effectiveness, we are left with anecdotal evidence (stories of individual children who did or did not get better), our combined clinical experience with many such children who did or did not get better, and common sense.

Speech and Language Therapy

All children with ASD need help to develop their communication skills. In most cases, speech-language pathologists (SLPs) are the most appropriate people to deliver this help. There is a good chance that the child with ASD included in your class is still getting (or should be getting) speech-language therapy, either within the school or outside. Speech-language therapy can be given anywhere from once a week for a half hour to several times every day (for the more severely affected or younger child). As with any other therapy, the special education team has to evaluate the trade-offs: more language therapy may be better, but missing more class time is worse. Sometimes the SLP will mix and match services; for example, he may see the child once a week for an individual session, once a week in a dyad (a twosome made up of the child and one other child with or without special needs) to work on interaction skills, and once a week in the classroom.

Some children with ASD need help with the same kinds of skills as other children with speech or language impairments, such as developing syntactically complex speech, improving articulation and intelligibility, or understanding rapidly presented auditory language. But there are needs that are special to the child with ASD, and therapy will be more effective if the SLP has expertise and experience with autism. Children with ASD are much more likely to need specific help with *pragmatics*, the social use of language. They need to be taught how to stay on topic, how to take turns in a conversation, how to make small talk and follow basic social routines, how much eye contact to make and how close to stand, how to be sensitive to others' reactions to what they're saying, etc. For many children with high-functioning autism, and almost all children with Asperger's, pragmatics will be a major focus of their language therapy. Chapter 9 discusses how you may be asked to support speech-language goals in the classroom.

Picture Exchange Communication System (PECS)

PECS is a basic communication system, usually designed and supervised by either a speech-language pathologist or a behavior therapist. In PECS, the child is given a set of pictures, either photographs of real objects (food items, car, toy), or a drawing that represents the object. The child is taught that when he picks up the picture (which may be velcroed to a refrigerator or, later, in a communication book) and hands it to a teacher or parent, he gets the desired item.

As you might imagine, PECS is most helpful for children who really do not yet understand basic communication with words. They may have the idea that they can try to communicate desires to an adult by vocalizing, crying, or pulling them to the desired object, but they do not yet understand that they communicate specific desires using a *word* that *stands for* the desired object. By making the picture noticeably resemble the word, tying the picture to the object in time, and making the activity motivating by using desired objects, the child can learn that the picture stands for the object. Some parents resist this method, because they fear that it will delay or prevent the use of spoken language. However, if PECS is successful at teaching the child the idea of referential communication, it can serve as a bridge to spoken language.

In general, PECS is used for children who don't yet use meaningful speech, or children whose verbal communication is quite unintelligible or very delayed. It may also be used with children who can say some words but who only use them to respond to others' questions or requests, rather than initiating conversation. If you have a student who uses PECS, his SLP should instruct you in the usage of the system.

FastForward

FastForward is a technique for increasing the speed and efficiency of language processing in children who have language impairments. It was not designed for children with ASD per se, but is used for them by some therapists. It is generally administered by SLPs, and is based on the theories of Paula Tallal, which hold that the basis of children's language impairment is slowed information processing, rendering the child unable to process the very rapid flow of auditory language.

FastForward consists of a set of computer games which help the child to process language (for example, discriminating sounds and words) and are geared to the child's language level, so that speed and difficulty can be increased as he masters the skills being taught. It is a rather intensive program, consisting of more than an hour per day for several months. (It is fairly expensive, too!) Research done by the authors of the program report success at improving language comprehension in children with ASD, but well-controlled studies done by investigators not involved in the program, or comparing it to other interventions, have not yet been published.

Applied Behavior Analysis (ABA)

There are a variety of names for behavioral interventions, including "the Lovaas method," "Applied Behavior Analysis" (ABA), "Early Intensive Behavioral Intervention" (EIBI), "Discrete Trial Training," or "Discrete Trial Intervention" (DTT or DTI). There are some real differences among these approaches, but for our purposes, they all share the same basic theoretical foundation, that of classical learning theory. The goals of these techniques can be broken into two main classes: teaching skills and eliminating interfering behaviors.

Teaching Skills

In order to teach skills, an analysis is undertaken in which the targeted skill is broken down into very small parts that can be taught individually and then strung together to produce the desired behavior. To take a very large and complex skill, namely using language, as an example, the child might have to be taught a series of skills such as looking at the speaker, sitting quietly, discriminating sounds and then words and then associating them with an object, moving from objects to pictures, motor and then vocal imitation, stringing words together to make simple sentences ("I want apple"), etc.

In general, each behavior is analyzed into these small bits of behavior. Then the child is taught each one, and when it is mastered, the next step is taught. Sometimes the child already has a component skill (e.g., eye contact) in his repertoire, but does not use it often. In this case, the frequency of the behavior can be increased by reinforcing it. In some cases, the behavior will not be in the child's repertoire to begin with. In this case, it has to be built. This can be done by physical prompting (e.g., teaching a child to make a pointing finger by actually forming the child's hand into the proper shape), or by transforming a similar behavior that already exists (e.g., for eye contact, getting the child to look at something interesting that is held near the adult's eye and then removing the object, so that eye contact with the adult results, and then quickly reinforcing that).

This is a staggeringly complex task. Typically developing children spend much of their first few years absorbing the complexities of language, a task for which the brain is hard-wired. How, then, is it possible to teach language in this way?

First, you have to start early. The literature says before the age of 5, but in our experience, to get a really good outcome you have to start as early as possible, preferably before 4. Then, work has to be intense—20 to 40 hours a week, with additional practice and rein-forcement of skills by families. Given this intensity of treatment, some children reach a point, usually within one to two years, where they start learning faster and faster, and start to pick up language just from hearing it, without having to be taught every specific word or gram-matical form. These children have a chance to catch up to their peers, at least approximately. Others continue to need step-by-step teaching of everything we want them to learn. Although they will probably learn faster and more with this method than with other methods, they may not catch up.

Changing Behavior

The other main goal of ABA is to eliminate behaviors that get in the way of the child's learning, relating, and being accepted by oth-ers. These behaviors include some that are specific to autism, such as repetitive behaviors (staring at lights, smelling things, twiddling objects), and behaviors that are not specific to autism (inattention, noncompliance, aggression, tantrums, escape behavior). In order to eliminate or lessen these behaviors, the ABA therapist first does a func-tional behavior analysis. This consists of taking baseline data on the undesired behavior. Every instance of the behavior is recorded, along with what happened just before (antecedents) and what happened after (consequences) with no attempt yet to change the behavior.

This is sometimes called the ABCs of behavior analysis – Antecedents, Behavior, Consequences. The goal is to discover possible functions for the behavior. Common functions of behavior include:

- to escape something (such as work that is too demanding or a sensation that is unpleasant);
- to receive attention; or
- to get access to a desired object or activity (such as a specific toy or a turn on the swings).

An analysis of Miguel's tantrum pattern may demonstrate that 50 percent of his tantrums occur when materials appear that signal the beginning of a language lesson, and that his tantrum is followed by escape from the lesson. Or it may turn out that his tantrums often occur around 3:00, which may mean that he is getting hungry, with no way to communicate this.

A program is then designed with the presumed causes in mind. In the first instance, the therapists may halt the language lessons for a week or two, be sure that ongoing lessons are made easy, fun, and rewarding, and then slowly and subtly reintroduce language material, keeping lessons short and easy. In the second instance, a snack may be given at 2:00. The intervention that's tried depends on the conclusions we draw about the function being served by the behavior.

How ABA Is Provided

Often, experts in ABA who have autism experience may be needed to set up either kind of program (teaching skills or decreasing negative behavior). However, once the programs are set up, teachers, aides, and other therapists may be able to carry them out, with periodic oversight and modifications by the ABA expert.

Data continues to be taken throughout delivery of the services. When a child masters a skill, he practices it in multiple settings (generalization) and then is tested every so often to make sure the skill is still mastered (maintenance).

The ideal method of delivering ABA for the typical child with ASD might be to start with 20 to 30 hours of treatment when the child is under age 4 or even 3, with additional hours delivered by parents in a less structured way. When the child has gained some language skills and is starting to get interested in other children, he might continue to get ABA treatment at home for a half day while spending the other half in a preschool, accompanied by one of his ABA therapists. As he continues to master social and language skills, the percent of time spent in a group setting could be increased. Eventually he may be able to attend preschool or kindergarten with only a part-time aide. Some children, however, continue to need the aide well into elementary school or beyond, in order to facilitate social interaction, help keep them on task, interpret language that is beyond them, and preteach and review academic material.

Several well-done studies on ABA demonstrate its effectiveness, and our clinical experience amply bears that out. One often-cited study by Ivar Lovaas compared children receiving 40 hours of ABA to a group receiving 10 hours. The former group made rapid and striking grains and about half were able to be included in first grade with no support; the children in the 10-hour group did not make this dramatic progress. However, the definitive study, in which children are randomly assigned to ABA vs. a contrasting treatment, with equal intensity and quality of services, and blind ratings gathered, has not been done. Therefore, it can't be stated categorically that ABA is the best treatment for all young children with ASD. Furthermore, most attempts to replicate the Lovaas study often report striking gains in the ABA groups, but *not* to the extent reported by Lovaas (that half the children are indistinguishable from typically developing children, for example). However, one recent study (Nov. 2005) in the *American Journal on Mental Retardation* did report exciting results comparable to those of Lovaas.

If you have a student who is on an ABA program, it will be important for you to understand what is being worked on and how the program is set up, so that you can participate as much as the ABA consultant or behavioral psychologists requests. For example, you might be asked to note instances of negative behavior (e.g., whining, distress, noncompliance with lessons), or give your student a positive reinforcer (praise, sticker, checkmark on a chart) in response to a successful behavior. Even if the child's one-on-one aide is responsible for doing this nuts and bolts work, it is important for you to know what behaviors are being reinforced and which are being eliminated, so that if the child is successful, you can add your praise, and if a certain negative behavior is being deliberately ignored, you can be consistent with that method.

For a good basic overview of ABA methods, you may wish to read *Right from the Start* (Harris & Weiss), listed in Suggested Reading.

Verbal Behavior

"Verbal behavior" is a variant of ABA that has become very popular in the last five years or so. It is associated with the techniques of Vincent Carbone, and of Mark Sundberg and James Partington (see References). Verbal Behavior, based on the work of classic learning-theorist B.F. Skinner, stresses the function of the child's communication, rather than just the mastering of the specific words or gestures. Teaching is delivered in a more natural environment, with behavior allowed to reap its own natural consequences. For example, if the child points to something, he gets it; if he asks another child a question, he gets that child's attention. Another aspect of teaching that is stressed is "fluency," in which skills are taught to the point of being overlearned so that the child can do them without conscious attention or effort. This makes them seem more natural and enables the child to use them in multiple situations that demand attention.

There are behavioral experts who identify themselves as using the "Verbal Behavior" method. However, many first-rate ABA therapists who don't call themselves "Verbal Behavior" specialists also use many of these and similar techniques, so you may get an excellent ABA consultant who uses a wide variety of similar methods even though he's not a "Verbal Behavior" specialist. See the book by Mary Barbera and Tracey Rasmussen in Suggested Reading for a good introduction to the Verbal Behavior approach for laymen.

Floortime

Floortime is a developmental intervention based on the work of child psychiatrist Stanley Greenspan and his colleague, Serena Weider. They have several books on the subject. The focus of Floortime is on developing the motivation for the child to communicate. It takes its name from the position in which it's usually done—getting down on the floor with the child to play, rather than the more controlled, adult-directed sitting at a table that ABA often uses. Floortime strives to develop "circles of communication" in which the child says or does something, the adult responds by speaking, playing, giving something, touching the child in a pleasant way, and encouraging more communication. The goal is to increase the child's pleasure in relating to others, and to foster reciprocity in his interactions.

In many ways, Floortime is theoretically the opposite of ABA approaches. It is child-focused and child-driven, whereas ABA is adult-directed. It strives to enter the child's world, whereas ABA can be seen as pulling the child into our world. It assumes that the primary goal is to develop the motivation to communicate and that skills will follow, whereas ABA assumes that the primary goal is to teach specific skills and that motivation to use them will follow.

There are a few studies of children who have gone through Floortime programs, but as with most other approaches, they have been done by the principal proponents of Floortime, and have not been done blind or by comparing Floortime to contrasting approaches. Therefore, hard evidence for its effectiveness compared to other programs is lacking. In our clinical experience, although we have seen some children do well with it, we have also seen other children make virtually no gains. ABA approaches are more likely to push the children along faster and may therefore produce a better long-term prognosis.

We have found that when Floortime is not beneficial for a child, it is usually neutral, rather than detrimental. One exception might be if you have a student who has recently had Floortime and is therefore used to being allowed to engage in his own preferred activities rather than follow an adult's direction. If you have trouble directing him or his behavior is not under good control, consult the school psychologist or behavior consultant, and let them know a behavioral program is needed.

Relationship Development Intervention

Relationship Development Intervention (RDI) is a relatively new treatment approach for autism which has attracted a great deal of attention, especially from parents. It focuses, as the name suggests, on the development of social relationships, with particular emphasis on *experience sharing* (a broader category that includes joint attention, described in Chapter 2). In a series of books and workshops, Steven Gutstein, the main developer of RDI, has described the stages of social interaction in typical development, how to assess the individual child in terms of these stages, and a series of exercises that parents (and teachers) can do to develop skills along this continuum. This assessment scale is specifically designed to be school friendly and useful in designing social goals for a child's IEP and assessing progress in meeting these goals.

No well-controlled studies assessing outcome for children who receive RDI training have been published yet, but the content of the program looks to us sensible and well thought out, and, in many ways, not that much different from other social skills programs. We do find some recent claims for very high success rates to be a bit dubious. More information can be obtained through Gutstein's website (http://www.rdiconnect.com). This treatment is likely to be done outside of the classroom by parents, or occasionally by a school psychologist, counselor, or SLP, but parents or therapists might share with you which aspect of the treatment is currently being worked on, and ask you to reinforce this in the classroom, if possible.

The TEACCH Approach

TEACCH (which stands for Treatment and Education of Autistic and related Communication-handicapped Children) was developed by Eric Schopler, Gary Mesibov, and their colleagues at the University of North Carolina. It forms the basis for the state-wide North Carolina autism services and has been adopted by many other schools and systems throughout the world, including many cities in Japan. The TEACCH method is an individualized program, devised by parents and teachers together, that develops goals for the individual child. It is mostly considered a classroom model, used in self-contained classrooms for children with autism spectrum disorders, although it can also be adapted for the home and for individual teaching.

The primary methods are based on the fact that most children with ASD find it easier to process visual information than auditory information. This preference is capitalized upon by organizing the classroom into work stations where a physical location is associated with a task or skill, using picture organizers and sequences to let the child know what his schedule is, and letting the child use a picture communication schedule when necessary. It also takes the child's idiosyncrasies into consideration. For example, if a child has an extremely negative reaction to unexpected changes in routine, his schedule is posted in a series of pictures, with changes from the usual routine clearly marked.

There is little direct evidence comparing TEACCH to other methods and not much research into its efficacy. Some of its methods, such as a picture schedule and visual organizers, clearly help children with ASD focus and learn, and have been incorporated into non-TEACCH classrooms and ABA programs.

TEACCH is unlikely to be used in your regular education classroom, especially if you are outside North Carolina. If you are asked to use some elements of it for a particular child, just ask for help in setting up specifics—you won't find it difficult.

Eclecticism

A few years ago, proponents of TEACCH, ABA, Floortime, and other such intervention programs held rather rigidly to their own theories and techniques and had little use for the opposing camps. Not so any longer. More and more, good therapists are drawing on techniques from all of these approaches. For example, a primarily ABA therapist will use Verbal Behavior techniques, may play with the child on the floor to encourage emotional and social reciprocity, will make visual schedules, etc. The Eclectic approach is in. For you as a teacher, this means that you need to be flexible and open to learning about new approaches. You may be asked to use an entirely different set of treatment approaches with the student with autism you have this year than you used with a student several years ago.

Sensory Integration

Sensory integration therapy (commonly known as SI) is usually provided by occupational therapists, sometimes in school, often outside of school. It is based on the theories of Jean Ayres, which hold that children with various developmental disorders, including autism spectrum disorders, have difficulty with integrating sensory input from various modalities (smell, touch, sight, etc.), as well as making movements in response to sensory input. Consequently, they are unable to interpret sensations correctly and over- or under-react to such input, often responding with inappropriate behaviors. Sensory reactions in ASD are described in Chapters 2 and 3. In brief, children with ASD may have three types of sensory abnormalities:

1. **Under-reactivity:** ignoring or showing slow arousal in response to sensory stimuli in any modality (for example, ignoring people speaking, ignoring loud sounds or bright lights that would grab another child's attention).

2. **Over-reactivity:** reacting as if the stimulus were stronger than it is. For example, they may find sounds unpleasant that other people ignore, or find light touch unpleasant, and therefore dislike people touching them, getting their hair cut, or wearing certain kinds of clothes. Some children can appear to be underresponsive but, in fact are in a "shut down" mode due to overstimulation.

3. **Sensory-seeking behavior:** behaving in a way that seems designed to provide the child with particular kinds of sensory input. For example, a child might seek visual stimulation by twiddling his fingers in front of his eyes, staring at lights or shadows, looking along straight lines, or looking at things out of the corners of his eyes; auditory stimulation through repetitive vocalizations or humming; and vestibular (movement) stimulation through rocking, spinning, or head shaking.

These sensory abnormalities often interfere with learning, mood, behavior, and interacting, and are the focus of SI treatment. SI therapy involves providing specific sensory and motor activities that challenge the child to respond more normally to the input. These sensory and motor activities are thought to promote the ability of the nervous system to process and integrate sensory and motor information.

SI has become very widely used, and many parents swear by it. They report that their children are calmer and more attentive after their SI sessions, and better able to handle overwhelming environments (e.g., airports, Chuck E. Cheese's restaurants) after their SI treatment. All evidence for SI, however, is anecdotal. There are no published studies of research in which SI was given to some children and similar but non-SI activities such as gross motor activity or relaxation exercises were given to others, with behavior rated by adults blind to what treatment the children were receiving.

Whether SI works, and if it does, why, is currently unknown. Proponents of SI hold that it has direct therapeutic effects on the nervous system, but it might have any of its therapeutic effects through other means, such as by providing children with a break from academics, a set of positively reinforcing activities to do with an adult, and a chance to engage in gross motor activity and discharge some of their energy.

If a student in your class is receiving SI treatment, he will usually be removed from the class to get his SI. Sometimes, the OT delivering the treatment might ask you participate in some specific ways, such as by giving the child a chance to go into a small space or to wear a weighted vest either at prescribed times or if he appears to be getting distracted or distressed.

Medication

Many medications are prescribed for children with ASD. But here's the key: although they can help reduce specific symptoms (described below), they can't cure autism. They can help with symptoms such as attention and sleep problems, but they don't generally help the core symptoms of autism such as difficulties with language, communication, and social interaction.

As a teacher, you may or may not be informed if your student is taking medication. Parents may want to start their child on medication and only later ask you whether you have noticed any changes in behavior so your observations won't be influenced by knowing that your student is on a new treatment. Or, parents may ask you to report side effects or changes you observe in behavior. If so, ask the parent to give you clear guidelines about types of information they want you to collect.

Some medications (such as stimulants) work right away if they're going to work, while others (such as antidepressants) may take weeks to show an effect. Below are the main categories of medications that are often prescribed for ASD symptoms.

Antidepressants. Antidepressants include the selective serotonin reuptake inhibitors or SSRIs (e.g., Prozac, Paxil, Zoloft). These medications can be helpful in reducing stereotypies (repetitive behaviors), compulsions, aggression, and self-injurious behavior. They may improve moodiness, anxiety, irritability, and sleep problems, especially (but not only) if a child has someone with depression in his family. If mood problems or compulsions were interfering with social interactions, the medication may improve sociability.

Dopamine Antagonists. These medications (e.g., Haldol, Risperdal) are heavy-duty medications sometimes used to treat adults with serious mental illness such as schizophrenia. These can be helpful for children with severe disturbances of behavior, such as self-injury, aggression, or hyperactivity. Be aware that they can cause sleepiness and lack of responsiveness.

Stimulants. Stimulants (e.g., Ritalin, Dexedrine, Adderall, Concerta, Metadate) and other nonstimulants often used to boost attention (Celexa, Strattera) are best known for their use in treating AD/HD. While children with ASD who also have attention problems respond less predictably and positively to these medications than other children do, some of them do respond well to these drugs. These medications are often prescribed when attention, impulsivity, irritability, and hyperactivity are interfering with learning and social interactions.

Opioid Antagonists. Opioid antagonists (e.g., Nalaxone) are used to offset the effects of heroine in addicts. Some pharmacologists have tried them with children with ASD to treat self-injurious behavior, stereotyped movements, and hyperactivity. Some studies have reported some success, but later studies reported less benefit, and these drugs are not often used in autism.

Anticonvulsants. These medications (e.g., Depakote, Tegretol, Phenobarbital) are usually used by neurologists to treat seizures. They can be used with children with ASD who have seizures, and also to improve mood.

Sleep Aids. Many children with ASD have difficulty sleeping. Some parents find that melatonin (over-the-counter) helps their child get to sleep, and Clonidine is also prescribed by some physicians for sleep problems.

Several large-scale studies of medication with children with ASD are currently being conducted. A few have been completed, but many of these used small samples of children or were open-labeled trials (raters were not blind to whether the child was taking the medication). So, at present, medication decisions are largely up to the clinical skill, judgment, and experience of the doctor.

Physical Therapy and Occupational Therapy

Physical therapy (PT) and traditional occupational therapy (OT) are prescribed for children who need help learning or relearning motor (movement) skills. In a school setting, PT's generally provide adaptive physical education or physical therapy to help with gross motor problems—that is, with those involving the arms, legs, trunk, or other large muscle groups. For example, they might help a child develop better strength or balance or more coordinated movements. OT's generally teach fine motor skills such as cutting, writing, drawing, as well as self-help skills.

Although there are no well-done randomly assigned treatment studies of the benefits of using OT or PT with children with ASD, these treatments have "face validity." In the words of a well-known pediatric neurologist, Dr. Martha Denckla, "What you teach is what you get." In other words, you're not teaching the child to crawl differently in hopes that that will stimulate language. If the child can't hold a pencil, you teach him to hold a pencil. If his balance is poor, you give him practice keeping his balance in various situations. As any dancer knows (remember your childhood dancing lessons?), balance can be taught and practiced. OT's and PT's also have standardized motor tests that can quantify how delayed a child is in different motor skills.

If your student has school-based OT and/or PT, he may leave the room to receive this therapy, the therapist may work with him in the classroom, or the therapist may consult with you about ways to help him meet the movement demands in your class. For example, the therapist might recommend a pencil grip or slanted desk that will help with his handwriting or seating adaptations that will help him sit more comfortably at his desk.

Alternative Therapies

Alternative therapies are treatments that are not generally accepted by mainstream physicians and psychologists. Some have been tested and shown not to work. Some have not been rigorously tested. As with any treatments, the first goal is to do no harm. Therefore, if parents are considering any of these treatments, they should consult with their pediatrician to make sure that, even if the treatment is not yet proven, it at least has no significant risk to the child's health. Rarely, parents might ask teachers for their opinion, or what their experience has been. Although you should not offer an opinion about the safety or validity of these treatments, it is always a good idea to suggest that parents discuss all such possible treatments thoroughly with the child's primary doctor.

Vitamin Therapies

Over the last several decades, parents and others have tried a number of different vitamin therapies in an attempt to ameliorate the effects of autism. At present, some people believe that large doses of pyridoxine, magnesium, thiamine, or calcium have beneficial effects on social behavior, mood, and language. To date, there have been no definitive studies showing that these treatments can reduce a child's autistic symptoms. In addition, parents have to be careful that they are not giving their child a dose of vitamins that is so far above the RDA that it could endanger the child's health.

Gluten/Casein Free Diet

In the last few years, many parents of children with ASD have shared information about using the gluten-free/casein-free diet on the Internet. Families following the diet eliminate all foods containing gluten (a protein found in wheat, rye, barley, and their derivatives) and casein (a protein found in dairy products) from their children's diets.

At the height of this diet's popularity, as many as 30 to 50 percent of children who came into our offices were being tried on this diet. Many parents reported behavioral improvement, but this was often hard to document objectively. Parents also often reported that when their child inadvertently ingested some forbidden foods, they would see an increase in negative behaviors. The diet seems to be waning in popularity, as parents increasingly conclude that it has no significant benefit over the long run, despite their impressions of short-term changes in behavior. No controlled studies have yet been done, but one is under way.

The diet has a downside, too. Some nutritionists worry that so many foods are eliminated and some of the substitutes so unpalatable, that children may not get adequate nutrition. In addition, not being allowed to eat gluten and casein means no pizza, ice cream, or birthday cake, which can result in social isolation and deprivation. (With sufficient advance warning, however, gluten- or casein-free varieties of these childhood delicacies can be purchased or made.)

Of course, you must respect parents' wishes concerning their child's diet, and try to let them know ahead of time if a snack will be served that their child cannot eat, so that they can provide a substitute. As mentioned earlier, if children are curious about why James can't have the cupcakes, it can be explained in terms of certain food being unhealthy for certain children, and James can be asked what his favorite (allowed) foods are, to reassure the children that James can still have treats.

Secretin

A digestive hormone called secretin has also received a great deal of attention as a potential treatment in the last ten years or so. The interest began after one child with autism was reported to have miraculously improved after he was given a GI test that involved receiving a dose of secretin. Many children with ASD subsequently received this hormone as treatment, even though it was not approved for this use. Some received it repeatedly, some just one time; some as injections, some orally. Several recent controlled studies report minimal or no benefit to the children.

Auditory Integration Training

Auditory integration training has also received a lot of attention, although the number of parents trying it for their children with ASD seems to be waning. The theory is that children with ASD cannot tolerate certain frequencies of sound, so they respond with challenging behaviors and withdraw from the sounds. The treatment consists of the child wearing headphones for several hours a day for several weeks, listening to sounds that have been altered to modulate and control the unpleasant frequencies, with the goal of allowing them to tolerate these sounds better. A review of treatment research in the *Journal of Autism and Developmental Disorders* concluded that there was no, or, at best, inconclusive support for this treatment.

Facilitated Communication

Most of the alternative treatments discussed in this section are done outside of school. In contrast, facilitated communication (FC) was once used with some regularity within the classroom, and classroom aides and even teachers were often asked to use the method with their students. Although use of the method is now definitely on the wane, FC has been studied a great deal over the past twenty years.

The idea behind facilitated communication is that children with autism do not really have the severe social and language deficits they appear to have. Instead, the problem is that they cannot control their movements and therefore cannot show what they know or reliably communicate what they want to say. In order to allow them to communicate, they are given a keyboard or letter board. The "facilitator" usually holds the individual's hand with the index finger sticking out, to form a pointer. The individual is then asked questions, and "answers" by pointing to, or typing out, letters to spell out words.

There were some amazing early stories of the success of FC. For example, a nine-year-old with severe mental retardation who had no spoken language and whose developmental age consistently tested at around twelve months, suddenly spelled out things like "Tell Mom I've always loved her and appreciated everything she does for me, and I'm so glad that now I can tell her how I feel." This strained credulity. Also straining credulity was the fact that the individual with ASD often did not appear to be looking at the letter board, while the facilitator did.

Fortunately, FC is easy to test and has been tested many times. In research studies, when the individual with ASD is given access to certain information (for example, a picture on a card), and the facilitator is given different information, the answer spelled out reflects the facilitator's information and not the child's. The typing appears to be a "Ouija board" effect, where the facilitator is unconsciously guiding the child's hand to letters that make sense.

Unlike other alternative treatments, FC is not harmless. First, it can lead to a huge waste of valuable time. Imagine putting the nine-year-old with severe mental retardation in fourth grade for a year, where he apparently took tests along with the rest of the class, but in actuality was staring around the room for a year, learning nothing. Second, parents who had made some sort of adjustment to having a child with significant disabilities got unadjusted. (Nick isn't autistic or mentally retarded; he just needs help to express himself.) Then, when the FC communications turned out to originate with the facilitator and not with Nick, the parents had to adjust all over again. Third, several parents were accused of sexually abusing their children with autism, through FC. One father actually spent several months in jail before the FC was shown to be invalid.

FC is certainly an interesting social phenomenon. Why did it catch on, when it certainly seems implausible, and requires us to abandon everything we've learned about autism since the 1960s? It is easy to see why parents flocked to it; how much easier to handle a movement disorder than autism or mental retardation in your child. For some special educators, it was a validation of the philosophy they adhered to, that all children are inherently equal, even though they may be different. All abilities are equally valuable. Some children are just "differently abled." Well, unfortunately, disabilities are real. Some children really cannot talk, really cannot think the way others can, really cannot communicate. FC, in our view, fed and supported the denial inherent in the view that children with autism or mental retardation are not really disabled. And denial does no one any good in the end.

In the unlikely event a parent asks you to use FC with a child in your class, you should refer the parent to the special education department or principal (since parents heavily invested in FC are unlikely to change their mind on your say-so). Of course, if a parent asks for your honest opinion, you should give it, but be tactful.

Chelation

Chelation is a well-accepted treatment for children who have high levels of heavy metals such as lead in their bodies. It is administered through intravenous or intramuscular injection or by mouth, depending on the medication and the metal it is given to remove. The treatment has significant physical risks to the child, and is not to be undertaken lightly.

Recently, chelation has become another trend in treating autism. We have seen several children who were undergoing chelation treatment for autism, with no documented high levels of heavy metal in their blood or bones. Some parents are giving their children "chelation creams" on the skin. As we are finishing this book, the first report of a child with autism dying during chelation has just appeared in the newspapers, although chelation advocates argue that it was administered improperly.

The Bottom Line for Alternative Therapies

As we said earlier, this list of alternative therapies is not exhaustive. Other alternative therapies, such as hyperbaric therapy and cranio-sacral therapy, not only have no evidence to support their use, but are based on theories that strain credulity to the breaking point. Be skeptical. Use your common sense.

Some activities tried as alternative therapies, including swimming with dolphins, riding horses, listening to music, or creating artwork, can be therapeutic for all children, and children with ASD are no exception. Some of these activities can benefit a child in rather subtle ways. For example, they might stimulate creativity, create a connection with an animal, get the child pleasantly excited and therefore motivated to communicate, and teach him physical skills—but they do not cure autism.

If a parent tells you that his or her child is receiving an alternative therapy, be supportive, but emphasize that you can best help the child by focusing on the goals in the IEP. If you see any behavioral deterioration or significant change, be sure to let the parents know.

Part 2 | The Student in Your Classroom

6 | Educational Placements

As described in the Introduction, in 1975, the U.S. Congress passed Public Law 94-142 (The Education for All Handicapped Children Act). This law mandated a "Free and Appropriate Public Education" for all children, regardless of their disabilities. After several revisions, the law is now known as the Individuals with Disabilities Act of 2004 (IDEA), and mandates that federal money be given to the individual states to fund special education. The states, in turn, disburse some of this money to individual school districts, which create and fund special education services for each resident child with special needs. The special education laws, the budget, and common practice vary from state to state, and from district to district. You can contact your state Department of Education to get copies of the current laws in your state.

The variability in services available to students with ASD is striking. It is not the case, as you might imagine, that the most affluent towns necessarily have the best services. Sometimes larger public school systems have more children with ASD and get more special education help from the state government and can therefore afford to set up special programs that a smaller district cannot afford. Furthermore, parents who have the means to move sometimes relocate to areas with the best reputation for special education services, placing more strain on the school system's budget.

There is no doubt that good quality special education services are *expensive*. Sometimes a program for an individual child will cost the equivalent of a full time teacher, or more. This can lead to resentment from the school, taxpayers, or parents of typical children in overcrowded classrooms. However, if you put yourself in the parent's place and ask yourself whether you would try to get your child with a disability the best possible services, you will probably answer "yes." The ability to see the parent's perspective will be an important tool in your building a relationship with the parent, a relationship which will be a crucial contributor to a successful year for the child.

One element of the law that often creates dissension is that it does not mandate that the child get state-of-the-art services, but only that she get an "appropriate" education. Sometimes, what a school sees as "appropriate," a parent sees as inappropriate or inadequate. On the other hand, what a parent sees as "appropriate," the school administrators, who are balancing this child's needs against the needs of all the other children in the district, may see as inappropriate, or as a Cadillac of services that they cannot afford.

Parents understandably want the Cadillac for their child with ASD. They rightly perceive that the typical child, who is resilient, may recover from a less than terrific year in school, but that for a child with ASD, every year, especially in the early grades, may either help the child catch up or widen the gap. They may feel a sense of urgency and even desperation that causes them to make demands that the school personnel see as entitled or unreasonable. Try to keep this in mind as you develop your relationship with each parent. Again, if you find yourself getting annoyed with a parent's demands, ask yourself what you would do if it were your child.

Does this mean that all children with a diagnosis of ASD qualify for special services? No, because services are supposed to be driven by demonstrated need, and not by a particular diagnosis. In some cases, a child with ASD may have very mild special needs that can be addressed by some simple classroom modifications or teacher strategies that don't necessitate formal special education. However, a diagnosis of an autism spectrum disorder usually *will* get the child more attention and a higher level of services than another diagnosis. For example, a particular child with ASD may need and benefit from exactly the same services as a child with mental retardation, but the ASD diagnosis is more likely to "buy" her the needed help.

How Does a Child Get into Special Education?

The short answer is that the child is formally evaluated and is found to have a disability that affects her ability to learn. A team of professionals and parents is then formed to develop the plan (Individualized Education Program) that lays out exactly what the child needs special education for, what services she needs, and where she will receive them. (This is discussed in more detail below.)

Many children with ASD are identified as needing special education before they enter elementary school. A parent, preschool teacher, doctor, relative, etc. may realize that the child is not developing typically and recommend that she be assessed to determine whether a disability is causing her developmental differences.

Other times, especially if the child is more mildly affected by autism or has Asperger syndrome, he or she is not identified until kindergarten or later. In this case, a classroom teacher may be the first to realize that the child needs special help.

You might observe a child in your classroom who has not been identified as having ASD or any other developmental disability. However, she is struggling socially with peer interactions, with controlling her behavior, or with learning the material. You feel that this child needs additional support, so you make a referral to the Committee on Special Education for evaluation and consideration of an IEP. The parents, or other professionals in the school, may also make a referral for evaluation, potentially leading to the development of an IEP. In any case, you will need to meet with the parents to discuss your concerns. The referral must be made in the form of a written letter, which includes the child's name, date of birth, and reason for the referral. The letter should be submitted to the principal of the school or to the director of special education. Once a referral is received, the district must set up a meeting within ten days to explain the evaluation and IEP process and to gain the parent's formal consent to start the evaluation process.

The Evaluation Process

As explained above, before a child can receive special education services, she must be evaluated and found to have a qualifying disability. (She also must be between ages 3 and 21.) A qualifying disability is one that is: 1) listed in the federal special education law, IDEA, and 2) is determined to be significant enough that the child needs special education and related services in order to access the curriculum (i.e., the disability adversely affects educational performance).

It is important to remember that there is a difference between diagnosis and school classification. A given child may be diagnosed as having an autism spectrum disorder but not be classified by the school system as autistic if she does not require special education intervention in order to access the curriculum. The school usually believes the outside diagnosis is correct, but does not classify the child when the child does not qualify for an IEP.

Under IDEA, there are 13 disability categories that can qualify a child for special education services. They include:

1. mental retardation (cognitive disability)
2. hearing impairment or deafness
3. speech or language impairment
4. visual impairment or blindness
5. emotional disturbance
6. orthopedic impairment
7. autism
8. traumatic brain injury
9. other health impairment (e.g., AD/HD, epilepsy, Tourette syndrome)
10. specific learning disability
11. deaf-blindness
12. multiple disabilities

In addition, at their discretion, a state or school district may choose to use the term "developmental delays" for children aged 3 through 9 instead of one of the above categories.

If a child has not previously been identified as having an autism spectrum disorder or other disability listed in IDEA, she needs an initial evaluation to determine her eligibility for special education. Once a child has been found eligible for special education, the federal special education law, IDEA, requires that she be periodically reevaluated to determine whether she continues to qualify for special education, as well as to gather information about her abilities that will be helpful in setting goals and choosing services for her.

Initial Evaluations

An initial assessment or evaluation will involve standardized tests, including checklists or questionnaires for parents and teachers, direct observation of the child, interviews with parents and teachers, and review of the child's history. It is important that you make certain that the child is observed in the school environment in which the deficits are most apparent. For example, deficits in social interaction with peers may be most obvious in less structured situations such as the cafeteria during lunch.

The evaluation must include multiple procedures to assess all areas related to the disability, and be sufficiently comprehensive to identify all special education needs.

The areas that must be considered include:
1. academic achievement, functional performance, and learning characteristics;
2. social development;
3. physical development;
4. management needs.

Usually professionals from many disciplines evaluate children who are suspected of having an autism spectrum disorder. Professionals involved may include:

- *Psychologist or neuropsychologist:* to assess the child's level of intelligence and functioning in such areas as reasoning, memory, attention, and executive functioning;
- *Speech-language pathologist:* to evaluate the child's speech and language abilities;
- *Occupational and/or physical therapist:* to determine whether the child has gross or fine motor difficulties and perhaps to determine whether she has any abnormal responses to sensory input;
- *Audiologist:* to evaluate hearing, if there is a concern that the child is not responding to speech or other sounds;
- *Special education teacher:* in the case of older children, to administer academic achievement tests and determine whether the child has been keeping up with grade level work;
- *General education teacher:* in the case of children who have been attending school in a general education classroom, to report about the child's social, emotional, and work study skills and any concerns in the classroom.

Sometimes, immediately following the evaluation, there is a meeting to report the results of all of the evaluations to all other members of the evaluation team and to the parents prior to the IEP meeting. Sometimes the evaluators will meet with the parents individually; other times, they don't meet at all. It is best to provide feedback to the parents regarding the evaluation prior to the IEP meeting. One important reason is that it is not fair to expect parents to immediately digest and cope with possibly adverse evaluation results and then move on to planning their child's IEP at the same meeting. In addition, if the parents feel that the evaluation is not an accurate reflection of their child, they have the right to request an independent evaluation. This must be paid for by the school district and performed by a qualified professional mutually agreed upon by the parents and the school district (unless the school district can prove that its evaluation was adequate). Once the evaluation is complete, the IEP meeting is then scheduled (see below). The maximum amount of time from the beginning of testing to the IEP meeting is 120 days.

Reevaluations

Another important provision of IDEA is that the child is entitled to a full evaluation every three years, which must include validated tests to address aptitude and achievement, functional and developmental status, and ability to be involved in and make progress in the general curriculum (or whether and what curricular modifications are necessary).

What assessments constitute a thorough work-up depend on the child's age and abilities. It also depends, more than we would like, on what assessments are available, or what the school or a parent's private health insurance is willing to pay for. In general, for the comprehensive work-up that IDEA requires every three years, there should be a competent assessment of cognitive ability, usually done by a psychologist or neuropsychologist, including basic cognitive processes such as language, attention, memory, visuo-spatial skills, reasoning, fund of information, and other executive function skills. The child's reading, spelling, writing, and math should also be assessed. This can be done by a child psychologist, neuropsychologist, educational psychologist, or special education teacher. A speech-language pathologist should perform a comprehensive evaluation of the various aspects of language. If fine or gross motor issues are noted, an OT and/or PT should assess these areas.

What about medical evaluations? In addition to seeing a pediatrician, many children with ASD see a neurologist and/or psychiatrist on a regular basis. This is especially important when any of the following are known or suspected: seizures or other frankly neurological symptoms, coexisting psychiatric disorders such as depression or obsessive-compulsive disorder, the need for medication. In our opinion, every child with ASD should see a neurologist at least once (after all, autism is a neurological disorder) and the neurologist can decide whether ongoing neurological supervision is indicated.

What about the other years, in between the triennial evaluations? If everyone agrees that the child is doing well and there are no strong disagreements about placements or services, the child may not need interim evaluations. On the other hand, an outside evaluation may be very helpful if the child is not doing well (in the view of one or more members of the special education team, including parents), or there is serious disagreement about placement or services, or the child is quite young and her symptoms are changing rapidly. Sometimes parents simply want someone to take an independent look at their child and give them an opinion about her rate of progress. This is quite reasonable. We see many children for a yearly evaluation, because parents come to depend on a consistent outside view of the child's current status and prognosis. Sometimes, we suggest that a yearly evaluation is no longer necessary, but some parents feel better knowing that a yearly objective evaluation will be made by someone not involved with service delivery and not involved with the child on a daily basis.

Sometimes these evaluations confirm what the parent already thinks about good progress or not-so-good progress, and sometimes, unfortunately, parents have to be told that their impressions (or those of the school) of rapid progress are not borne out in the evaluation. When people are involved with the child on a daily basis and are invested in the outcome, they sometimes focus on small gains and interpret them as meaning that the child's behavior and cognitive skills are becoming more like those of typical children than is really the case.

The Teacher's Role in Evaluation

If you are lucky, the child in your classroom will have received excellent and thorough assessments, and the full results will be available to you to assist you in planning the child's education. (Sometimes parents or school administrators feel that it is better for the teacher not to be privy to the child's medical diagnosis or evaluation reports because they might lead to lowered expectations or fixed attitudes about the child's capability, either consciously or unconsciously. Not knowing this information can certainly make your job more difficult.)

If you, the teacher, attend the IEP meeting, there is a step where the team discusses whether or not the child qualifies for special education, and if so, under what disability category. In addition, the child's "present level of performance" (PLOP) is summarized—and this includes results of any standardized testing (IQ tests, achievement tests, etc.) as well as how the child is doing in all areas for which there are special education goals. So, at a minimum, you will know the child's qualifying classification (autism) and see a summary of her evaluation results.

In our view, the teacher should be given as much information as possible about the child, including access to assessment reports that may help her adapt instruction or materials for the child. For example, if a teacher knows that a child has good verbal memory, but that multiple repetitions are necessary for the learning to occur, that may save both the child and the teacher frustrating moments. Conversely, if assessments reveal that the child seems to learn easily but that retention is problematic, the teacher will know that he or she cannot assume without checking that Emily has necessarily retained what she learned yesterday.

In some cases, you as the teacher will be part of the actual evaluation process—for example, by giving the child standardized reading or math assessments during the school year. These results will sometimes be considered part of the assessment data used to determine whether the child is making sufficient progress toward her academic goals.

The IEP

Once a child has been evaluated and has been found to qualify for special education services under IDEA, the next step is to develop an Individualized Education Program (IEP). This may occur at the same meeting where the evaluation results that first establish eligibility are discussed, or at a separate meeting.

An IEP is a legally binding document that spells out:

- evaluation procedures,
- the child's classification (which may not be the same as the child's medical diagnosis),
- the child's "present level of performance" (PLOP), or behavioral, language, cognitive, and motor functioning,

- long-term goals and, for children with more significant disabilities, short-term educational objectives for each area in which the child needs special educational help,
- clear and measurable criteria for assessing progress in achieving goals,
- services that are needed to help the child achieve her goals (e.g., speech-language therapy, a one-on-one aide, instruction from a special educator in math),
- accommodations needed by the child (changes in the setting, instruction, or how material is presented to the child that don't alter academic expectations, such as seating at the front of the class or extra time on tests)
- modifications needed by the child (changes in what the child is expected to learn that do alter academic expectations, such as giving her math problems on a first grade level instead of third grade level),
- the least restrictive placement appropriate for the child, and
- a determination of whether the child requires an extended, twelve-month, school year to prevent regression.

The IEP is developed by the child's special education team over the course of one or more IEP meetings (see next section).

What Is the Special Education Team?

Each child with ASD typically has a number of school staff members assigned to her IEP team, in order to meet the requirements of IDEA. Each member generally takes primary responsibility for addressing one aspect of the child's needs as determined through the evaluation process (e.g., speech and language skills, academic skills, social skills) and for establishing goals to be written into the IEP for those areas.

For a child with ASD, the core of the intervention team is often comprised of the parents, classroom teachers (general and special education), a speech-language pathologist, resource room teacher, an occupational therapist, a physical therapist, and a school psychologist or guidance counselor. Each of these core team members not only addresses the child's needs but also provides advice to other staff members with regard to their area of expertise. It is important that all school staff that interacts with the student be apprised of the student's goals.

The Teacher's Role in IEP Meetings

It is beyond the scope of this book to go into great detail about what occurs in an IEP meeting. Instead, this section focuses on the parts of the IEP where you, as a teacher, are most likely to be asked to provide input.

As a general education teacher, you are required to attend the IEP meeting of any student who is in your class for all or part of the day or who *might* be placed in your class (that is, placement in a general education class is an option that will be discussed for the student). As a member of the student's special education team, you may also be asked to:

- participate in the discussion of what the most appropriate placement for the student would be (see section on placements below);
- help write appropriate goals for academic subjects the student will be working on in your class (see below);
- provide suggestions about accommodations or modifications needed by the student (e.g., visual presentation of the material, use of computer for written work, copies of all class lecture notes provided to the child, extended time for tests; see the chapters on academics and cognition for other suggestions). As a teacher, you will probably have more input about the accommodations that would be helpful for your student than about the related services;
- provide suggestions for specific teaching methods you feel will work for the student in your classroom;
- participate in the discussion of who will deliver each special service the child needs, including who will modify work and lessons for the child and give her special instruction.

Writing Goals

At the heart of a student's IEP are the goals that she is expected to reach during the course of the school year. Goals must be written for every area in which the child is determined to need special educational help. These goals, which must be objective and measurable, state what specific skills the child is expected to learn in each area that is affected by the child's disability.

Each child with ASD should have academic goals, speech/language goals, and social skills/behavioral goals.

For example, academic goals might include:
- Ethan will increase his reading comprehension level to the 5.5 grade level as measured by teacher-made assessments and standardized tests.
- Sonya will learn to tell time to the half hour on an analog clock.

Speech/language goals might include:
- Jorge will say "Help, please" to request assistance in the classroom.
- DeWanda will increase correct use of the personal pronouns "I," "he," "she," and "they" to 90% of the time.

Social skills goals might include:
- Tim will use appropriate eye contact 8 out of 10 times when talking with peers.
- Amanda will initiate an interaction on an on-going topic in play and conversation.

Often the child's team will draft goals prior to the actual IEP meeting, usually with input from the parent. Your role is to participate in the discussion, understand what is to be accomplished by the child in your classroom, and to develop specific academic and social/behavioral goals with the aid of the special education teacher. The team, including the parent, will likely have many goals in mind. Part of the process of developing an IEP is to prioritize goals and include those that are most important. If too many goals are included, meeting them can overwhelm you and the child's other education providers. In addition, the goals should be specific. A goal such as "Jenny will interact appropriately with peers" is unacceptable because it is non-specific. Better goals are "Jenny will appropriately initiate play with a peer" or "Jenny will ask a question about a topic under discussion, listen to the answer, and ask a related follow-up question."

Discussing Related Services and Supplementary Aids and Services

After a student's goals have been agreed upon, the special education team discusses what **"related services"** will be needed to help the student meet those goals. A related service is a service that is "required to assist a child with a disability to benefit from special education" and includes: OT, PT, speech-language therapy, counseling, etc. In other words, related services help a child achieve her individualized goals in the areas where her disability affects her learning.

The team also discusses needed **"supplementary aids and services."** These are "aids, services, and other supports that are provided in general education classes or other education-related settings to enable children with disabilities to be educated with nondisabled children to the maximum extent appropriate…." These may also be referred to as **accommodations.** In short, they are changes to materials, the classroom, or instruction that do not change what the child is learning, but make it easier for her to access the regular curriculum. For example, accommodations might include: using a keyboard instead of cursive writing to complete compositions or take notes; being given preferential seating at the front of the room; teacher assistance in recording assignments and scheduling long-term projects; extended time to complete assignments and tests.

Some of the services your students with ASD might receive as part of their IEPs are:

Speech-Language Therapy. The speech-language pathologist helps to develop a child's receptive and expressive language skills. Intervention is geared to the needs of the child and may address language at the levels of phonology (speech sounds), grammar, vocabulary, and pragmatics (social use of language). This member of the team teaches and helps the child practice strategies to improve his or her social communication skills and processing of complex language. These strategies (such as graphic organizers, discussed in Chapters 9 and 11) then have to be practiced in other settings, such as the classroom.

Counseling. The school psychologist or guidance counselor may provide counseling in individual or group settings. For children with ASD, he or she is often the team member who provides social skills intervention (although social skills training is also provided by speech-language pathologists, guidance counselors, and special education/resource room teachers).

Physical or Occupational Therapy. Work on motor skills is the primary responsibility of the occupational and physical therapists. The occupational therapist is responsible for developing fine motor skills, particularly those that are required in daily life (such as dressing and toileting) or in the classroom (such as holding a pencil and cutting). In younger children, handwriting and drawing skills are often a focus of intervention. As children get older, more emphasis may be placed on teaching them to type. In addition, work in OT addresses sensory motor integration, coordination of movement, balance, and motor planning. Occupational therapists may also work on helping the child with organizing her materials and daily routines in the classroom.

The physical therapist helps the child develop gross motor skills, such as running, hopping, ball play, and balance. When PT is provided as a related service at school, the emphasis is on developing the skills the child needs to benefit from her IEP, so recreational skills are less likely to be the emphasis than skills such as sitting at a table or desk well enough to use the hands to write.

Individual Assistant or Aide. Frequently, a child with ASD in your classroom will have an individual assistant (also known as an aide, paraeducator, or shadow). You as the teacher supervise this staff member with support from the special education teacher and the rest of the team. The assistant helps the student to focus and sustain her attention to task, and to have social interactions, and follows through on accommodations and modifications in the curriculum for the child. For example, the assistant will help the child to follow her visual schedule, provide warnings prior to transitions, help her employ learning strategies, and to become a more motivated and independent learner over time.

You may not have had the opportunity to work with an aide before and have many questions. You and the special education teacher are responsible for determining the methods used to meet goals and the initial teaching of any concepts. You will meet with the aide and discuss what you want to accomplish with your student with ASD and the methods by which the aide will reinforce the child's attention and concepts that you teach. An aide is hired by the school for the child. Aides usually do not have a great deal of training in education.

You will need to instruct the aide. You will need to be very clear about what you want him or her to accomplish. At the same time, it is important to hear what she says about your student with ASD and the child's response to teaching. The aide will work so closely with the child that she may have insights that you do not. However, the aide should not ever take over primary responsibility for teaching the child. Under the No Child Left Behind Act, all students are supposed to have "highly qualified" teachers, and aides are not highly qualified teachers.

You are responsible for communicating with the child's parents, and, although the aide should ideally be present at meetings with you and the parents, she should not communicate with parents on her own. Aides are often paid hourly and the school often won't pay for them to come to meetings after school.

At times you may find that the aide does too much for the child. For example, she might continue to write the child's homework down or collect all of the child's materials to take home, when the child clearly has developed the skills to do so independently (or could develop the skills if she were required to be more independent). You will need to help the aide to help your student with ASD to become as independent as she can be (see Chapter 8 for more specific information).

Making Decisions about Classroom Placement

The decision about where the student will be educated is one of the last steps completed in an IEP meeting. Only after the special education team has written and agreed upon the goals for the student and determined what related services and accommodations she needs is classroom placement supposed to be determined.

In other words, teachers, parents, and others are not supposed to arrive at the IEP meeting with preconceived notions about what classroom or school would be most appropriate for the student, or the amount of time (if any) she should spend included in a general education classroom. In practice, however, team members often do have preconceived ideas. Frequently, team members will already have suggested placements to the parents, or even told them what placement(s) their child "qualifies" for on the basis of her diagnosis, test scores, etc. Or, parents may have their own ideas about what placement is right for their child, and may have gone to observe various placements to determine which one would best fit their child's needs (in their opinion). And, if a child has already been receiving services in a particular program of a particular school, the assumption is often that the child will remain in that placement.

Given this tendency of special education team members to assume prematurely that a particular placement is right for a child, your challenge as a teacher is to keep an open mind about placement decisions until after your student's goals and services have been agreed upon. As a team, you are then to consider, starting with the "least restrictive" (most inclusive) options, which placement would be most appropriate. Under IDEA, the special education team is supposed to choose the placement where the student can best achieve her individualized goals and access the general education curriculum while having the maximum contact with typically developing peers.

What Specific Placements Are Available for Children with ASD?

As mentioned in Chapter 1, IDEA mandates that a continuum of educational placements be available to students with special needs, including:

- general education classes,
- resource rooms,
- self-contained special education classes in the public school,
- special schools (public or private),
- home instruction, and
- instruction in hospitals or residential schools.

The student in your general education classroom may be using some of these services now, such as resource room help, and may have received home instruction or placement in a special class or school in the past (and for some children, these placements may lie in their future), so it's beneficial for you to have a working knowledge of the range of educational opportunities available to the child. The placement options below are listed from most inclusive (least restrictive) to least inclusive (most restrictive).

Full Inclusion in General Education

A child who is fully included receives all her education in a regular classroom. The child receives special services such as speech/language therapy in the class. In practice, children who spend most of their time in general education classes but are pulled out for therapy or tutoring no more than a few times a day are still described as being in "full inclusion." Depending on the child's cognitive and behavioral challenges, she may need a one-on-one aide to benefit from the regular classroom.

The advantages of such a placement for students with ASD are many, and include opportunities to:

- develop long-standing relationships with typical peers,
- model the behavior of typical peers,
- be tutored by peers,
- be exposed to or master grade-level curriculum and classroom routines,
- learn in a group.

The general education teacher, in concert with the special education teacher who is responsible for the child with ASD, must individualize the child's curriculum and methods of teaching. Some children with ASD will be able to learn some material (perhaps science, for example) with the rest of the class, but will need small group or even individual instruction for other material (language lessons, for example).

There are also disadvantages to full inclusion, and, despite the current beliefs among some educators, we do not believe that full inclusion is right for everyone. Some children with ASD have such severe behavioral challenges that it is impossible for them to conform their behavior to the demands of the classroom and tolerate the activity and stimulation of the classroom there.

More commonly, however (since behavior can be modified), cognitive challenges may make it difficult for a child to achieve her goals in a general education classroom. In the younger grades, it may be possible to modify the curriculum in meaningful ways, but as the child gets older, the material and skills she needs to learn may become so discrepant from her same-age peers that she would make more progress in a resource room or separate class (see below). The idea is to place the child in a school setting that will allow her to achieve her potential. To take a rather extreme example, it may make more sense for a child who needs to work on toileting, dressing, basic communication, and pre-vocational skills to be in a separate setting where she can work on these skills, rather than spending her time in a fourth grade classroom, sitting through science or social studies lessons she does not understand, waiting for a chance to erase the board to show that she is improving her ability to follow verbal instructions.

This is not to say that the goal of inclusion is always, or even usually, for the child to keep up with grade level material. It may be that mastering simplified material a grade, or even several grades below the class, is possible in an inclusion setting. But if the cognitive gap between the child and the rest of the class is too large, as in the example just described, a full inclusion setting will probably not be the place where the best progress toward appropriate goals can be made.

Partial Inclusion

A child who is in partial inclusion receives a significant part of her education in the regular classroom, often with a one-on-one aide. Her "home base" may be the general education classroom, or a self-contained classroom (or, more rarely, a resource room). The special education teacher who is responsible for this child's program and for the resource or self-contained room, together with the rest of the team, will decide how much, and which activities, can be done in inclusion.

A Note on Terminology

Mainstreaming is a term that can mean full or partial inclusion; it has gradually been replaced by the inclusion terms. Although there is no formal definition, *mainstreaming* sometimes refers to the gradual process of inclusion when the child has demonstrated her ability to profit from the general education class, while *inclusion* may refer to a placement in general education regardless of the child's growth and development. Advocates of *full inclusion* for all students oppose the idea of *mainstreaming* because they feel that it reduces the child to visitor status in the regular classroom.

Similarly, *integration* is sometimes used synonymously with *inclusion*, but at other times it refers to placement in a class (often a preschool class) that contains both typical and special needs children in roughly equal numbers.

Reverse mainstreaming (or inclusion) refers to placing one or more typically developing children into a special education class (usually in pre-K or early grades) for part of the day to give the special education students a chance to interact with typical peers and model their behavior.

Some children might only be included for social times, such as lunch and recess, or during specials such as PE, art, and music. Other children might be included for some academic subjects, but go to a resource room or self-contained class for others.

If a student with ASD will be partially included in your class, it may help her to feel more comfortable socially to use "reverse mainstreaming" before she makes the transition. Have some of your students visit her in her current classroom and play and work with her prior to the first day she will enter your room. Once she starts coming to your class, let her know in advance what she will be doing in your room each day.

It is important that you are completely aware of the child's goals so that you can support them. Let your other students know that even though your student with ASD only attends class some of the time, they need to help her feel welcome. Give your other students specific ideas of what they can do (e.g., say hi, give compliments, help the child when she wants help or if you ask the other students to help).

Resource Room

A resource room, usually run by a special education teacher, is separate from the general education classroom but in the same school. The child with ASD (or other disability) can come to the resource room, with or without her one-on-one aide, to receive instruction in subjects where she needs special help, if she is learning material below grade level, or if she needs different teaching methods or one-on-one instruction. Children can spend anywhere from half an hour a week to several hours a day in the resource room, with the rest of the day usually spent in regular education. It's always a challenge to strike a balance: learning may be more efficient in the resource room, but a social and academic price may be paid for time spent out of the classroom.

Substantially Separate Class

These are self-contained classrooms, usually within the regular public school, for children whose IEP teams have determined that they can best achieve their goals in this setting. Often these classrooms are for children with more significant disabilities who are considerably below grade level in academic subjects. However, there may also be self-contained classrooms for children who have the ability to learn on or near grade level, but who need more individualized instruction and attention than is available in the general education classroom. In some school districts, for example, there are self-contained classrooms for children with Asperger syndrome and for children with learning disabilities who are working on the general education curriculum in small classes.

Self-contained classrooms may be comprised of children with a single disability, such as autism, or a mix of children with autism and other disabilities, such as language disorders, emotional disorders, intellectual impairment, physical handicaps, or multiple handicaps. They typically (and hopefully) have small class size and very favorable student to teacher ratios (2:1 to 5:1) and are taught by special education teachers. The goal is usually to move the child toward inclusion, if possible.

Depending on the severity of the children's needs, they may be working on basic self-help, communication, and pre-academic skills, or they may be working on academic material on grade level or at grade levels lower than the children's chronological age. Therapies (PT, OT, SLP) may be delivered in the class or as pull-out services. Some students may take advantage of *partial inclusion*, as agreed on by the team, or typical peers may visit the class for peer tutoring or social interaction (*reverse mainstreaming*).

Public Separate Day Program

This is a publicly funded, self-contained program, similar to the self-contained classroom, but comprised of an entire program rather than just one class. It may contain multiple classes to accommodate children of different ages and ability levels, and education focuses on communication, self-help skills, social interaction skills, behavior control, and some academics. It will usually offer special services (e.g., speech therapists, behavioral specialists), prevocational, and vocational programs. Most instruction is in small groups, but programs are (hopefully) individualized for each child.

These programs are often funded by a combination of federal, state, and local monies, and are run by a consortium of neighboring towns; they are sometimes called "collaboratives" for this reason. Because they are publicly run, they are sometimes housed in local public schools, which gives the children a chance to participate in general education inclusion as they can.

Private Separate Day School

These are separate schools that are privately run but approved by the state. Most tuition is paid for by the local school district in which the child lives, but parents may pay privately if they have the means and cannot get the school district to pay. (Transportation is often as expensive, or more so, than tuition.) These schools may offer services very similar to those of the publicly run separate schools described above. One advantage they have for parents is that parents may have more control (sometimes, in fact, setting up and running the schools themselves). They also tend to be more "ideological" than public programs, sometimes using exclusively ABA, or TEACCH, or other specific methods (see, for example, websites for some private schools in Massachusetts to get a flavor of this: New England Center for Children, Higashi School, May School).

Parents sometimes strongly advocate for one of these programs, as opposed to a "collaborative," because they have more highly expert staff or are better able to teach very challenging children, or because there are no local collaboratives with autism programs or expertise.

Residential School

Most residential schools are privately run but approved by the state department of education, although a few are public. These schools are generally reserved for children who present severe behavioral challenges and cannot be served adequately in a day program. Family factors play a very significant role in deciding whether or not this placement is appropriate for a child. Not only are some families more averse to the idea of placing their child outside the home, but some are better equipped to manage difficult behavior in the home. Some families cannot cope with the child's behavior, because the child is so relentlessly aggressive or destructive, because they have other children who need special attention, or because the child needs 24-hour-a-day supervision.

Residential programs are quite expensive, although they may end up costing the local district no more than a good day program because state governments share the bill. Sometimes as a child with ASD gets older, residential programs may be considered if the child has intense needs for adaptive skills and vocational training in addition to difficult behavior. Residential programs typically have day school programs, followed by extended programming in the living facility that concentrates on adaptive skills (housekeeping, cooking, shopping) and leisure/recreational skills (outings, recreational activities). They are usually run year-round with a few week or two-week breaks;

children may only go home during these breaks or may visit home as often as every weekend.

Hospital Programs

Hospital programs for children with ASD used to be fairly common, with the children put in inpatient psychiatric facilities for treatment, but this is quite rare now. Most children with ASD who are in psychiatric or other hospital settings have other severe psychiatric or physical disorders for which they are hospitalized, and they attend a day school within the hospital setting. Children are rarely hospitalized for ASD alone unless their behavior is dangerous and out of control and they are being medicated.

Home Programs

Home programs are common for very young children with ASD, but become less common as the children get older. Many preschool children are in full- or part-time ABA programs run in their homes, while simultaneously attending play groups or part-time preschool classes. The actual therapy is delivered by ABA therapists, but parents observe and participate, and can carry out additional teaching when the therapists are not there. Such home programs can run from 5 to 40 hours per week, or even more. The goal of most such programs is for the child to be readied for learning in a group setting, such as a regular preschool or kindergarten class. For older children in the early elementary grades, the IEP team may decide (usually in accord with the parents' wishes) that the child needs an additional year or two of home programming before she is ready for a group setting. Occasionally, a parent will reject all autism programming that is available in the district and will want to home school his or her child.

Who Makes the Decision about Educational Placement?

Again, this is the job of the special education team, including the parents. Often, the team can agree on a placement, but occasionally the parent and one or more professionals disagree with the rest of the team. Usually, this is in the direction of the parent wanting an outside (and more expensive) placement for the child (separate day

Where Do Most Students with ASD Go to School?

To give you an idea of how many children with ASD you might find in each of these placements, the following are figures given for 2005 (taken from IDEAdata.org).

Placement	Percentage
General education classroom (outside of regular classroom for less than 21% of the day)	31.3
Resource room (outside of regular classroom more than 21% of the day but less than 60% of the day)	18.2
Separate class (outside of the regular classroom for more than 60% of the day)	39.8
Public separate school facility	5.2
Private separate school facility	4.4
Public residential facility	0.1
Private residential facility	0.6
Homebound/hospital placement	0.4

or residential program). Occasionally, parents want a more inclusive placement for their child than the other team members believe is appropriate. If negotiation fails, this disagreement may have to go to mediation, or a due process hearing held by the state Department of Education. Since IDEA requires that children be educated in the least restrictive environment where they can meet their educational goals, whichever party wants the child included has an edge to start with. However, parents are often able to show that the child will not have an appropriate education without being placed in a highly specialized facility.

Special education placements and procedures in other English-speaking countries, including Canada, the UK, Australia, and New Zealand, are quite similar to those in the U.S. (Waltz, 1999). Additional information about special education in Canada can be obtained at: http://www.patientcenters.com/autism/news/Canada.

What Happens after the IEP Meeting?

Once the IEP is established, parents are entitled to, and should be encouraged to, take a look at the classroom setting that was recommended by the IEP team and to get information on the other children who would be in their child's class. If the parents disagree with the team's recommendations they should inform the district in writing. Within 15 days of notification, the district must schedule a meeting with the parents to try to resolve the conflict. If an agreement cannot be reached, the parents have the option of either going to mediation or to an impartial due process hearing. An impartial hearing officer, not employed by the school district, conducts the hearing and must render a decision within 30 days of the hearing.

You may be called on to testify at an impartial hearing. If you are, you should expect to be asked questions about how the child is functioning in your classroom and about your opinion of what the child needs.

Once the IEP is agreed upon, it must immediately be implemented. A team of service providers is established. They may have been members of the evaluation team, but can be other staff members. In the following chapters, we will describe your role in implementing the IEP, as well as how you might work with other service providers to help your student achieve his or her goals.

7 | Getting Started

A Recipe for Success

Under what circumstances does inclusion for a child with an autism spectrum disorder lead to a happy and productive year for everyone? Let's be realistic: there will be ups and downs, challenges and problems, and a wonderful teacher still can't "cure" autism. Furthermore, there may be developmental, medical, or family factors affecting the child that are totally beyond your control. But—in most cases—you can help the child have a successful inclusion experience.

What do we mean by "successful inclusion"? We do *not* mean that the child will be on grade level for all, or even necessarily any, academic skills, although if this is an achievable goal, you should certainly work towards it. "Successful inclusion," to us, means that you have a productive year and:

- the child learns important academic skills, improves his social skills, and feels successful;
- the child's peers increase their understanding, acceptance, and helpfulness; and
- what the child accomplishes in your class maximizes his chances for success in the next year.

So, how do you get started?

First, you should understand some of the *characteristics of children with ASD that generally predict a greater chance for successful inclusion.* This does not mean that children without these traits cannot succeed in your class. However, the chances are that you will have to do more curriculum modifications and that the child will probably make slower social and academic gains if he doesn't have these characteristics:

- Cognitive abilities that test in or near the average range;
- Communicative language present by the age of 5;
- Absence of seizures (because seizures tend to be associated with more cognitive impairment);
- Diagnosis of autism in the preschool years or earlier and placement in intensive intervention (except children with Asperger's disorder or mild autism may not be diagnosed until kindergarten or later and still have an excellent chance for success).

This doesn't mean that for a successful experience, the child has to have all of these characteristics, but research and clinical experience shows that each one is a factor associated with better outcome.

Second, there are *characteristics of school programs that promote successful inclusion:*

- The teacher has training in the behavioral characteristics, needs, and learning style of children with autism spectrum disorders.
- Classmates are made aware of any special skills or expertise the child with ASD has.
- Parents are kept informed and support the program.
- Special and general education staff are optimistic about the success of the child's inclusion and committed to doing whatever they can to making it work.
- The special education team meets regularly to consider the child's progress.
- The general education teacher receives adequate consultation and supervision.
- The teacher has enough time to make needed modifications to materials, or has an assistant who can make them.
- The teacher fosters a classroom atmosphere of group cooperation and acceptance of everyone's differences.
- The child with ASD is placed in a classroom with a high teacher-to-student ratio.
- The class has only one or two children with ASD or other significant disabilities that require intensive adult support.

■ If needed, the student is provided with a trained one-on-one assistant, either a paraprofessional or behavior therapist. (If the child's needs are milder, and he can sometimes follow a group lesson, do his seat work, and interact with other children without support, then a shared classroom aide may be sufficient.)

■ Support services and therapies are available (PT, OT, speech-language therapy, behavioral consultation, school counselor for social skills).

■ Adaptive or assistive devices are available as needed (keyboards, computers, calculators).

Again, if these features are not all in place, don't despair—you can still have a productive and successful year with the child with ASD. But you should be realistic about whether you're being given adequate support.

Getting Off to a Good Start

Besides the characteristics described above, which are not under your control, there are also some simple procedures which *are* under your control and can maximize the chances of a *getting off to a good start*. You won't be able to use them all, however; pick and choose, or suggest some to the appropriate parent or therapist.

Preparing the Student with Autism before the First Day of Class

■ Take pictures or videos of the classroom areas, lunchroom, bathroom, teachers, and some students for the child, so he knows what to expect. Try to make sure the people and things you photograph will still be there when school starts.

■ Therapists or teachers should use Social Stories (see Chapter 11) to prepare the student for the transition to the inclusion class, as well as for special activities throughout the year. This story should explain the main events that will occur on the first day of school and some key classroom rules.

- Invite the student's parents to bring him to school when it is empty so he can find his way around with no pressure.
- Prepare the student for your class in a 1:1 setting. Let him meet you ahead of time, discuss some expectations and rules, answer his questions or concerns, reassure him that you expect a great year. If possible, meet him in the classroom you will use and show him around.
- Provide the parent, aide, or a therapist with some of the class curriculum as far ahead of time as possible. This way they can start to prepare the child for some of the material he will encounter early in the year.
- Create picture schedules/picture books that the child can review before the year starts or early in the year, so he knows what the daily routine will be.
- Give each child his own desk so that the child with ASD has some feeling of control over his environment. If you rearrange the room from time to time, let the child with ASD (or all children) take their own desks with them to the new spot. If the child becomes anxious or distracted when in close proximity to other children, try to position his desk so he is not forced to face another child.
- Children with ASD do better when they know where things are kept. If possible, keep his math materials in one place, his reader in another, the chalk and scissors in another, etc. If the child is old enough, let him pick a spot for each set of materials; otherwise, you pick, but be sure to explain the system to him.
- Make sure you tell the child with ASD, as explicitly as possible, what is expected of him. If he can read, you might provide him with a copy of classroom rules when he comes to meet you in class before the beginning of the year. Unlike some other children, many children with ASD like rules and take them quite literally.
- If the child is moving from a self-contained classroom to a more inclusive one, use reverse mainstreaming to help him gradually get used to the new classroom. Handpick two or three peers to come into the separate class to talk about what the inclusion class will be like, for several visits. Discuss with the peers what they would like to say

AUTISM IN YOUR CLASSROOM | **131**

and go over some topics, such as classroom rules, special activities, classroom jobs, etc.

- Transition slowly. If the transition is expected to be difficult for the child, start with an hour a day and work up to full-time inclusion (it's a balance between keeping the child's emotional equilibrium and not missing too much).
- If standardized testing is necessary (for example, for reading placement), it is helpful to do it before school starts or within the first few days. That way the child with ASD can get into his school day routine as soon as possible.

Procedures to Use All Year

So, the school year is under way. Here are some additional general principles that will be important all year:

- Keep in frequent communication with parents about what's happening at home and at school. Let parents know what concepts or skills are being focused on so they can reinforce them at home. Discuss whether the homework load is too big, too small, or just right. (Communication with parents is described in Chapter 4.)
- When you introduce a new unit and materials related to it are kept on display or accessible, make sure you explicitly teach the child with ASD where these materials are to be kept.
- Be sure to have some fun and educational small projects put away for the child. Children with ASD do better when they are kept busy with interesting activities; they tend to drift into their own world when left alone.
- Present the work in manageable chunks. The child with ASD can easily feel overwhelmed and begin to engage in resistant or avoidant behaviors. Provide lots and lots of reinforcement for effort, whether the child is successful or not.
- Let the child do one thing at a time. Children with ASD are often terrible at multitasking. They tend to focus completely on one thing at a time (not always, of course, what you want them to focus on). Use every trick you know to help them focus on the task at hand (visual supports,

reinforcers, high-interest material). Then, if the child is on task, *don't* distract him. (While he's working on his math sheet, don't say, "Oh, Billy, don't forget to take your lunchbox home today.") See Chapter 8 for more information on difficulties with attention.

- Multi-sensory presentation (visual, auditory, movement) will often help keep the child with ASD focused and interested.

- Teach rules and provide opportunities to practice. As you try to help the child with ASD fit in better with his peers and develop his social and communication skills, your basic technique will be to teach him some simple rules (start *very* simple) and then give him lots of opportunity to practice these rules. We outline many of these rules in the chapters that follow; pick the ones that your child needs the most and can probably master. Don't do more than a few at one time.

- After a period of work, or if the child with ASD is getting restless, give him (and perhaps all the children) a gross motor break. If only the child with ASD needs it, you can ask him to erase the board, water a plant, pass out supplies, or deliver a message. It's much easier to forestall disruptive behavior than to deal with it when it arises.

Adjust Your Own Behavior

Here are some additional general guidelines addressing how your own behavior can help or hinder the child with ASD from doing well in your classroom.

Keep Your Cool

Stay cool, calm, and collected. Don't take negative behavior personally. Put things in a positive way. Children with autism spectrum disorders (like other children, but more so) do not respond well to emotional arousal in others. They may not understand why you are angry or frustrated, they are not very empathic about your frustration (but what child is?), and they may become very anxious around raised voices.

Stay cool, calm, and matter-of-fact, as much as humanly possible. Remember, in the vast majority of cases, the child with ASD is not being deliberately disrespectful or provocative, or challenging your authority, even though this may be your immediate reaction. He truly does not understand the emotional reaction he provokes in others by apparently disrespectful language because to him it may just be language that is literally true ("your shirt has a funny smell"). You may have thought he understood some behavior rule of the classroom but he didn't really get it. His ability to inhibit impulses to speak or act is weak. He can be stressed or made frustrated, confused, or anxious by what other children take as normal classroom noise or movement. So your response should be authoritative but calm ("Let's figure out a nicer way to say that so other people's feelings aren't hurt." "I think you can be a good hand-raiser. Let's see if you can raise your hand the next time you want to say something." "You know a lot about this subject. Let's give the other kids a turn, and then we'll come back to you.")

As with every other child, the behavior and progress of the child with ASD in your class will depend to some extent on his relationship to you. He needs to feel respected, understood, and valued, even while he knows that you will keep his behavior in bounds.

Provide Consistency and Predictability

Your student with ASD depends much more than most children on consistency and predictability. This is part of the syndrome. As he gets to know the classroom routine, he will come to depend on it, and on the consistency of your reactions to his behavior. If a change has to be made, whenever possible, prepare him for it in advance. Let him know what will happen and why. Prepare for the unexpected: let him know that every so often there will be a fire drill, but that you won't know ahead of time. Let him know why it is actually important that people not know ahead of time about fire drills. Give him simple, specific directions about exactly what to do in that situation, and if he can handle it, maybe some specific responsibility like raising the window shade.

Give him a rule with which to comfort himself when the unexpected happens (maybe even printed on a card), like "Expect the unexpected" or "Sometimes surprises happen. That's OK."

Give him five-minute warnings before he must stop an activity. Don't surprise him with the end of the activity with no warning. He may also have trouble letting go of an unfinished activity. Make a plan ahead of time for what you both will do if the project doesn't get finished (as his perfectionism or slow processing makes sometimes likely). For example, he could take it home to finish or finish tomorrow, or you could give several alternative stopping points on a worksheet so he can feel he was finished even if he wasn't.

Give the Child Time

The nervous system of the child with ASD sometimes needs extra time to do things. This is particularly true of language-related tasks. He may need extra time to think about a question you asked or to read a passage. He needs extra time to shift his attention from one topic or activity to another. On a larger time scale, he may need more time than the other children to adjust to the classroom; it may be several months before he's really comfortable with the rules and procedures.

See the Child's Strengths

An autism spectrum disorder is a disability. It comes with limitations and challenges. But it also comes with a certain cognitive and personality style that can be a real asset in many ways. The child with ASD is seldom deceitful or manipulative. (Of course, he may try to get out of unpleasant tasks by engaging in behaviors that have been rewarded with escape in the past, but he's not playing with your head.) Children with ASD tend to be quite honest (sometimes *too* honest). Their preoccupations can lead them to have real passions for subjects (music, astronomy, insects, rocks) and they can become highly expert in their preferred subjects. They're not too concerned with the subtleties of their peers' reactions to them (although many children with ASD very much want to be liked by other children) so they're not mindlessly conformist. They like and understand rules, so if you can get them to understand and accept basic classroom rules, they are likely to abide by them.

Let the child know that you see his strengths; compliment him often on these traits and on his attempts to master new skills as well as on his successes. When you are getting to know the child, observe whether he responds well to great enthusiasm, or whether he responds better to quiet and moderate praise.

Try to Understand the Child's Motivations

This is difficult. We've been working with children on the autism spectrum for many years and we often don't "get" what's driving them to do some of the things they do (part of what keeps us fascinated).

One way to try to understand behavior is to consider the old psychological theory about why people work. It often applies nicely to other behaviors as well. The three motivations are suggested to be *power, affiliation, and achievement.*

Do you work or pick a specific job (aside from the need to pay the rent, of course) because you like to be around other people, have others to talk to, and form relationships with others (affiliation)? Do you work because you like the authority and responsibility; the chance to control others and tell them what to do (power)? Or do you work because you like to really get things done, get projects finished, see the completed work done right (achievement)? We can all think of people who have a balance of motivations tipped to one or the other of these. Well, children with ASD are usually big on *achievement.* If your student seems bossy to other children or demanding of adults, it is quite likely that this is not, as it might seem, a matter of trying to get power over others. He's just trying to keep things on the right track, make sure things are going the way they should, and maximize the chance of the expected or desired outcome.

What Teaching Strategies Work in Inclusive Classrooms?

There is a small but well-done set of studies on some teaching strategies that promote success of students with autism spectrum disorders in inclusion classes. We present a summary here (adapted from a research review by Joshua Harrower and Glen Dunlap; see References).

Use Pre-practice or Pre-teaching Liberally

Expose the child ahead of time to activities or materials that you anticipate he will find difficult. If you're discussing the calendar or the weather in circle time, have his aide or one of his therapists prepare him with this material the day before or just before circle time, so he's familiar with the material and will find your language easier to understand as it flows by in real time. Also, preparing him with an answer will enable him to volunteer an answer (maybe with a prompt). Obviously, you won't be able to pre-teach everything—that would double the child's school day! Pick the most difficult activities for the child (or if they're really too difficult for him, give him something else to do during those activities, and focus on the material he has a better chance of getting—the material of intermediate difficulty).

Provide Prompts

Expect that the child with ASD will need more prompting to stay on task, provide correct answers to questions, and interact with peers than typically developing children do. If the child is off-task or does not know the answer to a question, provide prompts of increasing specificity, giving the child as much opportunity as possible to return to task or give a correct answer on his own.

For example, if your student is supposed to be doing a worksheet and appears to be off-task, a hierarchy of prompts might be:

1. strolling down the aisle and making eye contact and a smile,
2. reminding him quietly of the time left,
3. reminding him quietly of the incentive he's working for in staying on task and completing work,
4. asking him if he needs help with a particular problem,
5. providing help with the problem he got stuck on.

Prompts can be of other types, too. Researchers found that putting a vibrating device (like a cell phone with the ringer turned off) in a child's pocket, timed to go off at intervals, served as a prompt to the child to make a social initiation to another child, such as inviting him to play, or asking a social question. Artificial as these prompts may seem, they can help to make appropriate behaviors more habitual and give the child opportunities to get reinforced for success. Then, over time, he will be able to generalize the behaviors (use them in other settings with other people) and become independent of the prompts.

Use Positive Reinforcements, or Incentives Very Liberally

This is absolutely key to keeping the cooperation of the child with ASD and managing potential behavior problems and is discussed in Chapter 12. See what the child likes (or ask his parents) and then individualize the incentives you use. For the child with more behavior or impulse control difficulty, use immediate reinforcers; provide an incentive (even if only a smiley face) for a small piece of work successfully completed. For the older or higher functioning child, use delayed incentives. Let the child earn points on the way to a larger reward that may be given at the end of the week (e.g., a chance to visit the office, a sheet of gold star stickers to take home).

School work and social interaction can be very difficult for children with ASD. Don't wait for success; reinforce your student's effort and attention.

Use Picture Schedules

Picture schedules can help the child know what to expect on a typical day, and on unusual days, warn him about events he should be prepared for ahead of time. Using schedules is discussed in more detail in Chapter 12, and books that can be helpful in making and using visual supports are listed in the Suggested Reading list at the back of this book.

Help the Child Monitor His Own Behavior and Reinforce Himself

If the child is able, teaching him to monitor his own behavior can be very valuable. For example, have him keep track of the number of times he remembered to raise his hand before speaking, and the number of times he didn't. Have him reinforce himself by helping himself to a gold star from the dish on your desk and bringing home a chart full of stars at the end of the week to show his parents. When possible, use natural consequences. For instance, say: "You got all your worksheet done. Great! Now you have time to work on that puzzle." Your praise and the opportunity to do a favorite activity in his free time are natural consequences—unlike saying something like: "You got all your worksheet done. Great! Here's an M & M." (Although food rewards can work wonders, too, when you're pressed!)

Use Functional Analysis of Problem Behaviors

As Chapter 12 discusses, you may need to request a functional behavior analysis (FBA) if your student has frequent or disruptive problem behaviors, especially if it's not clear what is triggering these behaviors. These analyses, which are usually completed by the school psychologist or behavior specialist, can pinpoint why a child is persisting in using a problem behavior. Problem behaviors generally don't arise from nowhere. Keeping a record may reveal, for example, that Derek starts to make noises or distract the other children when lessons are too difficult for him, or when his feelings have been hurt, or when he's bored. Once you know the underlying reason for a behavior, you can change the precipitating factors or the way that you respond to the behavior to make it less likely to occur. For more information about FBA, see *Functional Behavior Assessment for People with Autism* by Beth Glasberg.

Use Peers as Tutors, "Peer Mentors," or "Peer Buddies"

Tutoring by peers can increase the child's motivation and attention, and has been shown to result in improvements in reading comprehension and math. Teach the peer mentor to initiate play with the child with ASD and keep him socially involved on the playground (see Chapter 11). Peer mentor systems work better when at least three typical peers are used, either in a rotating system, or with different tasks. Peer mentors or tutors should be selected based on their social maturity, willingness to help, and patience. They should be given clear guidelines about what to do for the student with ASD and instructed to ask for help when they are confused about what to do. Training and supervision could be provided in a lunchtime mentor club. See Chapter 11 for more information on peer mentors.

Use Small Cooperative Learning Groups

Put the child with ASD in a learning group with one or more peer mentors or tutors, who are instructed to make sure he stays involved and is given a task he can do. See the section on "Peer Tutors, Mentors, and Lunch Buddies" in Chapter 11 for details on how to do this.

Give the Child with ASD Choices

If possible, let him choose which assignment he wants to do for tonight and which tomorrow night. Let him choose which incentive he wants to work for. Choices (whether apparent or real) can greatly increase the child's motivation and involvement. However, if the child struggles to make decisions and the process of making a decision makes him very anxious, limit the decisions you ask him to make to the simple ones.

Use High Interest Materials

Motivation is absolutely key for children with autism spectrum disorder. (It is for all children, of course, but the child with ASD may be less driven by the need to acquire and demonstrate mastery of skills to you.) So, use high interest material as much as possible. If he's obsessed with Pokemon (or Thomas the Tank Engine, Neopets, etc.), use Pokemon characters in your math examples, or ask the aide or speech therapist to prepare some reading paragraphs about Pokemon characters.

Work with the Student's Parents

Parents are a critical part of the special education team. They can provide insight into the child's behavior, needs, and thinking. Although they are not usually education "professionals," they know their child better than anyone else does and observe him in the widest range of environments. Parents often have an excellent intuitive sense of what will and will not work for their child. They need to hear your observations and be helped to implement strategies you are using in your classroom at home.

Parents will also have many questions for you. They will ask for your advice and you will be called on to explain how their child's educational goals can be achieved in your classroom. You will sometimes need to explain why certain methods of intervention or curriculum modifications have been chosen. The rest of the child's team will help you do this.

You will help the parents to follow through with interventions at home, along with other members of the team, to encourage generalization of skills. It is, however, important that the parents are allowed to remain the child's parents and not expected to become the educators, especially if cognitive and academic work is causing friction between the parents and child. The main idea is to help the parents help the child complete homework and to teach the parents about their child's cognitive style and the way he processes information. The parents should only take on cognitive work, beyond that required for school, if it can be done in such a way that it will not interfere with their relationship with their child. See Chapter 4 for a fuller discussion of family life with a child with ASD, as well as information about effective ways to communicate with parents.

How Do You Know That Inclusion Is Working?

As the year goes by, some *indicators of successful inclusion* to watch for are:

- The child is able to generalize what he learns. For example, if he's taught social interaction skills with specific peers, he starts to use these skills with others.

- You find you can gradually fade out some of the child's reliance on his one-on-one assistance.
- The child becomes increasingly capable of independence in some areas of functioning.
- The child is winning acceptance from peers.
- The child is making good progress toward meeting his IEP goals and is learning at a rate commensurate with his abilities.
- The child is happy and likes coming to school.

On the other hand, *indicators that inclusion is having limited success* include:

- The child continues to show full reliance on one-on-one assistance.
- The child continues to need a very high degree of supervision and has few independent successes.
- The child is alienated from peers or stigmatized by them. (In this case, you should get the school guidance counselor or school psychologist involved in helping classmates understand and accept the child.)
- The child cannot generalize what he learns to new situations or new material.
- The child is mastering a limited amount of new material—less than might be expected from a student with his cognitive abilities.
- The child is unhappy and resists coming to school.

Remember, in some cases, the child's limitations, or limitations on available support and resources, may make limited success the best that can be achieved. However, if any of the above indictors of limited success continue for several months, you, the parents, and the other members of the IEP team should meet to discuss your concerns. There may be additional supports and services available for you and the child that could help him have a more successful experience in inclusion. These supports might include consultation from an inclusion specialist, school psychologist, or behavior therapist, or more individualized assistance for the child in the classroom. Alternatively, members of the IEP team might agree that it would be better for the child to move into a less inclusive setting, at least temporarily.

Remember, inclusion is not an end in itself. The purpose of education is to enable the child to learn to his or her potential and to experience academic and social successes. When this can be accomplished in an inclusion setting, that's great, but the child's welfare should be paramount. This may necessitate flexibility in making decisions about placement.

8 | Cognition and Motor Issues

Cognition refers to all of the mental processes that allow a person to come to know something. These include attention, organization and planning, memory, and learning. Chapters 2 and 3 introduce information about cognitive strengths and weaknesses often found in children with ASD. This chapter talks about how teachers can help a child with ASD to learn more effectively. It does not focus on specific academic skills (that comes later, in Chapter 10), but rather on more general learning issues such as using a child's strengths to compensate for her weaknesses, enhancing attention to material, and increasing the ability to organize, plan, and remember information. We also include a discussion of the fine and gross motor skills that are important for students with ASD in inclusive classrooms to develop, since these skills can contribute to, or detract from, a child's success with some of the academic and social skills needed for successful inclusion.

Cognitive Profiles

Autism spectrum disorders are not defined by overall intelligence. In fact, children with ASD can have intelligence that tests anywhere from severely mentally retarded to very superior. In this book, we use the term "high functioning ASD" to refer to children with intelligence in or near the normal range. High functioning individuals with ASD, except for some with Asperger's disorder, tend to be strong in processing visual and spatial information. They tend to be weak in auditory and language processing. Children with Asperger's syndrome may have nonverbal learning disabilities, where visual and spatial information processing are weaker than language skills. Everybody with ASD (including those with Asperger's) has relative strengths in processing and remembering simple and concrete material (including language). Everybody with ASD shows weaknesses in handling complex and abstract language, memory for complex ideas, and in organization and planning.

Effective teaching uses a child's cognitive and linguistic strengths to improve or compensate for her weaknesses. Simple visual information that can be memorized should always be used to support learning. This includes some combination of pictures, written language (if the child can read), and concrete visual demonstrations. A strength in simple rote verbal memory can also be used to help the child learn through repetition, verbal rehearsal, and talking through the steps to complete a task. Some children may need more repetition of auditory information than of visual information because auditory information is fleeting, whereas visual information stays put until it is processed. In addition, the child may have impaired attention to sounds, impaired discrimination of sounds, and slowed processing of sounds.

Even for children with Asperger's, processing of auditory information should be supported by visual information. It is important to remember, however, that because children with Asperger's have impaired visual processing, visual information needs to be simple and very clear. Also, since children with Asperger's may show relative strengths in verbal skills, it is important that they learn to talk through all visual material including such things as math problems, diagrams, maps, and visual sequences.

Children with autism think and learn in a way that is quite different from the average person. They seem to learn first by rotely memorizing and only later do they understand the material. For example, a child with autism may memorize the words in a story without complete comprehension and only understand it completely once taught what it means. Another example is when a child with autism memorizes and uses a social rule she has been taught but does so in a rote way and does not initially understand when to use the rule or how the social behavior functions for her. She only comes to understand the meaning of the behavior after she has used it many times or the function has been directly taught to her.

It is important to be explicit about every step of a process, and every important concept, in what you are teaching. Don't assume the child understands all of the material just because she can repeat it. Direct teaching of what may seem obvious to you will result in less frustration for the child with ASD and less frustration for you. Do assume that the child will naturally pay more attention to the details of what you are teaching but may entirely miss the main point and concepts. You will need to explicitly differentiate the essential from the nonessential parts of the information for her.

Attention

Difficulties with attention is one of the most frequently reported problems for children with ASD in the classroom. The attention style of a child with ASD can be baffling. On the one hand, the child may have an almost incredible ability to attend to her own agenda. In fact, many children who turn out to have ASD were first brought to a doctor because their parents thought there might be something wrong with their hearing. They often do not respond to their name, and parents say that when the television is on "a bomb could go off" and the child wouldn't notice. On the other hand, ability to sustain attention to what you are teaching or to peers can be very limited.

In order for a child to effectively learn in your classroom, she must pay attention to what you are teaching. Understanding the attentional deficits that are common in children with ASD (especially high functioning ASD) will help you to intervene in a way that has the best possible chance of working.

A good way to describe the attention of a child with ASD is that she has trouble managing it. In other words, she has difficulty putting her attention where it needs to be. She may have trouble sustaining her attention or sticking with something once she has started to pay attention to it. She may have trouble selecting out the important things to pay attention to. She may have trouble shifting or moving her attention from one thing to another, or she may shift her attention to the new thing, only to derail and move her attention back to something that is more important for her (her own preoccupations, or the last thing she was doing).

Children with ASD often have a unique attentional profile: They do have the ability to sustain their attention to at least certain types of information (usually their own repetitive interests). However, in interacting with children with ASD, it is clear that they often have trouble sustaining their attention to information outside their areas of interest. It turns out that ability to sustain attention is far more related to the child's motivation to pay attention to the material than to her ability to attend. (Some researchers think this is also true of children with AD/HD.)

Optimizing Attention for Children with ASD

To enhance attention it is important to motivate the child through effective reinforcement. What is reinforcing to the child with typical development may not be reinforcing to the child with ASD, however. You must determine what is most reinforcing for each individual child. One child with ASD may require immediate reinforcement with a favorite treat or "stars." Another child may be reinforced by breaks away from social interaction or by being allowed to engage in her own preoccupations for a specified period of time. See Chapter 12 for more information. In addition, a good guide for more in-depth information on using reinforcement with children with ASD is *Incentives for Change* by Lara Delmolino and Sandra Harris.

Use Visual Strategies

The modality (auditory, visual, kinesthetic, etc.) through which the material is presented can enhance attention and make it easier for a child to process it. It is best to present information through the stronger modality in concert with the weaker. Many high functioning individuals with ASD are actually better at making visual discriminations and faster in searching visual material than their typical peers. In addition, concrete visual information can enhance attention simply by virtue of the fact that it sticks around longer than auditory information, giving the child a chance to process a piece of information she initially missed.

There is evidence that neural processing of auditory information is abnormally slowed in high functioning children with ASD, while the speed of processing visual information is largely normal. So their processing in these two modalities is out of synch. It is important to help the child develop her ability to put visual and auditory information together.

You should give the child lots of visual cues. Draw pictures and write on the board. Give her notes or graphic organizers so that she can look at the visual information and follow along with your lecture. It is important that the visual and auditory information match. It will be very confusing if you talk about one thing and your written notes present different information. Query the child to make certain she can show you where what you are discussing is in the notes. In addition, allow her time to process auditory information. Resist the impulse to repeat auditory information over and over or to quickly restate what you are saying in other words if it looks like the child does not understand. Wait the child out and supplement with clear visual cues, making sure to direct her attention to where it should be.

Make Sure the Child Knows Where to Focus

Many children with ASD do have the ability to focus their attention if they are told where to focus. The classic test of focused or selective attention is called the cancellation task. In this task the child is required to quickly cross out a specific target letter or number every time she finds it on a page filled with letters and numbers. People with ASD are just as good at this as people with typical development. Still, it is important to explicitly direct the child's attention to where it needs to be. Research shows that the speed with which a child with ASD responds to visual information is better when she is told what she is supposed to be attending to. Point to where her attention should be or remind the child of the topic under discussion by stating it and writing it on the board or on a piece of paper to place on her desk. Be aware that this strategy only seems to work when there are no significant distractions around.

Minimize Distractions

When there are distractions around, it is often difficult to get the child with ASD to focus her attention on schoolwork. Therefore, the environment should be set up to remove distractions and the child should be taught how to ignore distractions, if possible.

Use Preferential Seating. One of the easiest ways to minimize distractions is to seat the child close to the teacher so that there are not many people or objects between her and the instructor to distract her. One teacher in a mainstream class said that she and the individual assistant of a child with ASD could not get him to attend to the lessons in her class even though he attended very well in resource room without a lot of structuring by the resource room teacher. A classroom observation revealed that the child had been seated in the middle of the room by a large fish tank, which was both visually and auditorally distracting. A change in seating, along with the efforts the teacher was already making to orient his attention to the important information, greatly improved his attention to the lessons.

Remove Visual and Auditory Clutter. To the extent possible, remove visual clutter.

- Do not seat the child near an interesting bulletin board, classroom computers, or the class pet.
- Seat the child where she has a clear line of vision to you.
- Keep the child's desk free of extraneous materials.

If the child is distracted by background noise, there are other strategies you can try:

- Reduce the noise of chairs scraping on the floor by putting casters on the chair legs
- Seat the child as far away from the hall as possible if people walking by distract her

An FM audio system can be used to boost the signal of your voice relative to the background sounds in the classroom, as well. If you think an FM system may be necessary for the child, consult your SLP about it. (See Chapter 9 for more detail about this methodology.)

It is also important to consider whether certain smells are distracting to the child. Although in our experience this is not that common, if the child appears distractible, query the parent about the kinds of things that are particularly distracting to the child, including scents. Perhaps a staff member is wearing a fragrance that distracts or disturbs her.

Help the Student Stay Focused on a Task

Once distractors are reduced, it will be easier to let the child know where she should place her focus. Again, it is important to visually cue the child:

- You can write down (with words, symbols, or pictures) what she should be attending to on the board or on a sheet of paper and place it on her desk.
- You can prearrange nonverbal signals with the student that signify that she needs to focus and where she should put her attention (e.g., a touch on the shoulder followed by a point to where she should be attending).

■ Get feedback from the child and give frequent feedback. Ask the child to repeat what you just said and ask simple questions about the task at hand. Importantly, be sure to use a nonverbal signal like a pat on the back or "thumbs up" that tells her she is doing a good job.

Study Buddies: You might have a typically developing student act as the child's study buddy and cue her as to which page the class is on in a book or what materials are needed to complete a task during your lessons. It would be helpful to involve different study buddies from day to day. Be sure to observe the interaction between the study buddy and your student with ASD in case the buddy becomes too directive or either student becomes too frustrated in the interaction. The interaction should always be positive and supportive. Later the child with ASD can be taught to look at other students in the classroom on her own to discover what she should be doing and to check with you if she's not sure what she's supposed to be attending to.

Help the Student Shift Focus to a New Task

When you are shifting the focus of attention from one task to another in your class, it is essential to keep in mind that:1) the student with ASD often may not shift without specific cuing, and 2) it takes more time for a child with ASD to shift her attention, even with appropriate cuing. It is also important to understand that the child must completely shift her attention to process what you are presenting. Children with ASD have what has been called a narrow spotlight of attention. They are not multi-taskers and cannot generally focus on more than one thing at a time. If they don't completely shift their attention to where it should be, they will miss information that you present. It is difficult for children with ASD to flexibly allocate their attention or move it around.

Auditory and visual warnings, visual schedules of activities, or visual lists of the steps required to complete a task can cue a child that a shift in attention will soon be required. You can say something like, "Soon we will start the next part of the lesson." Then when you are going to start the next activity say, "Now it is time to do the next part of the lesson. We will _____." Make sure to write and point to the next activity on the board or on paper on the child's desk.

Attention is aided by expectation. If the child expects something to happen, her attention will get there more quickly when it does happen. You want to prime her for what is coming next.

Minimize Down Time

It also helps to keep down time to a minimum. With too much down time it can be easy for a child's attention to derail and go to something that is more absorbing for her such as her own preoccupations, or she may perseverate on (inappropriately keep attending to or repeating) a previous task or even a phrase you used during teaching that is still in her head. One of the greatest difficulties in the classroom can be to get a child with ASD to move her attention from her preoccupations or internal concerns (such as anxiety) to the task at hand or to her peers.

It is easier to limit preoccupations if the child is talking about what she is thinking. You can say "We are not thinking about that right now. We are thinking about _____. You will have a chance to talk about it [the preoccupation] later." Be sure to specify when that will be ("after lunch" or "in 10 minutes"). It is harder to stop preoccupations when the child is just thinking about them, rather than talking. Watch for signs of internal preoccupation—a glazed look, moving lips as if she is talking to herself, stereotyped body motions such as rocking. Then you can ask the child if she is thinking about her "special stuff" and suggest she move on to the task at hand.

Keep the Student Engaged

Active involvement in class throughout the school day improves a child's ability to stay on task. Strategies for keeping your student engaged include:

- Give her special jobs to do to help in the classroom (for example, if she feels comfortable, have her point to information being presented on the blackboard).
- Ask her questions during each class activity. Make certain that she can be successful in answering. For example, if she is shy about speaking in class, ask questions that she can respond to with a nod or shake of her head. If she has trouble with verbal formulation (as most children with ASD do) ask the question in a multiple-choice format.
- Let her demonstrate her strengths (for example, by reading to the class).
- Try to incorporate her special interests into lessons sometimes. Give examples for concepts that relate to her special interests. If she is fascinated with dinosaurs, have

a couple of the math word problems involve dinosaurs. *(However, always keep in mind that the idea is to ultimately try to help her to attend to and complete assignments in the way that they are presented to all children.)*

■ Have her draw pictures related to what is being discussed as you present each lesson.

The key is to find ways to keep the child actively involved in the content of the lessons.

Set Time Limits: For some children with ASD who have trouble sticking with independent tasks, imposing time limits for completing a task can be effective. If the child does not complete her work within the time limit, she will have to do it during a time when she would typically be allowed to engage in her preoccupations and special interests (e.g., computer time). This type of procedure might lead to undue stress for some children who are not ready for it and should then not be used. Even when children are ready, only implement it in a light-hearted (and never a punitive) way with lots of reinforcement for success. Do not keep the child in from recess, as this is an important opportunity to interact with other children, practicing social skills. In addition, you may inadvertently reinforce slow completion of tasks if the social demands of recess are stressful and the child would prefer to miss it.

Individualize Your Strategies

As with all abilities in the child with ASD, she should be challenged to attend at a level where she will experience success most of the time. For example, you may want the child to work on completing her work independently. But if she is not ready to do it in your classroom, it may make more sense to have her do it in a situation where she has one-on-one attention and therefore continual feedback and structuring, such as in the resource room. However, the goal of helping her to move toward independence should be maintained.

In sum, children with ASD can sustain their attention when motivated. Attention to visual information is generally better than attention to auditory information. It is important to not have too much down time. Explicitly telling the child where she should put her attention is helpful but only if the environment is free of distractions. Children with ASD need more time than other children do to disengage their attention from the current focus and move it to a new place. The major ways to improve the attention of a child with ASD in your classroom are to:

- reduce distractions,
- provide appropriate reinforcement to motivate,
- explicitly tell the child where to focus her attention,
- give the child time to shift her attention through warnings and expectations,
- provide visual cues to help the child to maintain her focus and not derail, and
- keep the child actively engaged.

Organization and Planning

Children in your classroom with ASD will need help with organization and planning. Even those children with ASD who do very well academically have difficulty with organization and planning ahead. You will need to prompt the child to plan ahead. You will need to directly teach "plans" for multi-step tasks in school.

As you are teaching the child to plan ahead you will need to help her with organization. Children with ASD may forget to bring pencils, pens, notebooks, and textbooks to school and fail to bring home all of the materials they need to do their homework. Visual prompts and practice can help. For example:

- If a child consistently carries a notebook but always forgets a pencil or pen, pictures of a pencil and pen can be put on the notebook as a reminder.
- If the child has trouble keeping track of what she will need for each subject in school, the materials needed can be listed or pictured next to each activity on her schedule.
- You can help her remember to turn in her homework by giving her a brightly colored folder for homework papers. You might have her write the word "homework" on it and decorate it. Each night she should be prompted by her parents to place homework sheets in the folder and she should take out the folder as soon as she gets to school and place it on her desk.
- Subjects should be color coded with one color for the notebook, textbook cover, and other materials for each subject.

If the child cannot pack materials to bring home or back to school, she will need adult support in getting that done. However, the goal should be for the child to learn and ultimately implement plans for successfully carrying out these activities on her own.

Directly Teach Planning Ability

To develop planning ability, children should first be taught to follow simple plans for carrying out activities accompanied by visual cues. Parents should be encouraged to directly teach the child plans at home. For example, they can teach a general plan for creating something by having her participate in making things at home such as simple foods (e.g., pudding, a sandwich) or easy arts and crafts projects. The first step in making something is always to collect all of the materials that will be needed. The next step is to read the instructions or talk about the steps. As always, it helps to make the steps visual and concrete. If the child is not yet reading, pictures can be used. Next the child will follow each step, first, with prompting, as needed.

As the child is ready, prompting should decrease and then prompts should be dropped altogether and she should just follow the visual plan. In the beginning, the number of steps should be kept to a minimum (three at most). Over time, the number of steps can be increased. Ultimately rules for shopping, crossing streets, and taking transportation should be explicitly taught as well. For each project, the parents should take pictures of the child as she carries out each step. Later she can practice putting the pictures in the correct order and talk to people about what she did to complete her project.

To develop planning in school, it helps to directly teach plans for tasks that the child needs to do every day and for dealing with situations that often cause problems for the child in the classroom. For example, a child can be taught a plan for packing her bag at the end of each day (rather than just having the child's individual assistant do it). To determine the steps to be included in the plan, a task analysis will need to be carried out which considers what the child can and cannot already do.

For a child who does not yet have the reading and writing skills to record her own assignments, they can be written in an assignment pad accompanied by pictures of the materials needed. Then the child can be required to take out the materials and put them in her bag.

For a child who can read and write, the plan might look like this:

1. Teach the child to write down homework on a pad or in an agenda book.
2. After recording each assignment, the teacher or aide should help the student decide what materials she needs to complete each task.
3. She should write down needed materials on the pad next to each task.
4. Toward the end of the school day, the student should then collect the materials from her desk and check each one off on the pad as she puts it in her school bag. (In the beginning, be sure to allow plenty of time for this step so the student does not miss her bus or become anxious about missing her bus.)
5. She should practice this plan using other materials at home and in packing up her bag to go to school (suggest to parents that this be done the night before, given the usual morning rush).

In the same way, the child can be taught how to complete her nightly homework or develop plans for carrying out long-term assignments. It is important to make sure that the plans are always visual and concrete. You will need to help her break up the assignment into smaller units. You can teach by rote, writing out the general steps involved in completing any long-term report (e.g., decide topic, get topic approved, do some general reading on the topic, make general outline, etc.). You should even write into the plan "get help from teacher" during phases of a project that you know will be particularly difficult for the student (such as outlining). Encourage the child to memorize the plan, if possible.

The child should be taught to use her academic planner book or a large calendar to participate in making decisions about when she will complete each phase of a longer-term assignment. Communication with the parent in these matters is key. The child is unlikely to think of outside commitments in making her schedule with you and may then fail to meet her deadlines. Repeatedly failing to meet deadlines will allow her to feel that it is not important to meet commitments. To promote success, it is important to help her think realistically about her outside commitments when she is developing her plan. To do this, you will need to make sure you know what they are by communicating with a parent. You could ask the parent to write those commitments

Prompting

Types of prompts (from least to most intrusive):
1. Auditory verbal prompts (e.g., "Take out your math book")
2. Visual (with auditory) prompts
    a. Gestural (e.g., point to the child's math book)
    b. Model the behavior (e.g., Take out and hold up your math book; or take out and place her math book on her desk, put it away, and then have her do it)
3. Physical (with visual and auditory) prompts
    a. A touch (e.g., touch the child's elbow and the book to prompt her to get her math book out)
    b. Hand over hand teaching (e.g., gently hold the child's wrist and help her reach into her desk or backpack to get her math book)

If auditory verbal prompts do not help the child to be successful, add visual prompts and finally physical prompts. Give the child a few seconds to comply with a lower level prompt, then prompt at the next more intrusive level until the level of prompting required for the child to succeed is determined.

When the child is succeeding most of the time, begin to fade the prompts. Fade by prompting sequences of behavior rather than individual behaviors. For example, initially you may need to prompt every step in the process of packing up to go home (go to the closet, get your coat and bag, look at the list of books you need for homework, take out the first book, put it in your bag, check it off on the list, etc.). Over time and with success you will reduce the number of prompts until you are down to "pack up to go home." This means that prompts will be fewer and farther between.

Teach the child to seek visual prompts and to use them to prompt herself. For example, help her to look at what other students are doing if she is not certain of what she should be doing. Remember that most students with ASD have a relative strength in concrete visual processing so visual prompts will probably be helpful.

into the daily planner in a different color than the child will use to write down schoolwork.

The child should be given a great deal of practice implementing plans with the support and supervision of an adult so that she can become independent in implementing the plan. Exposing the child once or twice to a plan is clearly not enough. Even if the child can completely articulate the plan, she may still need prompting to carry it out.

Help the Child Generalize Planning Skills

It is essential to make a point of helping the child to generalize skills. As children with ASD learn a number of set plans for how to approach problems, they can be prompted to use these preplanned approaches when the same situations come up. Communication among staff members working with the child is essential so that each plan she learns is implemented the same way across settings. Using the same general plan in a variety of situations encourages generalization.

Don't be afraid to state the obvious when helping your student generalize skills. Plans learned and memorized by rote have to be generalized to new situations; this is helped by pointing out the similarities between the situation in which a plan was taught and a novel situation. For example, point out that the general steps in planning for a school project such as building a volcano are the same as those used for any craft or cooking project (i.e., find out what materials are needed, collect the materials, read through the steps for completing the project before you start, go back and read one step and complete it, then repeat for the next step, ask for help from an adult when you are confused or something is too hard, clean up all materials when finished). Another example is pointing out how the same graphic organizer you use in English class can be applied to writing in Social Studies and Science classes.

Teach the Child to Ask for Help

As the child is learning rote plans and organizational strategies for approaching tasks and applying them in a variety of situations, she also needs to learn the rule: "You will not have a rule for every situation." She needs to be taught to recognize completely novel or problem situations and to go to a trusted adult to ask for help in determining a plan to address those situations. You clearly cannot give her a plan for every situation she will encounter academically or socially. A very important coping strategy for her is to know when and how to ask for help. This will involve specifying who the child can ask for help with different problems and how and when the child should talk to that person. For example, children can be taught to ask to see a teacher for help and then ask, "When is a good time for me to get some help from you?" They also should be taught that they could use the phone to call someone to get help.

If a child does not typically ask for help or if she "requests" help in an inappropriate way (for example, by screaming or throwing her books on the floor), you will need to label the fact that she needs help. Then calmly tell her, "Next time, you can say 'I need help' instead." Write this rule down for the child. If a child is having these sorts of difficulties managing her emotions, try to anticipate her need for help and prompt her to ask before she does something inappropriate. For further information on developing a student's ability to modulate emotional reactions and ask for help, see Chapter 12.

In sum, organizing information is often a real weakness for children with ASD. As we said before, these children are not natural multi-taskers. They cannot flexibly move their attention around. They miss information and they may place undue importance on unimportant details at the expense of the overall idea. It is important to explicitly tell the child what the unifying or major concepts are that you are trying to get across and to show her how the details fit with those concepts. Then clarify the relative importance of each of the details. It will also be important to tell the child with ASD about the links between the information she is learning and real-life situations. Teach the child a general strategy for organizing everyday activities like long-term or multi-step projects, finishing homework or in-class work, and organizing her personal property and homework materials.

Memory and Learning

Many high functioning children with ASD have strong rote memory (memory for information exactly as it is presented) for both visual and auditory material, although memory for visual material is often better. In fact, memory for some types of information can be extraordinary.

Some children with ASD have remarkable memory for details, which is often associated with preoccupations such as travel routes, the makes and models of cars, sports statistics, facts associated with people (e.g., birthdates or the color house they live in), facts about the Civil War or another topic, or numerous tiny details associated with an event in their lives—anything that completely captures their attention. Some very verbal children on the spectrum can retell stories or material they read in a textbook almost verbatim. However, some children with ASD (sometimes the same ones who can easily remember details about their interests) have trouble remembering or recalling what they are taught.

Memory is influenced by a number of factors. If a child is not attending, the information does not get absorbed in the first place and so it is impossible to remember. As we discussed above, motivation plays a very important role in attention for children with ASD. So it is important to motivate the child to attend. This can be accomplished by:

1. making the material as inherently interesting as possible (see Chapters 10 and 12), and

2. by providing external reinforcers (breaks, stickers) for attending and learning.

Slowed auditory processing can influence memory as well. If a child processes auditory information slowly, by the time she has processed what she initially heard, she is hearing new information, which interferes with her ability to remember what was initially said. Presenting the material visually as well as verbally facilitates processing. Encouraging rote memorization of information presented through a multimodal approach to teaching is an excellent avenue via which children with ASD can initially acquire information. However, it is necessary to make sure that once a child has acquired information through rote learning, she learns the meaning of that information. Try not to talk too fast. Allow the child to register one idea before you move on to the next.

It is helpful to also teach the child mental visualization strategies. Specifically, it will help if the child learns to visually image the content of auditory information in her head. This especially makes sense if the child's visual memory is stronger than her auditory memory. To teach a child to visually image, you or the child's SPL can start by drawing (or having the child draw) pictures that represent auditorily presented stories. Once the child has experience with this, tell her to make the picture in her head and ask questions about what she "sees" to make certain that she is generating an appropriate visual image.

Whereas rote memory is usually a strength, memory for more complex, meaningful material is a relative weakness. Even children with good lower level language comprehension (such as comprehension of single words and sentences) have weak memory for complex information because they fail to use the strategies that children with typical development use to remember. Their learning style is to memorize details in a rote fashion. Soon, as they try to memorize all of the details, they exceed capacity and fail to learn or remember all of the information. In contrast, children with typical development use their understanding of concepts to aid memory. They understand the overall ideas and concepts and hang the details onto those concepts. Understanding how the details relate to each other and to the main point or concept promotes deeper processing, not just surface processing, as with rote memorization.

Deeper processing enhances memory for complex information. For this reason, you should directly teach your student with ASD to identify main ideas, extract basic concepts and main points in what she reads and hears, and learn to understand how the details she memorizes fit with those main concepts. A concrete visual approach to these skills is described in the chapter on language intervention (Chapter 9).

Mental Retardation

If you have a student with ASD who also has mental retardation (intellectual disabilities), the same profile discussed above is likely to apply:

- strengths in visual processing, rote memorization, concrete information, orientation to details;
- reliance on rules and procedures; and
- weaknesses in language and auditory skills, abstract or complex concepts, and making inferences.

The child will, however, have a greater degree of impairment across the board and less ability to use the compensatory strategies described above. In addition, this child will probably be learning material below grade level.

If you have a child with ASD plus intellectual disabilities in your class for all or part of the day:

1. There should be support available for the student and you from a special education teacher and perhaps an "inclusion specialist." Depending on how things are done in your school system, the special education specialist will most likely either:

    a. co-teach the class with you;
    b. be available to pull the student aside within the classroom to work with her and possibly other students on academics;
    c. work with the child in a resource room or other special education setting on certain academic subjects;
    d. take primary responsibility for modifying the child's class work and homework.

2. The student will most likely have modified goals in some, if not all, academic subjects, depending on her age and ability. For example, while the rest of the class is learning to divide decimals using pencil and paper, she may be learning to divide decimals with a calculator, or to divide whole numbers, with or without a calculator, or even how to write numbers.

3. Especially if the student's goals are significantly modified, it will be important to clarify who is responsible for teaching the student which academic content. Although by law, the IEP needs to specify who is responsible for teaching each goal, you may find that your student's IEP says that both the regular education and special education teacher are responsible for a given goal. Clearly, in this case, you and the special educator need to communicate directly about your individual roles in teaching the student. In addition, it is important to know that it is *never* the aide's role to teach the student a concept initially (unless the aide is a qualified teacher). That is up to you or the child's special educator. Although the aide may need to re-explain a concept, or watch the student working to ensure

she understands how to do something, educational assistants are not qualified to teach students with disabilities.

4. For your student with both mental retardation and ASD, the success of her inclusion experience will be measured by how well she achieves the goals on her IEP. Try not to get caught up in thinking that you have failed as a teacher if she does not "keep up" with the rest of the class in meeting grade-level objectives. What is more important is whether you and her IEP team think she is making appropriate progress toward her individualized goals. If you feel that the child is not making progress toward her IEP goals, and it seems that she is being educated in isolation in your mainstream classroom despite everyone's best efforts to include her, you need to bring this to the attention of the IEP team, including your student's parents.

Motor Issues

As mentioned in earlier chapters, children with ASD can have difficulties with some of the motor skills needed in the classroom. Most significant fine and gross motor issues are best addressed in occupational or physical therapy by specialists, but there are things you can do to help the child to develop better skills in these areas.

Handwriting

When a child with ASD has difficulties with motor skills, it often reflects a combination of problems with motor control and motor planning.

Motor control refers to the actual control over the pencil by the hand. Poor motor control can be seen in writing that's too heavy or light, too big, or shows unsteady, wiggly lines.

Motor planning refers to the child's ability to plan ahead. Poor motor planning can be seen in figures that don't fit within the space given, lines that don't intersect properly or that cut corners, and figures that are drawn or written too separated or overlapping. While a child may have the ability to draw simple vertical and horizontal lines, she may not be able to combine them to write a letter or draw a picture. In addition she may have trouble planning space on a piece of paper and begin to write something near the end of a line when it is clear, at least to you, that the word is not going to fit into the space.

Use Visual Guidelines. Children with ASD benefit from visual guidelines on paper when writing. At the most structured level, you can give the child dotted letters to trace. If necessary, you can use special paper with raised lines to write on or colored lines that help show the child where to start and stop writing. To help in planning space, you can draw rectangles on the page into which the child must fit each word she writes. When she gets good at this you can ask her to judge whether a word is a long rectangle word or a short rectangle word and whether she thinks it will fit into the space she has left at the end of a line. This approach helps the child to consider the size and uniformity of her writing and also helps her to slow down and think before she writes.

Use Cues. In teaching a child to write letters in the first place, it makes sense to capitalize on the child's strengths in simple rote auditory verbal memory and visual memory. You can directly teach a verbal plan for the movements involved in drawing shapes and writing letters. Although this certainly does not increase strength or motor control, it does improve motor planning. Once the child memorizes the verbal plan in association with the actual motor movements, she can use it to cue herself as she writes. These verbal cues can be simple descriptive ones (for 5: "down, around, go back, across") or more fanciful (remember the old cue for 5: "there was a child, he went around the corner, he put on his hat"). (A program like *Handwriting without Tears* found at www.hwtears.com may useful for many children with autism.)

Teach Keyboarding Skills. A child with fine and graphomotor (handwriting and drawing) deficits should learn keyboarding skills as early as possible. If the motor deficits are severe and she learns to type, she should be allowed to type her written work in school. Learning to type does not negate the need to develop better fine and graphomotor skills, since there will be circumstances in which the child will likely have to write things by hand. But give the child a chance to demonstrate her best work by typing, and then work on the handwriting as a separate issue.

Make Accommodations for Writing Problems. If a child is not typing, always take her slower writing speed into account when assigning written class work. If your student writes slowly due to significant graphomotor issues, she may need to take tests that require a significant amount of writing in the resource room. This way she can take additional time and not experience the pressure of needing to finish more quickly than she can in the classroom. This accommodation, if needed, should be noted in the child's IEP.

Some schools may provide the accommodation of a scribe to write down the child's thoughts and answers. However, the child should be required to complete some written work herself (possibly single sentences or single words or other work within her ability). If possible, the goal should be to have the child learn keyboarding skills. She must understand that she is responsible to the degree possible for her own work. Many times the use of a scribe backfires because the child begins to see the person who is scribing for her as being responsible for her work.

If you have to grade the student on handwriting, make it a separate grade from the grade for content, so she doesn't get penalized for graphomotor problems. And give lots of reinforcers (and good grades) for improvement and effort.

Some children with ASD have undue difficulty moving from printing to cursive writing (as do children with other learning disabilities). If learning cursive proves too frustrating for the child, forget it. Let her print. The point is to write legibly; how many brilliant adults do you know whose handwriting is illegible unless they print?

Physical Activities

It can be difficult to figure out how to include children with autism spectrum disorders in recess, physical education, and other sports activities. Many of the typical games and sports call for gross motor and social skills that the child with ASD has not yet mastered.

It is probably best to seek out alternatives to competitive sports for the child with ASD, at least until you are certain she has adequate skills. Some children with ASD are well coordinated and can participate in competitive sports, but they are distinctly in the minority. Lack of motor coordination and limited understanding of the overall idea of the game and details of how to play the positions and work as a teammate can produce significant frustration and distress as well as peer rejection.

Children with ASD can benefit from work with a recreational "sports coach." Parents often identify and work privately with a "sports coach" outside of school through a local gym. However, this role could be filled by the school gym teacher during adaptive P.E. (see below) or the child's special educator. This person works with the child one on one or in small groups, teaching the rules of typical playground games such as tag, running bases, and four square (aka box ball) so that it is possible for the child to participate on the playground if she wants to. In addition, the coach may teach the child rules for playing team sports such as soccer, basketball, and softball. In this safe and supportive setting, children can learn the rules of the games at their own pace.

Whenever possible, it helps to slow down the action and practice so the child can really learn. For example, play softball using a beach ball first because it moves slowly and is easy to catch and hit. This gives the child an opportunity not only to learn the skills but where to orient her attention during play and how to play as a team member. The child also needs to be taught that although there are basic rules for games, these rules change from setting to setting, so she should always check to see what the rules are.

Initially, when children with ASD start to play these games with their peers they may not handle the ball much. However, they will have learned to play their position and will not interfere with the play of their teammates, making them an acceptable addition to a recreational team. Physical games that have continual fast action, involve tracking the behavior of multiple other players, or require quick reactions (e.g., wall ball) are not recommended for most children with ASD, since it is hard for them to orient their attention quickly and respond fast. (Of course, if a child is really set on playing wall ball or basketball, she should be given the chance—sometimes she will surprise you!)

Sometimes children with ASD receive adaptive physical education instead of regular P.E. Adaptive P.E. involves adapting sports activities to the motor skill level of the child. The rules for specific games are also broken down into explicitly articulated steps. Adaptive P.E. is sometimes taught by a regular gym teacher and sometimes by a specialist. Adaptive physical education sometimes fulfills the role of recreational sports coaching for these children in schools. However, before you refer a child in your classroom for adaptive physical education, find out what the goals of the class are (assuming that your school offers such a class). The goals may be simply to work on developing gross motor coordination or to give the children with motor issues a place to safely engage in some physical activity. These are fine goals for a child with severe gross motor deficits. But if the child is just physically awkward and doesn't know how to engage in sports, she needs a sports coach instead.

If the parent of an awkward child discusses sports with you, you might suggest that sports that don't involve a lot of interaction among the players (e.g., swimming, skiing, track) make good choices for some children with ASD. But, as we said before, if the child is really motivated to try soccer, let her try. Especially if the child starts very young, when all the children are somewhat at sea and there is not a lot of competition, she may do well, and have fun.

Conclusion

In sum, while cognitive abilities vary widely in children with ASD, even high functioning children have cognitive issues in the areas of attention, memory for complex information, and organization and planning, including motor planning. Throughout this chapter we discuss explicitly teaching the child rules, plans, and strategies to optimize learning. Always keep in mind the goal of moving the child toward as much independence as she is capable of. Try to prevent the child from becoming too dependent on prompts from adults. Another issue in developing independence is helping the child to have insight into her own learning style and needs. Emphasize the child's strengths. Teach her about her strengths as well as her weaknesses and help her understand which strategies are most effective for her. Help her optimize the probability of success with situations in which she can use her strengths, and give her lots and lots of strokes for success!

9 | Language Issues

How well a student with ASD does in a mainstream classroom is strongly related to his language abilities. You will almost certainly find that language issues make it harder for you to teach a child, no matter what the subject matter. On the other hand, classroom teachers can play a major role in the development of speaking (expressive language) and understanding (receptive language). Teachers can work not only to reinforce skills taught by the child's speech-language pathologist, but also to develop additional written and oral language skills in the classroom. In this chapter we discuss the language issues of children with ASD and how they affect functioning in an inclusive classroom. We offer practical suggestions for how to address the language profile of children with ASD, including:

- problems with auditory processing,
- more impaired understanding of language than spoken expression,
- impaired ability to organize language, both comprehension (understanding how details fit together to form main ideas and concepts) and expression (such as telling a story or answering an open-ended question) in spite of relatively strong grammar, vocabulary, and articulation, and
- problems with pragmatics (social use of language).

Bear in mind that if your student is working with a speech-language pathologist (SLP), he or she will have the primary responsibility for helping your student improve his speech and language skills. However, the SLP should be willing to consult with you about difficulties you are having in the classroom, and suggest individualized strategies for you to try to support speech and language development and comprehension and expression related to content of the curriculum.

See Chapters 2 and 3 for more discussion of characteristics of language in children with ASD.

Some Basic Information about Language in Autism

Language and speech abilities vary tremendously in different children with ASD. Some children with ASD cannot speak at all. The majority of children with ASD speak late, with the exception of children with Asperger's syndrome. All young children with ASD, even those who appear highly verbal, have difficulty with language comprehension. Many children with ASD, especially when they're young, repeat the same things over and over. Some reverse pronouns (say "you" when they mean "I" and vice versa) and most use abnormal prosody (the melody of speech). Pragmatics, the social use of language, is universally impaired in children with ASD.

Language Acquisition Style

Children with ASD appear to have an unusual style of learning language. Verbal children with ASD sometimes appear to learn language in chunks rather than word by word. They often memorize and repeat entire sentences and may even use these sentences in appropriate situations, but without necessarily understanding the meaning of each word. For example, a child may learn to say "I want to go to McDonald's" as a way to request food. He may understand the meaning of the word "want" but not understand the meaning of "I" or "go" when used in different contexts, and may understand "McDonald's" to mean any kind of food.

Children with ASD may also use big words they don't really understand. Children who are typically developing usually understand words first and then use them in speech; children with ASD sometimes speak and only later figure out what the language means. For a teacher, this can be misleading. You might imagine the student's level of understanding is far beyond what it actually is. It is easy to assume that the child understands all of the class material you present because he can tell it back to you, but this may be far from the truth.

Some children with ASD have precocious ability to read (hyperlexia). Learning to read may even precede the development of speech. Development of the ability to read does not necessarily mean the child with ASD *understands* what he has read. On the other hand, some children with ASD *do* understand written language better than they understand oral language. You can check your student's decoding/comprehension of written language profile by comparing formal standardized testing of both skills.

Two Major Language Profiles in ASD

As you will recall from Chapters 2 and 3, various aspects of language have been examined in children with ASD. They include:

- **Phonology**—understanding and expressing the sounds of language;
- **Syntax**—or what most people would call grammar; involving word order and word form (such as how words change with past or future tense or in the plural form);
- **Semantics**—comprehension and expression of the meaning of language (single-word vocabulary and connected language);
- **Pragmatics**—the social use of language; involving gestures, eye contact, facial expressions linked with language, body position and voice, as well as the use of verbal communication, including turn-taking and staying on topic.

There are two basic language profiles you are likely to see in children with ASD. One profile involves pervasive difficulties in all the aspects of language defined above. The other common profile involves difficulties with the semantic and pragmatic aspects, and relatively normal phonology and syntax.

Pervasive Language Impairment

Some children with ASD have persistent deficits in syntax and phonology along with significant deficits in semantics and pragmatics. This pattern is seen not only in children with ASD who have mental retardation, but also in some children who have normal nonverbal intelligence—as indicated by at least average ability to do puzzles, put pictures in order, or understand which things belong to the same category (e.g., apples and bananas).

Children with pervasive deficits in all areas of language are seriously hampered in their understanding of language and in their ability to speak. What they can say is likely to be very limited. They have a small vocabulary, use single words or short and simple phrases or sentences, and their articulation problems may make their words hard to understand. These children need the specialized, intensive assistance of a speech-language pathologist experienced with autism.

The goal of school staff, including the classroom teacher, should be to help these youngsters establish meaningful communication skills and build language comprehension and vocabulary, as well as syntactically appropriate connected speech. Some helpful techniques are discussed below, but it is very important for you to work closely with the child's SLP. He or she can tell you what specific skills are being worked on, and how you can help try to reinforce these skills in the classroom.

Impairment Restricted to Semantics and Pragmatics

Most of the verbal children with ASD you're likely to have in your classroom will not be impaired in all aspects of language. They will not have fundamental problems in phonology and syntax, but almost invariably they will have problems with semantics and pragmatics. Their speech most often is not halting and effortful sounding. However, they may use words in a peculiar way, perhaps using words that are literally correct but seem wrong for the situation. For example, one child said, "All of the children may proceed to the classroom" instead of "It's time to go in." Their problems with pragmatics show up in such behaviors as inappropriately changing topics, talking endlessly about subjects they're interested in but the other children aren't, and not looking at people they're talking to.

So, all children with ASD, in both profile types, have deficits in semantics and pragmatics. Some of these children start out with only these language deficits. Others may have early impairment in phonology and syntax but get better over time. For example, it is not unusual for young, verbal children with ASD to make syntactic and phonologic errors in spontaneous speech but use perfect structure in their echoes (repetition of language), and then later develop normal phonology and syntax. However, for some children with ASD, phonology and syntax are not merely slow to develop but are persistently impaired throughout their development. You can observe this by listening: does your student make speech sounds that are as clear as his peers make? Does his language have the same grammatical complexity, and do his sentences seem as long as others his age use? If not, you should discuss his needs in these areas with the school's speech-language pathologist.

High functioning, verbal children with ASD do not have difficulty understanding and speaking single words, short phrases, or perhaps sentences, but have difficulty understanding and producing longer strings of language. This is true of written as well as spoken language. In fact, writing in response to a question or demand is often among the most frustrating and anxiety-provoking tasks required of a high functioning child with ASD. They will do better with simple, factual quizzes that demand a word or short phrase as an answer. Because of these language issues, multiple-choice exams may more accurately reflect what a child has learned.

All children with ASD focus their speaking and understanding on details and not the overall topic or main point. Children with ASD do not naturally organize language hierarchically according to overall topic, subtopics, and lower level details. They give details more importance than the main topic of the talk. In other words, they miss the forest for the trees.

With an overemphasis on details comes a failure to integrate details into larger concepts. In learning content material, children with ASD appear to attempt to memorize by rote what they read or hear, but they do not reorganize the information according to meaning or integrate the meaning of the language with their own experiences or world knowledge. This results in an impaired ability to understand cause and effect relationships and to draw inferences.

The stories and essays of verbal children with ASD are usually simple and lack a cohesive structure. When speaking, it often appears as if the child has memorized a (sometimes impressive) list of facts. Verbal children with ASD have difficulty sticking to the subject unless it is one of their specific interests, and when they shift topic in conversation they do not signal these shifts for their listener. The problem for them, in some cases, may be topic identification. It is impossible to maintain the topic if you do not know what the topic is. High functioning children with ASD can learn to stick to a topic when they know what that topic is. Therefore a major focus of intervention should be identification of topic.

High functioning verbal children with ASD sometimes have trouble with concepts at the single-word level as well. As stated above, they may not fully understand the vocabulary they use, and they sometimes understand the meaning of words without respect for the context in which the word occurs. It may be that they only learn part of the meaning of a word and then stick with that definition, so that they may use a hundred-dollar word when a five-cent word is more appropriate. These children have trouble using what they know about one word to understand a new word (e.g., seeing the connection between "help" and "helpful.") So, you may think the child *must* understand a given word because he understands a related word, but that may not turn out to be the case. Connections that are obvious to other children may not be obvious to him.

Word retrieval (easily finding the word to express what you want to say) is also often impaired. It may be slow or the children may sometimes simply fail to retrieve the words they are looking for. This makes sense given their deficient ability to organize words according to their meaning. A good analogy is a file cabinet. If your files are organized, it is easy to find something in the cabinet. If files are simply thrown into the cabinet or organized only by general category but disorganized within each category, it will be difficult to find what you are looking for.

How Do I Address All These Language Issues in the Classroom?

There are a number of key considerations in addressing the language issues of your student with ASD in your classroom.

Profile of Strengths and Weaknesses: The general goal is to improve language and communication via the child's strengths. The majority of people with ASD process information better when it is presented in a concrete, visual format than when presented in a purely auditory verbal format. Along with hearing a story, it will help the child to read along (if he reads) or see pictures that illustrate the action. Most high functioning individuals with ASD demonstrate strengths in rote memorization, while having problems with understanding complex or abstract material. Therefore, it is important that language be presented visually or with visual supports. In addition, the material or strategy you are teaching may need to be presented repeatedly to take advantage of the child's strength of rote memorization.

Overall Level of Cognitive Impairment: The more cognitive and language challenges a child has, the more modifications you will have to make in simplifying the concepts you teach him, and the language with which you communicate.

Learning Style: It is important to keep a child's learning style in mind in developing an approach in the classroom. As described above, many children with ASD appear to memorize language in chunks and are able to say it back before they completely understand it. Instead of discouraging these tendencies, take advantage of excellent rote memory by encouraging the child to memorize important rules, stories, facts, and definitions. Reinforce his attention and effort with praise or more tangible rewards (points, stickers). When rote material is solidly learned, you can then help the child to analyze the information and relate it to other concepts and facts.

Temperament: Rigid temperament and limited flexibility is typical in children with ASD. Therefore, consistency and predictability are important in developing a classroom approach to stimulating language. If you present information one way at one time and in a different way at another time, the child will probably not understand that the same concept is being presented. You should present information repeatedly in exactly the same way until the child has mastered it, and then encourage generalization by presenting the information in new ways (while relating it back to the original information, so the child knows that it's the same information). If a child is memorizing math facts, and is learning that "10 minus 8 is 2," but then you say that "10 take away 8 equals (or comes out) 2," or if you prematurely try to have him apply the information ("you have 10 nuts and you give your friend 8—how many do you have left?"), you may confuse the child with ASD.

Unlike other learners, where multiple forms of the information, and multiple examples, may reinforce the concept, the child with ASD may need a different approach. Try reinforcing a single presentation of the information (saying and writing the same thing) until it is learned. *Then* you can say "now let's see what happens with real things," and, again using repetition, explain how this applies to nuts and taking away. You may need to repeat this multiple times before moving on to some additional examples (pennies, stickers, circles). Generalization and mastery of the concept will happen eventually, but may need additional rote memorization and careful introduction of simple examples first. Predictability also appears to decrease the anxiety the child feels, and will allow him to learn more rapidly.

Long-term and Short-term Goals: Another major factor concerning the classroom approach is not to try to work on too much at once—to keep long-term goals in mind, but focus on achieving short-term goals first. Although short-term language goals in a young verbal child with ASD may be focused on developing more basic language skills (e.g., receptive vocabulary, syntax), it is likely that his problems with more complex skills such as conversation, story telling, understanding of a whole language lesson will persist. These may be goals for the longer term but should be addressed as soon as the child is ready.

All of these factors suggest that certain methods are most likely to be successful for helping the child to understand others and express himself. Fortunately, many of the specific methods described below not only support language development in the child with ASD but support learning in the typically developing children in your class as well. This is one of the many ways in which inclusion can benefit all the children in your class. We will now go over ways to help the four major deficits described above (auditory processing, language comprehension, organizing more complex language, pragmatics).

Addressing Auditory Processing Deficits

Children with ASD often don't process auditory information in the "typical" way. It often takes them an unusually long period of time to respond to auditory input or they may fail to respond altogether. Research we've done indicates that it actually takes the brains of children with ASD a longer time to process words than for their typically developing peers. This means that the child with ASD should be given a bit of extra time to process questions. He may surprise you by coming up with the answer after five or ten seconds, instead of the typical child's one or two seconds. It can be hard to tell when the child is actually working on the question as opposed to being distracted and thinking about something else. This is something you will learn as you get to know the child.

Since visual processing is a strength for most children with ASD, it is important that you support all auditory information presented in the classroom with visual information. One type of visual information comes from the speaker's lips, face, and gestures. Seat the child close to you during instruction (e.g., in the front row) so that it is easy for him to see you. Prompt him to attend to your facial cues. It may be sufficient to stroll closer to the child to regain his attention, or he may need more explicit instruction. During a private time, remind him that he should be paying attention to your face, and that if necessary you will remind him of that with a private signal (such as tapping your cheek or chin, or, if the child has a one-on-one assistant, she may quietly remind him where he's supposed to be attending). Research has shown that children with ASD look much more at people's mouths, instead of their eyes, compared to non-autistic children. This may be due partly to a dislike of meeting people's eyes, but focus on the mouth may also be an attempt to boost their comprehension.

If the child can read, you can use written language as a visual support. If not, the support must be in the form of pictures or real objects. Write all instructions on the board, and keep them simple. Use pictures and even role playing to support auditory processing of the most important concepts in content areas such as science and social studies. When an educational video or DVD is shown in school or at home, turn on the closed captioning if the child can read, as this along with the video will support auditory processing and help keep attention on the material. (This can help the attention of other children in the class, as well.) Importantly, this type of presentation not only facilitates auditory processing but also helps the child to develop comprehension of what he hears.

Some children with ASD only have trouble with auditory processing in a noisy background environment. It is important to find out whether this is the case for your student; the speech-language pathologist can test for this. If the child does have particular trouble with noisy environments, then he and your classroom can be evaluated for a sound-field FM system. An audiologist typically carries out the evaluation. This system enhances the sound frequencies of the teacher's voice relative to the frequencies of the background noise. The teacher wears a lavaliere microphone when he teaches and the sound of his voice is amplified and presented through speakers. A sound-field system, where audio speakers are mounted to the walls in the classroom, is recommended over a system with speakers on the child's desk so that the child is not singled out.

Addressing Language Comprehension Issues

The best advice regarding language processing in children with ASD is always to assess their comprehension of what you present. Remember, don't be fooled into believing that the child understands something just because he can give it back to you word for word, or because he has a sophisticated vocabulary of single words. (It is easy to assume that he understands "Now we're going to compare some different shapes to see which ones have the most sides" because he can accurately say "This is a dodecahedron and it has 12 sides.")

You can assess understanding informally. Check the child's comprehension of what you just taught by:

- asking him to tell it back to you in different words, or
- having him answer questions you put to him (this is better for a child who has difficulty formulating oral expression), or
- asking him to pick out the pictures that show what you taught.

You may want to ask the child's speech-language pathologist to sit in on a lesson with the child, and assess his comprehension afterwards. Remember that if the child has trouble finding the words to tell you what he is thinking, testing his knowledge through a multiple choice or true-false format may be more effective.

Again, don't assume that because a child can decode the written word it means he understands what he has read. Children with hyperlexia who read the *New York Times* at the age of four clearly haven't a clue as to the meaning of the material. However, the ability to decode the written word can be used effectively to help develop the child's language comprehension by pairing written language with auditory language and a visual representation of the meaning of that language. Keep the written language simple, read it aloud with the child, and present it with a picture (e.g., "the bird is eating the yellow apple"). For more capable students, consider providing written material (such as an outline) to the individual child, as well as putting it on the board, to reinforce the most important concepts in content areas and pair that information with pictures.

Children with ASD require visual representation of the meaning of concepts to support comprehension of both written and auditory language. "Comic books" can be effective tools. Even the most capable children with ASD need a great deal more work than your typically developing students on understanding cause and effect, drawing inferences, making predictions, and making appropriate connections between life experience and the content of the language they are reading or hearing. As the classroom teacher, you will need to make a point to directly articulate these connections for the student and write them on the board as they come up in science, social studies, and reading. You may want to supplement class work through workbooks specifically teaching cause and effect relationships and drawing inferences and enlist the aid of the child's parents to reinforce these skills at home. Graphic organizers (see below) are a method through which these relationships can be made concrete and explicit.

Addressing Deficits in Language Organization

Children with ASD tend to learn words and concepts as isolated facts and do not naturally see the connections among concepts. They often memorize stories as a list of facts, giving each fact the same level of importance. They give details more importance than main ideas, and may completely miss the main idea.

Topic Identification

One of the first areas to address is topic identification—teaching the child to see the common thread among a variety of details. There are a series of activities you can use to accomplish this goal. It is important to start from a point already within the child's ability.

The first activity could be identifying the shared category for a list of words (e.g., BIRD for "robin, chickadee, crow, sparrow"). The next step is to label the commonality among a group of words that do not fall into an established category (e.g., CLASSROOM for "teacher, books, desk, blackboard").

After the child can give a topic label for a list of words such as yeast, flour, oven, kneading, and rising, the next step is coming up with a topic label for a group of sentences in a paragraph. For example: "The baker added yeast and water to the flour. Then he kneaded the dough for ten minutes. After letting it rise for an hour he put the dough in his favorite pan and put it in the oven to bake. It smelled wonderful." For both, the topic is "baking bread."

The next step is to teach the child how to identify the main topic of a written or spoken paragraph. Finally, the child is taught to read a book and identify the main topic and the subtopics represented in the book. Books about animals are good to start with. The main topic is the name of the animal, and subtopics may be habitat, food, predators, etc. Once the child can do this, then he is ready to learn to represent the meaning of auditory or written language in a graphic organizer (see below).

As the child learns to identify topics, he can begin to work on organizing his speech. Organizing spoken language will primarily be done by the speech-language pathologist (although you will work on this when the child needs to give an oral report in your classroom). You will help more with organizing written output. You can give the child the name of a topic and teach him to generate topic sentences about it. At first, the topic sentences can be very simple. For example, if the topic is gorillas the child can say, "I like gorillas." Later it is important for the child to think about what he wants to say about a topic. Once a child can generate topic sentences, then he is ready to use graphic organizers for expression.

Graphic Organizers

Since most verbal children with ASD have relative strengths in nonverbal problem solving and visual memory, using graphic organizers is a good way to develop their expressive and receptive language organization. A graphic organizer is a concrete, visual representation of the organization of language. It is a diagram that organizes information on a page so that it is easier for the child to see the relationships in meaning between ideas (see figures 1 through 7). Children with ASD benefit from being taught specific rules. This method lays out rules for how to hierarchically organize verbal material. It teaches children to give the main topic more weight than secondary themes and secondary themes more weight than details.

Graphic organizers can be used to improve reading comprehension for both factual and fictional material. They force children with ASD to reorganize material and make it their own in a way that they cannot if they simply depend on their strength in rote memory. Graphic organizers can be used to integrate information from a number of sources, including their own experience, and aid ability to draw inferences. Graphic organizers can also help with topic maintenance and the ability to answer questions in conversation.

Here, we summarize several types of graphic organizers that we have found helpful for children as young as 4 years of age. We use five graphic organizers to concretely and visually represent the organization of language. We also use this method to outline other material, such as pictures that tell a story, or social situations observed by a child.

Below, we summarize the 5 main types that we have found cover many language situations:

1. Description Organizer (Figure 1)

The description organizer, also known as a web, can be used to define words, and to describe as well as to help in understanding accounts of people, places, objects, and simple and complex events. The description organizer can be used for writing essays. The central node is the main topic and nodes connected to this central node represent subtopics. Each subtopic has lower level details attached to it. The

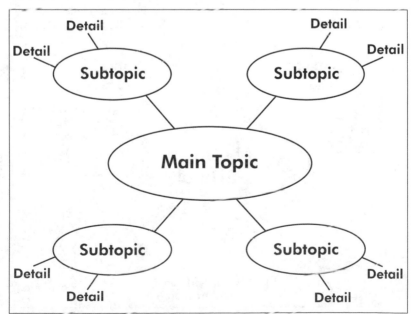

Figure 1. Description Organizer

relative weights of the main topic, subtopics, and details are signified by the size of the node.

Expression: Figure 2 below presents an example of a web for describing a day at school. When the child is first learning to use the organizers, he initially generates this web by brainstorming with an adult. Each branch of the web contains one subtopic and its corresponding details. The main topic and subtopics can be determined by an adult or by the child. An adult may make the determination to teach a child, for example, how to talk to his parents about his day at school at the end of each day. When the child talks or writes from a web, he first generates a topic sentence for the main topic. Then he decides the order in which he will talk about the branches and talks out one branch at a time, starting with a topic sentence about the subtopic and then adding at least one sentence about each detail, never jumping from one branch to another. It is important to make sure that the child sticks to the web and does not go off on a tangent.

In addition to mapping real life events, you can use the description organizer to map fictional short stories, single chapters, or full books using predetermined subtopics. A "who" branch refers to char-

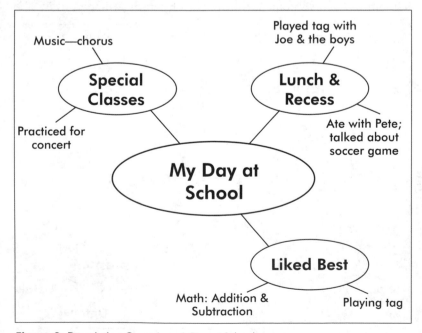

Figure 2. Description Organizer: A Day at School

acters, "when" and "where" branches to setting, "why" to the central conflict, "how" to the resolution, and "what" to the plot. A sequential organizer (see below) charts the plot. It is not necessary to describe the entire sequence of events but rather to identify the three or four pivotal events in the story. A description organizer based on a book can aid a child in retelling a story orally and in the writing of a book report or summary.

Description organizers can be used to help children formulate definitions. This is an important activity in making sure that the child understands the full meaning of words in his vocabulary. Each definition involves identification of the category to which a word belongs and characteristics (e.g., form and function for nouns). In this case, the main topic in the description organizer is the word itself and the subtopics are "category" and "characteristics."

To aid the development of expressive language, your student should rehearse definitions or stories based on his graphic organizers (especially stories about his life). His parents can be involved in helping him rehearse as part of homework. Rehearsal should be carried out in different ways based on the child's strength(s). For example, if the child has a particularly strong visual memory, he can be taught to visually image the organizers in his head and speak from them. If the child has a strength in rote verbal memory, he can rehearse stories aloud. It is helpful to write out each of the child's stories and definitions based on his graphic organizers and to compile them in a book along with the graphic organizers. This will aid rehearsal at home with his parents. He should be encouraged to tell others (grandparents, friends, etc.) his stories.

Comprehension: Using a web to map fictional stories as described above not only aids the child's ability to retell the story but also aids comprehension. Mapping factual material in content areas (e.g., a social studies chapter summary) also aids comprehension of the concepts in that material.

At first you may need to make the webs for the student. Later, to further develop comprehension, it will be important for the child to generate the webs for himself. First, the child identifies the main topic and then the subtopics. Only after this is accomplished should he fill in the details that fit with each subtopic. This teaches the child to think about the general concepts he is to learn and how the details fit with each basic concept. This is a critical skill for learning in the future.

Identifying subtopics is probably the most difficult part of organizing thematic material. You may need to help your student identify subtopics by listing all of the details on index cards, then group these into common categories, and then label each category/subtopic. Factual material is easier to organize than fictional and should be attacked first. Once the child can outline factual material with a description organizer, you can then teach him to outline fictional material.

Graphic organizers can also be used to develop a child's ability to answer "wh-" questions. An adult can ask a question about the material that has been mapped, and if necessary point to the detail in the map that is the answer to the question.

2. Comparison Organizer

Comparison organizers are used to teach a child to articulate and understand the similarities and differences between two main topics (Figure 3). The subtopics in this case are "similarities," "differences in topic 1," and "differences in topic 2." Figure 4 is an example of a comparison organizer examining the similarities and differences for spiders and insects.

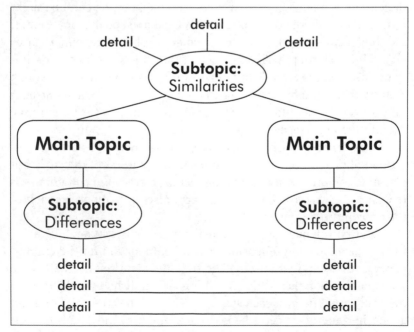

Figure 3. Comparison Organizer

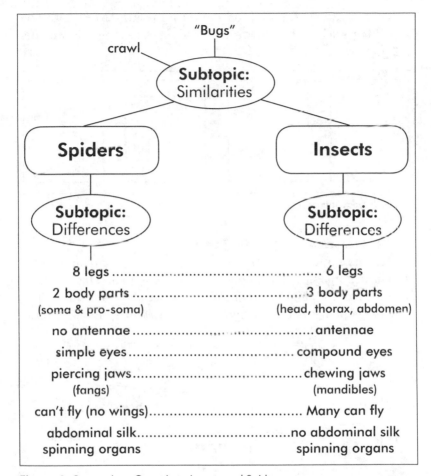

Figure 4. Comparison Organizer: Insects and Spiders

For younger, less experienced students a simpler form of the comparison organizer can be used. The comparison organizer for older or more advanced students is more complex, involving identification of common dimensions along which the two topics differ. For example, in Figure 4 the dimensions are number of legs, body parts, etc. (adapted from Parks & Black, 1990). With practice, students can use comparison organizers to help them write a five-paragraph theme.

3. Sequential Organizer

A sequential organizer helps a child to talk about an event or process in sequence, and consists of a series of linear components.

This organizer can be used for expository writing to explain how something is done—the steps in a procedure. An example is provided in Figure 5.

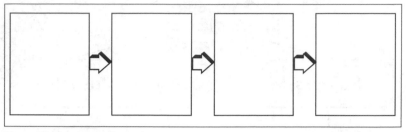

Figure 5. Sequential Organizer

4. Cause and Effect Organizer

A cause and effect organizer (Figure 6) helps a child identify what in an initial situation produced the final situation. This organizer helps to focus the child on the question of cause and effect, in addition to helping him figure out specific connections. Our analysis of stories

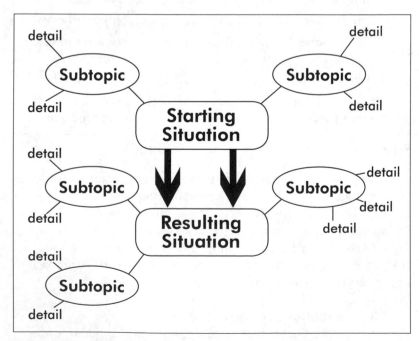

Figure 6. Cause and Effect Organizer

produced by high functioning children with ASD (one by Beth Kelley at the University of Connecticut) showed that the children seldom bothered to think about cause and effect relationships, preferring instead to simply describe a sequence of events.

The organizer is comprised of two description organizers. The one on top describes the initial situation and the one on the bottom describes the resulting situation. Once this organizer is filled in, the child can look at the concrete visual representation of the information and make a decision about what in the initial situation caused the resulting situation. This type of organizer is helpful for understanding and talking about cause and effect in science and social studies and even in social situations. These organizers are used for expository writing to explain why something happens.

5. Cyclic Organizer

This type of organizer is actually rarely used but effectively represents scientific concepts in which one event predictably leads to another, which then results in the original state of affairs. For example, this organizer can be used to represent the water cycle or the nitrogen cycle. An example is provided in Figure 7.

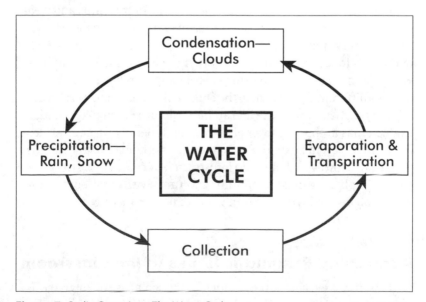

Figure 7. Cyclic Organizer: The Water Cycle

Promoting Success by Individualizing the Approach

Your student should participate in making the graphic organizers to the extent that he can, from the beginning of the teaching process. The ultimate goal is to have the child produce the organizers independently. The steps required to help your student with ASD independently generate his own graphic organizers might be the following:

1. Provide the student with a graphic organizer that is already filled out; go over it with him, explaining how you read it.
2. Provide the student with a graphic organizer that is partially filled out with main topic and subtopics. Work with him to fill in the details.
3. Have the student decide the main topic, help him decide the subtopics, and have him fill in the details.
4. Finally, have your student generate the entire organizer on his own.

Once you have introduced all of the organizers to the student, give him practice identifying the appropriate graphic organizer for the situation.

The format of the graphic organizers used with a given child depends on the child's neuropsychological profile of strengths and weaknesses. For example, if a child has problems with visual sequencing, the sequential organizer would not be used. Organizers can be color coded in order to focus the child's attention. If the child is having difficulty with topic maintenance, coloring each subtopic and its corresponding details a different color can help the child stick to each subtopic. If a child is having difficulty with the hierarchic structure of language, and, for example, has a tendency to emphasize a single detail over central ideas, the main topic can be one color, subtopics another color, and details a third color. However, if the child is distracted by color, stick to black and white. Graphic organizers containing pictures with or without written words can be used with children who are not yet reading.

Addressing Pragmatic Issues in the Classroom

As discussed above, pragmatics, or the social use of language, is a universal stumbling block for children with ASD. Pragmatics is where social skills intersect with language. Pragmatic problems can affect all the social aspects of language; some of these are discussed in Chapter 11. Some are dealt with in social skills curricula such as *SOS, Skillstreaming,* and the *Walker Social Skills Curriculum* (see Resources.)

Conversations with Peers

The biggest problem that many children with ASD have is in holding conversations with their peers. Well after most other language issues have gotten better, conversation remains difficult. Most of the suggestions in this section are therefore geared toward helping you help the child with his conversational skills. Hopefully, the child will be getting help from the speech-language pathologist on this skill. Find out what he is working on and look for natural opportunities in the classroom for him to use what he's learning in therapy. Just knowing what specific social or pragmatic skills are being worked on may enable you to quietly reinforce the child for using the skill, or hint that this is a good chance to use a skill.

You might encourage the child to tell stories about his experiences, mapped in graphic organizers, to others in the class. When he is listening to others, help him identify the main topic and then engage in simple conversation on that topic.

The child must be taught the types of speech acts people use to maintain the topic under discussion (such as asking questions, adding information, and commenting). You can prompt him by quietly asking him or the whole class to name the topic of the talk and then to think of questions to ask to keep the conversation going.

Many children with ASD have issues with conversational turn-taking. They speak a lot but don't listen much. They lecture, offer information, or ask questions to which they already know the answer. Becoming a good listener and knowing that it is important to talk about others' topics are crucial in becoming better liked by other children. Older children may be able to understand that being a good listener is a key to being liked. Some very well-liked children and teens do little more for a conversation than murmur sympathetically, repeat what the other just said ("Oh, you went to the beach!"), or agree ("Oh, I think so too."). Children can be taught to ask a question, listen to the answer, and then make an appropriate comment, as in the game described below.

Keep the Conversation Going

There is a great game that the student with ASD can play with his peers during free time that develops conversational skills.

To play the **Keep the Conversation Going Game:**

1. Make a set of index cards with a single topic written on each (e.g., sports, school, recess, my last trip with my family).
2. Make a stack of 21 cards, 7 of which say, "ask a question" (e.g., "where did you go?"), 7 say, "make a comment" ("that sounds like fun!"), 7 say "add information" ("my cousin went there, too").
3. Put the 2 stacks of cards face down on the table.

Play: Player #1 chooses a topic card. The other players each choose a card from the other pile. Player #1 generates a topic sentence about the topic selected and then 2 detail sentences. After player #1 is finished, each child in the game does what his or her card says, in turn, to continue the conversation. When everyone's turn is over, then player 2 selects a topic card and play continues as above.

Eye Contact

Does the child maintain a reasonable degree of eye contact with other children and adults while talking to them? Does he stare too intently, or look anywhere but at the other person? You can have other children model a reasonable degree of eye contact, practice this in conversations between you and the child, show the child his own eye contact in video feedback, or have a peer buddy practice appropriate eye contact with him. You can ask the child to look at you so that he sees your gestures and facial expressions. However, don't push the child to look at your eyes. He may get more information from looking at your mouth than at your eyes. Visual information from lip movements can aid auditory processing.

Personal Space

Does the child know approximately how far away to stand from other children? Again, have him observe how far other children stand or sit from each other in different kinds of situations, and practice this with you or with a peer buddy, or observe himself in a video. (One arm's length is a good basic rule of thumb.) The commercially available Circles curriculum can be useful in teaching students about maintaining appropriate amounts of space depending on their relationship with the other person (see Suggested Reading).

Requesting Clarification and Help

Children with ASD may struggle through assignments or games where a little help from an adult or child might go a long way. They need to be directly taught and practice how to ask for clarification and help ("I don't understand exactly what you mean. Can you tell me more? Can you help me?"). This will reduce frustration when the child is having difficulty and a big plus is that just asking for help from another child may make the other child feel good and make the child with ASD better liked. ("You're really good at this game. Can you show me how to play?")

Manners

Most children with ASD do not pick up common courtesies just by tuning in to others' interactions. They may need to be explicitly taught: how to give a compliment; how to respond to a compliment or favor; automatic use of please, thank you, you're welcome; how to request politely; how and when to apologize; how to ask permission; how to politely decline an invitation; how to say goodbye (thank you for coming, it was nice to play with you, you're a good player, see you tomorrow); how to express concern for someone who's hurt or upset; how to introduce themselves to other children. You can make a point in your classroom to prompt all children to use manners. Posters are useful visuals to support the students' use of these skills. For more on how to teach these skills, see *Reaching Out, Joining In* by Mary Jane Weiss and Sandra Harris (see Resources).

What Do **YOU** Want to Do?

Many children with ASD have particular difficulty playing with or talking to other children because they are set on doing specific activities in a specific way or saying what is on their minds. Excessive talk on their own topics can be particularly annoying to other children. A skill that children with ASD need to be taught is asking other children what they want to do or talk about (perhaps offering some choices if it's their house or their materials), really listening to the answer, and going along with the other child's choice.

Not Saying Everything You Think

Children with ASD are not good at knowing when to speak and when to keep quiet. They have particular problems keeping quiet when something doesn't seem right to them, such as other children breaking rules, or when they are very angry or frustrated. They may be able to learn a simple rule such as "when you want to tell another child something negative, take three deep breaths, walk away, and think about it." Learning about the consequences of behavior (as discussed in Chapter 11) helps them understand the definitions of positive versus negative behaviors. Once the child is able to walk away, you can discuss what he can do as an outlet (since he may have trouble letting go of something he's been prevented from expressing). For example, he could write it down so he can tell his parent later, or get you alone and tell you privately.

Another area in which children with ASD have to learn not to say everything they think or feel concerns affection. It may be OK to give another child a compliment but to directly express affection, either physically or verbally, especially to a child he doesn't know well, is a no-no. If the child has started to do that to another child, give him explicit directions about what's OK to say and what's not.

Idioms, Metaphors, and Slang

Children with ASD have particular trouble with idioms, metaphors, and slang. They tend to be literal in their interpretations ("He has a GREEN THUMB? What's the matter with him?"). They don't understand trendy slang. This may make it hard for them to understand their peers, and may make them the butt of jokes when they say things wrong, or don't understand others. There's no shortcut for helping them with this problem. They need to understand that meanings can be slippery—that some words have many meanings, may mean different things in different situations, and may even mean opposite things in different contexts ("That's wicked cool!"). After they accept this as a general rule, you or the SLP can work with them on learning specific idioms, metaphors, or slang expressions one at a time.

Multiple Partners

If having a conversation with one partner is difficult for a child with ASD, imagine the difficulty he has in a three-, four-, or five-way conversation with a group of children. He doesn't always know who's talking, because it takes more time for him to shift his attention from one voice to another. The topics flow more freely and confusingly than in a simple two-way conversation. It's even harder to figure out when it's OK for him to speak, and whom the speaker is addressing. When possible, help the child develop conversational skills with one other child at a time.

Prioritizing Skills to Teach

As his classroom teacher, you will not be able to teach the child all of these skills. Look for what's giving him the most trouble with other children (or adults) and attack these. Talk with the parents and child about your desire to help the child understand how to talk to other children. Discuss whether you and the SLP want to help him by direct instruction, role-playing, videotaping him and reviewing the tapes, or using a peer buddy (see Chapter 11), or a combination of methods.

What about the Child with Asperger's Syndrome?

Most of the techniques described in this chapter will work quite well for children with Asperger's syndrome as well as children with other autism spectrum disorders. Children with Asperger's generally only have language deficits in the pragmatic realm. Their use of speech sounds, grammar, and vocabulary are generally quite good; their problems lie in:

- the socially appropriate use of vocabulary (using unnecessarily fancy words and complex syntax),
- picking up social cues from their conversational partners, and
- following the rules of conversation (turn-taking, staying on topic, talking about things others are interested in).

So, the methods for improving pragmatics described in this chapter as well as in the chapter on social interactions (Chapter 11) will be relevant to these children. They may, however, have difficulty with visual organization, so teaching them to use specific rules and scripts or how to outline may, in some cases, work better than the graphic organizers discussed above. However, the actual geometry of the organizers presented is quite simple, and therefore may work for these children. The only way to know is to try.

10 | Academics

Students with autism spectrum disorders who are included in a general education classroom for academic instruction can have a wide range of abilities. Depending on the individual child, academic work may require little or no modification to significant modification.

If a student with ASD who also has mental retardation is expected to learn some of her academics in your regular classroom setting, the special education teacher should be available to advise you on instructional methods, curricular modifications, and accommodations that will help (see Chapter 8).

If the child has average or close to average intelligence, more of the responsibility for directly instructing her and making modifications and accommodations will probably fall to you. Many high functioning children with ASD have strong basic academic skills, including strong decoding of written language, spelling, mathematical calculation, and ability to memorize content material. However, even these children usually have difficulty with reading comprehension, writing, relating newly learned content information to previously acquired knowledge, and drawing inferences. Other high functioning children with ASD have difficulty acquiring basic academic skills as well. In this chapter, we discuss strategies for developing academic skills and optimizing academic performance in children with ASD.

General Considerations

There are some general considerations in developing your approach to teaching academic skills and content material to children with ASD. *How you present information* to the child with ASD makes a big difference. In addition, you may need to *modify the amount or content of the information* you teach to the child.

Presenting Material

Material should be presented in a way that helps the child pay attention. As discussed below, orient the child to the most important concepts, and help her organize the material, making use of her processing strengths to facilitate learning. For example, for the majority of children with ASD, visual supports are essential. Whenever you present information verbally, be sure also to use visual cues, if possible.

Prepare the Child in Advance/Pre-teach

Get the child ready to learn during class by giving her clear expectations prior to the lesson regarding what she will be required to do and what she will be required to know. Pre-teaching content material in subjects such as science, social studies, or language arts can be very helpful. This can be accomplished by a resource room teacher, or the child's one-on-one aide.

In addition, the night before you are going to teach specific information in a content area, the parents can be enlisted to introduce the child to the material. It is helpful to give the child two sets of books, one for school and one for home. That way she will always have the materials she needs at home rather than needing to remember to bring them home. An outline (graphic organizer) containing key concepts and details can be sent home so the parent can go over those key concepts the night before. That way the child will be familiar with the material when you teach it. The child can even keep the outline on her desk to remind her of the ideas being covered and may follow along by pointing to each part of the outline as you discuss it. This approach gives the child the best possible chance of participating in the lesson and answering questions. Also, if written passages are to be used in teaching the material the next day, you can help by highlighting the most important passages in advance.

Auditory verbal comprehension will likely be a challenge for your student with ASD. Remember that it is very important to provide visual cues to help her process information being presented orally. In pre-teaching, you might give your student with ASD a graphic organizer that she can look at as you lecture on that material. For further information, see the strategies in the Reading section below on helping the child identify main ideas and organization of material, as well as Chapter 9.

Use a Predictable Routine

It helps to make use of routines while you are teaching the lesson. For example, always start by giving the child questions that she will be asked at the end of the lesson, then do the lesson, then have her answer the questions at the end. A predictable overall format to lessons can enhance attention. It is also helpful to give the child with ASD prior experience with the format of a test (teaching her about multiple choice, true/false questions, etc.) or assignments before they are given in class.

During the lesson, prompt your student at the level necessary for success. (See Chapter 8 for a discussion of types and levels of prompting.) If just a verbal prompt is not enough, use visual prompts to orient the child's attention. Physical prompts, such as a hand on the child's shoulder while giving an instruction, may be helpful too (as long as the child is not tactilely defensive). Also, don't be afraid to teach the obvious. Always articulate exactly what you want the child to learn from the lesson. Be as simple, clear, and concrete as you can.

Teach through the child's strengths. For example, if your student has visual perceptual strengths, always present information accompanied by visual cues. If she has verbal strengths, as do children with Asperger's, it is important to teach verbal scripts, taking advantage of language skills and verbal memory. For example, when teaching a child with verbal strengths how to solve math word problems, have her memorize a set of verbal rules (see the mathematics section of this chapter). When she is learning something like the water cycle, have her memorize the steps verbally, like a script.

If a child has poor verbal and auditory processing abilities, you need to teach all instructions and important concepts through a multimodal approach, always supporting auditory verbal information with visual information. As we discussed in previous chapters, it is important to present material to be learned concretely and visually using pictures, objects, and demonstrations. For example, when teaching new vocabulary, give the child a picture representing the meaning of the word, and, if possible, have her act out the meaning of the word. If the child can read, write out the most important information, including instructions. However, especially for children with language impairment, keep it simple. Avoid being wordy.

Charts and diagrams can be helpful, even to children with Asperger's disorder, as long as they are not too visually detailed. Use visual modes of presentation that will grab the child's attention (the computer or video) to reinforce the material. Sometimes it is easy to modify your presentation of material in this way as you teach. Other times you will need to modify the material itself to accommodate the child's weaknesses and teach to her strengths.

Post-teach

After the lesson is over, it is important to check the child's comprehension of key concepts and memory for details through post-teaching. This can be done by you (if you have time), by the special education teacher, or by the child's one-on-one aide. First, review the main topics of the material and then review the main concepts (make sure you use visual cues such as graphic organizers or pictures). Ask questions about the topics and main concepts as you go. If you find that there is a concept the student does not understand, use demonstration, other examples, and visual input to clarify. Finally, review the details that fit with each main topic and ask questions about factual details to make certain the student understands the details and how they fit with the concepts.

This sequence of events can become part of an established, predictable routine that is always used in teaching new material.

Modifying Material

Due to problems with motor and thinking speed, organization, and language comprehension, assignments may require modification or accommodations for the child with ASD.

Modifications involve changing the amount or type of information to be learned. For example, the language or concepts may be simplified. Or the child might be held responsible for memorizing fewer facts about the information presented. For example, when teaching about agriculture in ancient Egypt, your student with ASD might be required to memorize the main concepts (where and why the soil was fertile, how farming helps a strong civilization to grow) but not all of the details, such as dates and names of cities. Work should be challenging but within the child's ability and not so difficult as to be overly stressful.

Accommodations are adjustments made to the environment and to the way the material is presented to suit the child's learning style so that the child is able to learn the required material. The idea behind accommodations is not to remove the task demands but to help the child to meet them.

As always, the goal is to help the child to become as independent as possible in the future using her own compensatory strategies. For example, at first you or another adult in your room may need to help the child gather materials to complete a task and you will give her one step of a task at a time to complete. The next step in moving the child toward independence could be to provide checklists of materials and of the steps required to complete assignments, as well as schedules for getting the work done and have the child follow them. Further reduction of these accommodations can be achieved by giving the child a multi-step assignment, helping her identify the materials she needs, helping her break down the assignment into manageable chunks, and having her write everything out in a daily planner. If possible, the ultimate goal is for her to carry this process out independently.

Decisions about modifying material, and levels of accommodation, should be made by the child's team, including you, the parents, the psychologist, the speech-language pathologist, the resource room teacher, and occupational therapist, considering the child's overall pattern of strengths and weakness.

Adapting Language

Language may need to be simplified for the child to understand instructions and questions, as well as content material. You may need to rewrite some material using simpler grammar and vocabulary, including only the concepts you expect the child to learn, eliminating all extraneous details.

It is important to make sure the child fully understands verbal material. She should be queried to make sure she has understood. Accommodations to address the child's expressive language issues may be required as well. For example, in testing a child with significant retrieval or expressive organization/ formulation issues, it will only be possible to get an accurate assessment of the child's learning through a multiple choice recognition test format since she will not be able to fully formulate what she knows in language. It may also be helpful to provide "word banks" to help the child complete assignments calling for new vocabulary words. (A word bank is a list of the words that should be used in answering the questions for a given assignment.) Remember, as discussed in Chapter 9, graphic organizers can be used to teach the child how to summarize material and how to complete writing assignments.

Adapting Length or Time

Assignments and tests may need to be shortened. For example, you might assign your student half or a third of the math problems, as long as they represent all of the concepts covered. If it is necessary to complete the entire assignment for the child to learn the material, she may need extra time. In addition, the child may need the accommodation of extra time for both teacher-made and standardized tests.

For longer-term activities assigned to older students, it is helpful to give the child a choice among a number of alternatives so that she can, with help, reason out the assignment that makes most sense for her. For long-term and more complex assignments, make sure instructions are broken down into manageable, sequential steps. If possible, involve the child in breaking the assignment down and in planning when and how each step will be accomplished. Help her write down each step in a daily planner and monitor her progress. Involving parents in long-term assignments may be very helpful (depending on the child's needs).

Adapting Physical Layout of Page

It may help to change the visual layout of the assignment on the page—either to provide more room on the page for the student to write or to reduce visual distractions. For example, your child may need more space to write out math calculations, so you may need to put fewer problems and more white space on the page for her. Or, when matching words to their meanings, it might be too confusing for the child to draw criss-crossing lines, so you may want to reformat the worksheet to make it multiple choice instead. In addition, if you are using a textbook that has a lot of sidebars and illustrations on each page, you may need to number the sections of the page in the order that the child should read them.

Capitalizing on Special Interests

In adapting assignments, capitalize on the child's special interests when appropriate to motivate her to develop skills that are particularly difficult. For example, if the goal is to teach a particular type of writing, it may be all right for the child to write about any topic, including her special interests. This is the path of least resistance and will optimize learning. For example, if the child is obsessed with Nascar racing and the goal is to teach her various types of writing, she could write a description of one of the driver's cars, a biography of one of the drivers, a comparison of the lives of two drivers, or a story of one race.

Once she has experience with a particular type of writing, then she should use the same type of writing to focus on a topic that is not one of her special interests but rather one of your choosing. It can be very helpful to use special interests to motivate the child, but be careful not to foster obsessive behaviors. (See Chapter 12 on behavior for further information.)

Individualizing Homework

It is important to use homework to reinforce concepts taught in school, but homework assignments may need to be shortened and tailored to the needs of the child with ASD. Homework time may be needed for pre-teaching concepts or giving the child more practice with cause and effect reasoning, making inferences, or writing. Or it may be the time when the student completes class work she missed due to a meltdown in school.

Give homework that you know is possible for the child to complete in a reasonable timeframe (no more than an hour for elementary school age children). Ask parents to let you know if an assignment takes too long, and give them permission to shorten homework when necessary to keep the child from getting too frustrated. Parents may need advice regarding how best to help their child with homework and promote independence in getting it done. For example, many parents have found it helpful to break homework down into a series of small tasks, make a check-off schedule of the tasks including scheduled breaks, and set a timer using a reasonable time limit for each task so that the child can see how long a task does and should take.

It also helps to modify assignments to teach the child according to her natural learning style. For example, it may help to give the child a study guide and allow her to memorize the material by rote first and then work on understanding the main concepts. Main concepts should always be clearly highlighted and explicitly articulated. The child should be taught how the details fit with each concept.

Working in a Group

Working cooperatively on a group assignment can be one of the most difficult activities for a child with ASD. First, if the children are allowed to choose their own groups, the child with ASD is likely to be left out. It is best to pick group members out of a hat so that the entire class feels the group selections are fair. However, in some cases you may want to make certain that there is one child in the group who is kind and mature and will support the participation of your student with ASD in the group work.

Once in a group, children with ASD have a wide range of interactive styles. Some may try to take over the group with their own ideas and insist that things go their way. Others may be very quiet and not contribute at all or even resist sitting with the other children in their group when it is time to work.

Giving the child with ASD written rules can be very helpful in this situation. For example, rules may include: "Ask the group and the teacher what your job in the group will be. Ask what other students' jobs are. Ask if decisions in the group will be made by the leader or by group vote." In later grades it will be important to remind the child with ASD of the rules she needs prior to beginning a group project. (This reminding should be done in private.) Help her to understand that her ideas are important and that she should contribute those ideas but that ultimately the decisions are up to the group as a whole. An adult may need to sit with the child's group and provide reminders to the child. It will also be important to help the other children in the group to have some understanding of the child with ASD and to respect her contributions as they would respect the ideas of any child. (See Chapter 13 for a discussion of preparing other children in the class for a classmate with ASD.)

Getting Help

From the youngest age it is important to teach children with ASD to recognize when they need help and how to ask for it. Otherwise, they may learn to use inappropriate reactions when they are stressed out by task demands. If asking for assistance is a goal on your student's IEP, her speech therapist will likely be involved in teaching her this skill and can advise you on how to work on it in the classroom.

As the high functioning child with ASD gets older, it is important to explicitly identify the staff members who can provide support in various areas, such as academics and social skills. There should always be a point person who can direct the child to the person who will likely be of the most help. In addition, this point person can be the one who gets feedback from all of the staff members involved with the child to aid in planning accommodations at team meetings.

Set Goals with the Future in Mind

Future goals and expectations play a large role in determining what should be emphasized in the academic curriculum of a child with ASD. It is important not only to focus on development in the child's areas of weakness but in areas of strength as well. After all, it is the areas of strength that will be important in determining the child's future vocational possibilities. Often children with ASD demonstrate a strong interest and strength in computer skills. If a child's special interest could later reasonably become the focus in adult employment, it should be cultivated. For instance, a strength and interest in computer skills could lead to work in anything from data entry to programming, depending on the level and types of skills the child acquires. Strengths in visual spatial and construction abilities might be put to work in carpentry or architecture.

Specific Academic Teaching Techniques

Reading

Reading involves both the ability to decode the written word and to understand what you have decoded. Reading is a very important avenue for acquiring information, and, as stated in the chapter on language intervention (Chapter 9), it can be an important avenue for improving language in children with ASD as well.

Decoding

Many high functioning children with ASD demonstrate a strength in decoding. In fact, some of these children have hyperlexia, meaning they have a precocious ability to read words, usually in the presence of impaired reading comprehension. Despite strengths in decoding, however, most children with ASD, including those with Asperger's, have impaired reading comprehension at some level (see below).

The majority of children with ASD learn to decode via traditional phonetic and sight-word approaches. A popularly used approach with children with ASD is the Edmark Reading Program. It is recommended for children who are struggling with a phonetic approach. It is a sight word approach and teaches words from a list of the most common sight words in the English language (the Dolch Word List). The program also works on building the association between oral and written language and on story meaning. The program appears to work well for many children with ASD who have strong visual memory.

A subset of high functioning children with ASD does not learn to decode using phonetic or sight word approaches. These children usually have language impairment. Many have strong visual memory and yet cannot memorize sight words. These children: 1) may have both auditory and visual analysis or sequencing deficits (e.g., trouble seeing the details/individual components of visual material; perceiving them in the correct sequence or orientation) or 2) may have visual analysis that is strong on standardized testing, but poor in the context of reading. A possible explanation for the latter is that in standardized testing, the child's attention is focused exclusively on visually analyzing the material; therefore success on this task does not necessarily mean that visual analysis is an automatic skill. For some children, strong visual analysis breaks down during activities such as reading that require "multi-tasking."

In our clinical experience, some high functioning children with ASD who are not learning to decode according to traditional approaches can learn to decode via another route. That is, they can benefit from a sight word approach but with the visual complexity of the individual words reduced. With these children we use an approach where, instead of written words, the child is first taught to read a large number of single, visual, semi-representational symbols for words. Then words written in traditional orthography are taught by pairing them with these symbols.

The set of symbols used differs from child to child. Different children need symbols to be more or less *transparent.* Transparency refers to how easy it is to figure out what word the symbol represents. For example, Rebus symbols are completely transparent since they are little pictures of the actual objects, while Bliss symbols are not. Children with ASD learn to read Rebus symbols faster, but to help a child understand the symbolic nature of the written word, it is more helpful to use symbols that are not transparent, if the child is able to understand them. Figure 1 shows symbols for water and sun. As you can see, the symbol for sun is more transparent than the symbol for water.

Figure 1. Two examples of symbols, "sun" and "water", used to teach children with ASD to read.

We usually make up our symbols to suit each child. However, there are software programs that might be used to produce symbols. School SLPs often have this type of software. We then teach the children the names for the symbols, and, to aid comprehension, make index cards with the symbols and tape them to objects around the classroom and their house and associated with people's actions. The children read the symbols individually and in sentences (see Figure 2). In our experience, children with demonstrated strength in visual memory learn to read these symbols pretty quickly. Reading this type of material stresses neither the phonetic system nor visual analysis.

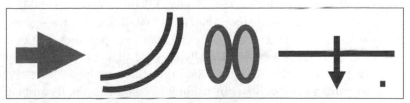

Figure 2. Sample symbol sentence that reads, "The water is deep."

To teach traditional orthography, we then pair each individual symbol with the same word written on a flashcard. The symbols are written in pencil and the words are written in marker over the symbol. As the child practices reading these each day, the symbols are slowly faded by erasing the pencil. The child then learns to read the words with traditional orthography.

Once the child has a corpus of sight words, she may be able to learn phonics skills if sight words are grouped according to features such as initial sound, final sound, and word family and if she is helped to analyze the words for separate sounds. Then she can use what she has learned to decode novel words. Throughout this process, "written" language can be used to help improve her language comprehension and expression.

The reading method described above is best implemented in a more structured situation such as the resource room, but can be effectively reinforced in your classroom. If such an approach is necessary, a reading specialist should advise you.

Reading Comprehension

Reading comprehension is often one of the most academically challenging areas for children with ASD. It significantly affects the child's ability to learn in all content areas (e.g., literature, social studies, and science). In assessing the reading comprehension of a child with ASD, assume nothing. Just because she can read something does not mean she can understand it. She may even be able to retell exactly what she read. Her excellent rote memory may make her sound like an expert on the subject. However, there are children like this who have frank language comprehension deficits and significant difficulty understanding what they read. These children require language therapy by the SLP to develop their general language comprehension.

Some children may be able to answer factual questions about reading material and therefore may seem to understand, but when you delve a little deeper, you will find that they are missing some of the basic concepts, especially those regarding cause and effect relationships. Even children with ASD who have relatively good language have difficulty extracting the main ideas and main point and assigning relative importance to details and main ideas in the material. Usually, they see all details as important and may give single details more import than the main ideas.

Reading Nonfiction. In reading factual material, it can help to teach children with ASD the method of looking at headings and subheadings in a text, turning them into questions, and then trying to answer the question after the passage is read (e.g., the heading is "Causes of the Civil War." So, you restate that as a question: "What were the causes of the Civil War?"). Unfortunately, some factual texts and most fictional material do not have headings, and if they do, the headings may not accurately describe the content of a passage. It is important to teach your student with ASD how to integrate individual ideas to find the main point of a passage.

In comprehending what they read, it is as if children with ASD process the material as a series of separate details and ideas. Since they do not naturally integrate all of these parts with each other and with world knowledge, it is difficult for them to draw inferences. Using graphic organizers to outline what they read, either factual or fictional material, can be an effective way of helping them to extract meaning, understand the relative importance of main ideas versus details, and understand the organization of the material (how the details fit with and support the main ideas). See the chapter on language intervention for details (Chapter 9).

In addition, in reading factual material, older children should be taught about the organization of the passage with regard to type of writing and its purpose (description, compare/contrast, sequence of events, problem solution, process, cause and effect).

Reading Fiction. A graphic organizer with the subtopics "Who" (characters), "What Happened" (plot), "When," "Where," "Why" (problem), "How Resolved" (resolution) can be used to structure questions that the child can ask herself as she reads fiction. (e.g., Who are the characters? What is the problem? What are the most important things that happened in this chapter (organized according to beginning, middle, end)? Is the problem solved?) It is good for the child to get into the routine of doing this.

Based on the organizers the student generates, she should paraphrase what she has read so that you can check her reading comprehension. Using an organizer is a great way to teach her to paraphrase. In talking from an organizer, she must generate novel topic sentences for the main topic and a subtopic before she generates novel sentences to recount the details attached to that subtopic. She does not retell the material exactly as it was presented through rote memorization. Therefore she processes the meaning more completely. Paraphrasing rather than exact repetition helps a child make the material her own.

In addition, the ability to visually imagine what you are reading about is strongly related to comprehension. It is important to encourage visual imagery. You can have the students draw a picture of what they "see" based on what was read or you can ask specific questions about visual attributes of characters or setting to encourage visualization.

Even the brightest children with ASD whose language comprehension appears quite good can have impaired reading comprehension. Not surprisingly, they have difficulty understanding relationships among characters, emotions, and the motives of characters in fictional material. They have difficulty discerning the author's purpose and making predictions.

High functioning children with ASD regularly make unusual associations to material they hear or read, and these associations certainly influence comprehension. These may be tangential associations or may result from their atypical view of their life experience. For example, a ten-year-old boy with ASD who lived in an affluent suburb of New York was reading the book *Shiloh* for class. His teacher asked why he thought the boy's mother in the book did not want the boy to adopt the dog, Shiloh. When it was clear that this student couldn't answer this question, the teacher tried to lead him to the answer by saying that the family lived in a poor, rural town in the south and were very poor. The student's response to this was, "Well, why didn't they move to New York? Then he could have the dog." In his experience, everyone in New York has plenty of money and his belief is that they have money *because* they live in New York.

As for every child, it is important to help children with ASD make material they read or learn their own. To increase their comprehension, they do need to make connections between the information and their lives, but it is important to make sure that the concepts they have developed about life are reasonable. Ask for the child's reactions while he is reading. You might ask the parents to have the child read to one of them and ask her for her association and reactions to what she reads. These questions should be framed in terms of what the child knows about what she read, what she would like to know, or what she learned. The parent should write the reactions in the margins of the passage and share them with the teacher. Not only does this activity help the child be an active reader but it can be very enlightening for you, the teacher as well.

To help the student develop cause and effect reasoning, point out causes and their effects as they are encountered in life or content material. Again, they can be visually represented in a cause and effect graphic organizer. For example, if the child with ASD behaves inappropriately with another child, explicitly explain the link between her behavior and the other's child's reaction ("You cut in front of Molly when it was her turn to slide. That's why she yelled at you."). She must be told that causes precede effects. It is remarkable how many very bright children with ASD do not understand this basic idea.

Written expression can also be quite difficult for children with ASD as well. Details of methods for addressing this issue can be found in the language intervention chapter.

Teaching in Content Areas

All the recommendations regarding reading and auditory verbal comprehension enumerated above apply to teaching material in content areas such as social studies and science.

Social Studies. Common problems children with ASD can have in social studies include:

- organizing the information;
- understanding abstract concepts such as culture, justice, and democracy;
- understanding the motivation of people or groups of people they are studying; and
- the cause and effect of historical events.

Having the SLP or special education teacher pre-teach some vocabulary and concepts and using graphic organizers can facilitate teaching this material in your classroom.

Science. Science clearly lends itself better to the use of visual supports and demonstration. Pictures and graphic organizers representing scientific concepts (e.g., the water cycle, condensation, systems in the human body, etc.) are essential. Hands-on experience through experiments and demonstrations should be combined with diagrams at every opportunity. For example, after presenting a diagram of how water molecules in warm air condense to form water droplets when they come in contact with cold air, the children should have an experience such as watching what happens to the outside of a cold can of soda on a hot day.

To help the child read maps and diagrams (such as the parts of a flower or a diagram of a cell in science), have the child color-code and talk through what she sees as she colors separate parts of the depicted material.

Abstract concepts such as formulating a hypothesis are best taught by having the child guess at the outcome of an experiment and then do the experiment herself. Teaching science concepts to your student with ASD in this way will be far more effective than reading the textbook alone.

Mathematics

Mathematical skills vary widely in children with ASD. Some have a real talent for math, while other children on the spectrum have significant difficulty. These problems may be related to:
- difficulty with concentration;
- difficulty organizing the material;
- trouble with abstract reasoning;
- difficulty with the language demands, especially of word problems;
- visual spatial deficits, especially in children who also have a nonverbal learning disability

Calculation

Simple calculations themselves are usually not a problem for children with ASD. That is, they usually do not encounter more problems in understanding the basic number facts and memorizing them by rote than would be expected, given their overall level of cognitive skills. If your student does have trouble, she should be helped to learn math facts using a method that is adapted to her learning style. For example, students who are auditory-verbal learners, such as those with Asperger's syndrome, can be taught to auditorally memorize math facts. The Semple Math program teaches rhymes, songs, and other mnemonics in a multi-sensory program to do this. (See Suggested Reading.) Or, you might want to try the "Memory Joggers" system, in which each number stands for a character and the number-characters are woven into short stories to aid in remembering the math facts (www.memoryjoggers.com).

Students who learn better through a visual, hands-on approach might learn number facts better through the Touch Math approach (www.touchmath.com), in which they learn to touch and count dots on numbers as an aid to calculation. Or, you might want to try teaching using some of the manipulatives described in *Teaching Math to Children with Down Syndrome and Other Hands-On Learners* by DeAnna Horstmeier. (See Suggested Reading.)

When problems with mathematical calculation occur, they are frequently associated with visual spatial deficits—for example, with keeping columns aligned. In performing mathematical calculations, these children benefit from fewer problems on a page and writing or having the problems written on graph paper so that they can keep the columns aligned and know where to write numbers when they are carrying (aka "regrouping").

When performing more complex calculations such as long division, these children may derail and lose track of what they are doing. When this is a problem it often helps to teach the child a set of verbal steps (write them down) for carrying out the calculations.

Word Problems

Related to their language impairment and attentional issues, some children with ASD can have difficulty with word problems. Typically, these children have a strength in visual problem solving and memory. The child should be directly taught how to convert the verbal problem to a visual problem. She should be provided with a list of written phrases or clues that occur in mathematical word problems that indicate the operation to be used (in all, total, difference, how many left, each, etc). Starting with simple problems, she can be taught to:

1. Find the word clues to figure out the operation (e.g., how many in all, how many left, the difference);
2. Write down all of the important numbers;
3. Use manipulatives (buttons, dots on the page) to represent the problems;
4. Convert the visual problem into a number sentence; and
5. Solve the problem.

It can be helpful for these children to reinforce math skills through the use of computer programs which visually represent the problems.

A Word about Spatial Skills

It is important to find out whether your student with ASD has visual-spatial issues. Children with visual-spatial issues will likely have trouble with areas of mathematics that call for spatial skills—number lines, the concepts of negative and positive numbers, clocks, and geometry (e.g., measuring and drawing angles, figuring out area or volume of 3-D shapes) as well as with reading graphs, maps, and diagrams. If your student with ASD has visual-spatial issues, we highly recommend that a special education teacher teach units taxing these skills. However, there are some strategies you can use in your classroom to support her learning in these areas.

In general, it is best to have children with ASD talk their way through these tasks and memorize verbal rules. For example, in learning geometry, your student should be encouraged to verbally memorize formulas and theorems. Simplify visual information, if possible, reducing extraneous details and modify (or let the child modify) so that it is easier to discriminate. In teaching the child to tell time on an analog clock, it may be helpful to color the hour and minute hand different colors. Then, begin by having the child completely memorize times that look most different (e.g., o'clock, :30, :15, :45).

Conclusion

In sum, you can facilitate the academic development of your student with ASD by knowing her profile of cognitive and linguistic strengths and weaknesses and teaching through the modality that capitalizes on her strengths. Be careful that you do not overestimate her comprehension of information based on what she has rotely memorized and can repeat. Help her organize information according to main ideas, subtopics, and the details that are connected to them. Concrete visual supports are essential, even for those children with visual perceptual deficits (although for these children they should be simplified and color coded). Preparing the child, and getting her into the cognitive mindset of what you will teach, can be effectively accomplished through preteaching. Using a predictable routine in your classroom throughout the day and specifically during lessons will facilitate her attention. Use modifications or accommodations to ensure that the material is challenging but puts success within your student's grasp.

11 | Social Skills

In this chapter we will provide an overview of approaches to social skills intervention in children with ASD along with a description of a comprehensive model for social skills intervention in schools. Our intention is not to provide an exhaustive review (this can be found in Sally Rogers's 2000 article, listed in the References). Instead, we hope to provide you with a description of the main types of social skills interventions and to give you some practical advice about interventions that are useful in a school setting. Other sources of concrete and useful information, including specific ways of teaching social skills, are the *Skillstreaming* books by Arnold Goldstein and colleagues, social skills curricula written by Jed Baker, *Inclusive Programming for Elementary Students with Autism,* and *SOS: Social Skills in Our Schools* by Michelle Dunn. See Resources. The Social Stories approach described below is also helpful.

As a teacher, you will not be responsible for implementing all of the interventions we present in this chapter. We are describing what we believe to be the most helpful components of social skills training in school. In the best situation, the school will be providing these services. If so, we want to help you understand the theory and practice behind these methods so you can help your student carry over his new skills to the classroom. If not, this information may help you advocate for a proactive, rather than exclusively reactive, approach to developing appropriate social behavior in your student with ASD by obtaining some of these services before there is a problem. Finally, some of these methods will be directly applicable to the classroom, regardless of what services the child is getting outside the classroom.

Introduction

Social interactions are a problem for all children with ASD, no matter what their cognitive level happens to be. The difficulties that children with ASD have with social interactions are described in more detail in Chapters 2 and 3.

Children with autism don't initiate interactions as much as typically developing children do. Even high functioning children with autism say that they have fewer friends, their relationships are less satisfying, and they are lonelier than their typical peers. Children with ASD have difficulty interpreting tone of voice, gesture, and body posture. They find other children's motives, intentions, and emotions difficult to understand. Their communication may be one-sided, repetitive, and lacking in true reciprocity. Some children with ASD may talk too much, while others may be passive and quiet. A pedantic, overly formal, style of speaking may be particularly noticeable in children with Asperger's syndrome.

Despite their social difficulties, nearly all children with ASD like to be around other children and want real friends. It is important to give them the opportunity to develop relationship skills, since these skills are strongly related to how they will cope as teenagers and in adulthood. During the teen years, children with ASD can become depressed as they become more and more aware of social and other limitations. Developing social and communicative competence in your student with ASD may be the most important educational goal for him to reach by adulthood.

Although social deficits are the hallmark of individuals with ASD throughout life, some school administrators persist in the view that social skills are not an educational issue. They feel that development of social skills is a parental responsibility. Others acknowledge that impaired social skills, just like impaired communication or motor skills, present a significant impediment to learning and to a successful, productive adulthood. They realize that even very high functioning individuals with ASD may fail to find or keep the kind of job they should be able to do because of their impaired social skills. Unfortunately, even when schools try to include social skills in the curriculum, it can be difficult to fit into the teaching schedule, and expertise is often lacking.

Schools are the primary social venue for children. Indeed, many children with autism are placed in inclusive classrooms in an effort to improve socialization. Often, parents prefer inclusive settings for their children once they reach school age. Some professionals advocate inclusion because they think the child's social behavior will improve, and the child will be accepted by peers, merely by being with the other children. This is wrong. Simply putting a child with ASD in your regular education classroom will do little to build social skills or acceptance by typical peers unless there is more direct social skills intervention for the child. To develop peer interaction skills, social skills training must happen in school, the setting in which children spend the most time with their peers.

Overview of Social Skills Interventions

Social skills intervention should begin as soon as the child is identified as having social skills deficits. Waiting will just result in the child establishing a negative reputation because of his or her socially inappropriate behaviors. Intervention should continue throughout school in every grade. At each stage of development there are new social challenges to meet. The social skills that work for building friendships in first grade are not the same as those needed for relationships in older children or adolescents.

Your role as a teacher will involve advocating for social skills intervention for the child in school and helping the child to learn and practice social skills. The help you provide will depend a lot on the assistance available to you, the presence of a one-on-one aide for the child, time built into your schedule to teach the child individually, the size of your classroom, the support of your administration for social skills teaching, the availability of a counselor, psychologist, or SLP to carry out the interventions, and your personal comfort in tackling these issues. We describe some methods below that you can adapt fairly easily to classroom situations; pick and choose what seems feasible to you and likely to help your particular student.

There are two major kinds of social skills intervention. One can be thought of as therapist mediated and the other as peer mediated. Optimally, both types of intervention will be employed in school.

Therapist-Mediated Interventions

In **therapist-mediated interventions** an adult therapist is focused on developing social skills in the child with ASD. This kind of therapy may be carried out by psychologists, guidance counselors, speech/language pathologists, etc. in individual or group sessions in school or in a private practice setting. You may find some of the methods and concepts helpful in your classroom. There are a number of formats for therapist-mediated intervention sessions. In some instances, an adult therapist simply provides opportunities for social interaction/play sessions in a safe environment. The therapist intervenes to increase the number of interactions or to troubleshoot bad interactions. These types of sessions provide a comfortable place for children with ASD to be with others. In other instances, the adult directly teaches social ideas and rules to the child and/or helps the child engage in social problem solving. Direct teaching of social rules and strategies, and, later on, active problem solving are more effective, as these approaches consider the attentional learning style of children with ASD.

Initially, the approach may involve teaching the child to avoid the types of interactions where his skill deficits are obvious, to prevent or lessen a negative reputation. Then the child should be helped to respond to the social overtures of others in an appropriate way and to participate in structured interactions with other children (e.g., board games). However, if the child's behavior is pretty consistently socially inappropriate it is best for him to limit interaction until he learns to be more socially appropriate. As soon as the child learns appropriate, adaptive skills, he should be continually encouraged to try them out with his peers.

Specific Goals and Methods

Therapist-mediated interventions address a variety of goals. Social skills curricula seek to directly teach and provide practice with a wide range of social rules. (See Resources, specifically those by Baker, Goldstein and colleagues, Gajewski and colleagues, and Dunn.) Some of these were developed specifically for children with ASD, while others were not, but can be adapted for the purpose. Often rules are taught in group sessions, although they can also be taught in individual sessions. Social skills groups can be made up of all children on the ASD spectrum or may include typically developing peers as well. Both types of groups can work.

Some interventions address limited goals such as teaching tone of voice and facial expressions, teaching the child to read "scripts" on cards to handle specific situations, or teaching about specific social situations through photos or drawings or pretend play scenes. The section below describes the social skills interventions you are most likely to encounter.

Social Stories and Comic Strip Conversations

Social Stories and Comic Strip Conversations (developed by Carol Gray) are two well-known, therapist-mediated methods for directly teaching social behaviors in real contexts to children with ASD.

"Social stories" explain and illustrate social rules and concepts. They are often written specifically for a given child to help him learn to deal more appropriately with a social situation that is problematic for him. For example, if Miles has trouble sharing art supplies when the class is working on group projects, a social story might be written starring Miles, showing or describing him sharing the art supplies and explaining why it is important to share. These homemade Social Stories are sometimes illustrated with photos or sketches of the child, or may be un-illustrated, depending on the child's likes and needs.

There are also books of prewritten Social Stories on universal themes that can be purchased. For example, they teach children with ASD about playing a game, going to a birthday party, riding the school bus, and making transitions. Obtaining some of the basic information about Social Stories (see Resources and Bibliography) will allow you to easily write your own stories for situations that arise throughout the year. They can be written with supporting pictures as well as words, whatever will make the ideas clear to the child, given his language level. Social Stories capitalize on visual strengths and allow the child to go back to the story and review it again and again. These stories not only teach a social rule for a situation but provide a context for using that rule. They include information about the child, his actions, the setting, and feelings of others.

Following is an example of a social story of the type you might write to cover a situation that the child is having trouble with—in this case, knowing how to behave at a birthday party:

Johnny was invited to Sam's birthday party. He and his mother went to a toy store to pick a present that they thought Sam might like. Sam likes sports, so they bought him a set of cards showing professional basketball players. On the day of the party, Johnny took his present. Mom drove him to the party. They rang the doorbell. Sam answered the door. Johnny said "Happy birthday, Sam. Thank you for inviting me to your party. Here's a present for you," and gave Sam the present. Sam put it in the pile of presents to open later. The children played games. Johnny watched the other children and copied what they did. Then Sam's mother told all the children to sit at the table and have pizza and birthday cake. Then Sam opened all of his presents, and thanked all the children. Sam liked the basketball cards and seemed very happy. Johnny wanted to help Sam open the presents, but he knew that these were Sam's presents, so he just watched and did not help. Then Johnny's mother came to pick him up. Johnny went to Sam and said "Thank you. I had a good time. See you in school."

Social stories can be written in many different ways. The story above may be too wordy or too complicated for some children with ASD. However, it includes the necessary components of any social story. In this example, you can see that the child is taught what the sequence of events is likely to be, what the proper behavior is, and how the other people are likely to be feeling and acting. Be creative in adapting this method to any classroom or playground situation, and have fun drawing pictures, or having the child draw pictures, to go along with your story.

Comic strip conversations, as the name implies, are actual comic strips of stick figures demonstrating each step in a conversation. They are very useful because they turn what is fleeting, auditory information in a conversation into a visual picture that the child can continue to look at until it is thoroughly understood. Again, they can be custom made for a particular child to help him with a particular problem related to conversational skills, or you can purchase books of comic strip conversations.

Social Problem Solving

Another goal in therapist-mediated intervention is often social problem solving. While it is very helpful to directly teach social rules, especially to younger children or those with more limited social skills, it is also important to teach a child how to think about choice and consequences in social situations and figure out what to do in a situation for which he does not have a rule.

Social Autopsies. One interesting approach developed by Richard LaVoie is called Social Autopsies. An adult talks with the child about his behavior in a particular social situation and helps him make connections between his behavior and its positive or negative effects on others and consequently on himself. Connections are also made to the causes of his behavior. These discussions can help children understand how their behaviors work for them and learn to anticipate others' reactions. With help from the adult, the child can plan more effective behaviors in the future.

This method was not developed with children with ASD in mind but it appears to help some children with ASD. Of course, you will not want to overwhelm your student (or yourself) by analyzing every behavior, but if you see the child in your classroom repeatedly making the same social blunder that provokes the same negative reaction in other children, you can point this connection out to the child (in a positive way). Then you can help the child come up with alternative ways of behaving. Observe his success at the new behavior and give him praise for success (so that even if the other children don't notice at first, he will be reinforced).

Personal Story Graphic Organizers. A similar approach to develop social understanding and problem solving, personal story graphic organizers (see Figure 1) were developed for children with ASD (Michelle Dunn, 2005). In this approach, the parent and child with ASD fill in a graphic organizer about a social situation that occurs, good or bad. The main topic, in the center of the organizer, is the event. There are three subtopics:

- The first is "What happened?" In this bubble, the parent and child fill in the most important details of what happened.
- The second subtopic is "consequences." Some examples of details for the consequences branch of the organizer are "The boy I wanted to play with ran away from me," "I didn't get the toy I wanted," "Mom felt angry," "My parents were proud," "I felt happy," "I got more time to play with my trains."
- The third branch contains details of a plan for how the child will approach the situation next time. Depending on

the problem solving abilities of the child, this plan can be a rule set up by the adult to be memorized by the child or an approach arrived at by adult and child together.

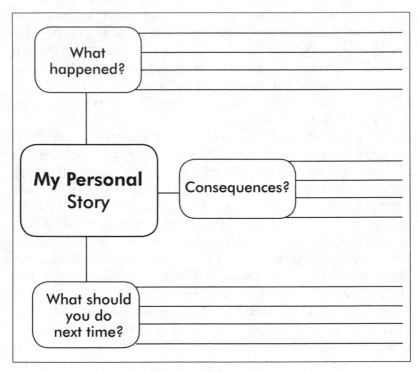

Figure 1.

Stories about appropriate implementation of a social rule or other social successes are just as important as those about social failures because they reinforce appropriate behaviors and clearly lay out the connection between those behaviors and their good consequences. For example, if a child successfully uses his script for stopping when he is beginning to become overanxious about schoolwork, the consequences might be that everyone was proud of him, he felt good about himself, he got his work done, and had extra computer time. Note that this also links social reinforcers with more tangible ones. What should the child do differently next time? Nothing. This approach teaches social rules that are particularly relevant to the child. Ultimately, it develops social problem solving and insight and also teaches the child that he will not always have just the right social rule for every occasion but that he can discuss ideas for what to do with a trusted adult or friend.

Video Self-Modeling. Another interesting approach to social understanding and problem solving involves videotaping the child while he is interacting with others and then using the videos to teach social skills. Of course, you would need to get parental permission before videotaping any child in your class. Watching himself on videotape allows the child with ASD to become an outside observer of his own behavior.

Videotaped self-modeling can be done in a number of ways. "Positive self-review" involves videotaping the child and then playing back for him only instances where he got the target behavior right, focusing on a single, specific behavior. In "video feed-forward" the therapist or teacher again edits out inappropriate behaviors and shows the child all social behaviors that were done well but with some editing so isolated behaviors appear strung together in a sequence. This teaches the child to use his isolated appropriate behaviors in sustained sequences. Watching these videotapes directly teaches appropriate social behaviors through a visual format. Editing videotapes to show only appropriate behaviors can be very labor intensive but may be quite useful for teaching one or two critical behaviors.

You might use an unedited videotape to facilitate a "social autopsy" as outlined above to teach social problem solving. The child can identify behaviors in the video that worked out well or poorly for him and plan future behavior. Children with ASD often have trouble identifying their own inappropriate behaviors but can easily identify inappropriate behaviors when they see others produce them. The videos allow the child to observe himself from an outside perspective. If you or the child's therapists decide to try this approach, it is important to clearly point out examples of successful behaviors as well as social mistakes. This approach works with children who have come to terms with their social difficulties and are highly motivated to change.

Videotaping methods make sense for children with ASD since most of them have stronger visual processing than auditory verbal processing. In addition, the child is helped by the opportunity to go back and look again at the same behavior. Video is also very appealing to many children with ASD and so they may pay better attention to material presented this way.

Social Perspective Taking

Some therapist-mediated methods address social perspective taking—that is, understanding another person's point of view (what the other is thinking, feeling, or experiencing). One such method is intended to teach "theory of mind" skills, or the ability to infer others' thoughts and predict others' actions. Sally Ozonoff and Judith N. Miller (1995) provided "theory of mind" training to a small group of children with autism. This approach was partly successful. After treatment, the children were better at "theory of mind" tasks, but these improvements did not translate into improved social interaction.

There is a very important message from this study. That is, children with ASD learn what they are directly taught. They don't easily generalize what they have learned to a new situation. So, as an example, if a child in your classroom does not seem to pick up on others' facial expressions, you or one of the child's therapists should teach understanding of facial expressions in a very direct and specific fashion. You can do this by having the class analyze facial expressions in photos (for the younger grades) and discuss situations that might evoke a particular emotion. If the child's peers are beyond this material, this lesson might be given by a SLP or by the child's one-on-one aide. It can also be done with role-playing, where the child and adult, or two children, model expressions for each other to guess. Then you may draw the expressions and articulate some rules about how to tell which emotion someone is feeling (e.g., eyebrows down, tight lips = anger).

The Teacher's Role in Therapist-Mediated Approaches

You may be able to use some of these methods in your classroom, but usually your role will be:

1. to know about these methods and your student's specific goals;
2. to collaborate in establishing goals for the child, providing feedback to the child and the therapist;
3. to reinforce social rules that are being taught in a therapist-mediated social skills intervention outside of your classroom (usually by a SLP, guidance counselor, school psychologist, or special education teacher). It is also important for you to understand the style of teaching social skills used in the social skills group so that

you can use a consistent approach in teaching appropriate classroom behavior.

Keep in touch with the child's social skills therapist, so he or she can tell you what skills are being worked on. You can help the child generalize the social skills he learns by helping to teach these skills in the classroom (reiterating the rules), and reinforcing any successes with praise.

As the child's classroom teacher, you will contribute important information about his social behavior in your classroom and you will help make the decision as to whether the child belongs in a social skills group or should have individual sessions. This decision will depend on your answers to the following questions:

1. Can the child pretty consistently stop doing something when asked to do so? Can he wait?
2. Does the child pay attention to other children and show some interest in what they are doing? Does he want to share their interests at least some of the time?
3. Does the child have any awareness and understanding that he is having trouble socially?
4. Does the child have enough language to benefit from a group situation with other children?

If the answer to these questions is generally no, then the child should start in individual sessions and the therapist can decide when he is ready to be in a group. If the answer to these questions is generally yes, then the child is likely to benefit from group sessions. The exception might be if he does not take any responsibility for his own behavior. If he completely blames others for his difficulties and does not understand that changing his own behavior can make his social interactions better, then he will not benefit from a direct approach to teaching social behavior in a group. Individual therapy sessions are more appropriate for a child like this until he understands that to change his social situation he will need to be willing to make some changes in his own behavior and that social skills group can help.

In some social skills group programs, staff evaluate the child's behavior first, and insist on implementing behavior programs to eliminate specific behaviors that will get the child rejected by peers, before children are allowed into the group program. (See Chapter 12 for a description of "Behavior Programs.") You can do the same in an informal way. If the child has specific behaviors that almost guarantee social rejection (nose picking, scratching unacceptable parts of the body, masturbating, aggression such as hair pulling, pushing, hitting, or kicking), let the school psychologist or counselor, as well as the parents, know that a behavioral program to eliminate these behaviors is urgently needed, so that the child has a chance of being accepted by his peers.

In addition, a child who needs to improve his reputation will be helped by peer-mediated approaches to social skills development, which tend to increase peer acceptance. We will talk about these approaches next.

Peer-mediated Approaches

Peer-mediated approaches are those that deliberately involve the child's typical peers in social skills intervention. Some peer-mediated interventions involve individual typical peers, such as peer mentors, tutors, or play buddies, while others involve groups, as in "Circle of Friends."

Research shows that peer-mediated approaches are more effective when peers are supervised and taught specific ways to interact with the child with an autism spectrum disorder, rather than being asked just to play with him. Peers can be taught to prompt the child for a specific behavior and to initiate social interactions with him. Trained peers produce greater social gains in children with ASD than untrained peers. Also, same age peers are more effective than older peers.

A word of caution: using peer-mediated approaches in isolation from social skills instruction for the students with ASD can be problematic. If your student with ASD does not understand how to respond to the initiations of his typical peers or is not taught social rules for interaction, he may be unwilling or unable to interact with his peers. At the very least, his social skills will not develop as effectively as if he had direct instruction in appropriate social behavior. Peer-mediated approaches are most effective when used in combination with therapist-mediated approaches. This gives the child with ASD the opportunity to learn more effective social skills, which he can then apply with other children.

Peer Tutors, Mentors, and Lunch Buddies

Involving typical peers as tutors, mentors, or lunch buddies can increase the interactions of children with ASD. Peer tutors interact with the child with ASD in academic tasks, helping to teach him and to focus his attention. Peer mentors engage students with ASD in social interactions (play and conversation), model appropriate social behavior, and reinforce social rules and problem solving with reminders and discussions. They may help the student with ASD to initiate interaction with others as well.

Peer mentoring and tutoring can result in the typical peers accepting the children with ASD more readily and interacting with them more. For the purpose of generalization it appears to be best to have multiple peers as partners for children with ASD rather than relying on just one trained peer. You might want to try to start a peer mentor club in your school.

In most peer mentoring programs, one child or a small group of children is selected from among the typical peers who volunteer to be peer mentors (of course with parental consent). Then, the peers meet with the child with ASD each day or on a weekly basis. They can meet as a group, or different peers can meet with the child with ASD on different days, either during lunch or during recess. Lunch meetings often focus more on conversation and verbal problem solving, while recess meetings can involve more play activities. Peer mentors may interact with the student with ASD: 1) in adult supervised groups, or 2) on their own during unstructured times of the day such as lunch, recess, and breaks or both. In one model, mixed groups of typically developing peers and those with ASD meet with an adult facilitator who monitors and steers the discussion or play, if necessary, keeping it in constructive channels. The meetings focus on helping the child with ASD to interact more effectively with peers and if possible to identify his social successes and challenges and help him come up with solutions to social problems. A school psychologist or counselor usually runs these meetings. Although the child with ASD does not have to be identified (and probably should not be) to the other children as "autistic," he does have to be identified as a child who needs some help with his social interactions.

In a second model, peer-mediation occurs during unstructured times of the school day without an adult facilitator. Assigning a lunch buddy each day to a child with ASD can be an effective method of building social skills. Each "lunch buddy" has lunch with the child with ASD once a week (or more) and prompts the child to interact with him and others. Children with more significant social deficits need their peers to tell them what to do to interact. More socially skilled children, who are already interacting with some success, benefit from social supports in the form of peer mentors. These are typical peers that the child with ASD can rely on to be there when social difficulties arise, to interact with him, and give him social advice. This type of approach tends to work for children who already have some knowledge of rules for appropriate social behavior and who are aware of and motivated to improve their weak social interactions.

Peer mentors should meet with an adult supervisor on a regular basis and discuss their interactions with the children with ASD. They get feedback from their supervisor and direction if they are confused about how to interact with the student with ASD. They could be trained and supervised by any staff member who is interested and understands your student with ASD, including the school psychologist, speech-language pathologist, guidance counselor, special educator, or even you.

The Teacher's Role in Peer-Mediated Approaches

You may be involved in recommending children in your class as appropriate peer mentors. Good candidates include children who have strong social skills, leadership skills, a desire to solve problems, and reluctance to blame others. You may even decide to start a peer-mentoring program. If you have no previous experience in peer-mentoring a book like *SOS: Social Skills in Our Schools* (M. Dunn) can be helpful.

What Makes Social Skills Interventions Most Effective?

As with all interventions for children with ASD, the form that social skills intervention takes should be guided by the child's cognitive strengths and weaknesses, as well as by his social skills deficits. The intervention should acknowledge the child's learning style, using his strengths to compensate for or remediate weaknesses. For example, children with ASD often have difficulty paying attention to the most important information in the environment and, even when they are cued to do so, do not automatically shift their attention. Consequently, direct rather than incidental teaching is more effective because it focuses the child's attention on the goal. And, since children with ASD are usually stronger visual learners, methods employing numerous concrete, visual cues are more effective. Likewise, since rote memory for simple auditory and visual information is typically strong, the method should take advantage of this strength in rote memory. For example, the child might be encouraged to memorize social rules through repeated exposure first, then later learn what the social behaviors really mean and how they function for the child.

Frank Gresham, George Sugai, and Robert H. Horner (2001) examined the characteristics of social skills interventions that make them effective. They considered three questions in evaluating interventions: 1) How effectively did the children initially learn the skills? 2) Did the children demonstrate the skills across different settings? 3) Did the children maintain the skills after a period of time? They concluded that to achieve these goals the necessary components of a social skills intervention program are:

- direct teaching of skills,
- modeling (demonstrating the correct behavior),
- coaching (watching from the sidelines and giving hints when necessary), and
- reinforcing good application of the skills (acknowledgement of success—this can be through praise, tokens, stickers, checkmarks, etc.).

The researchers concluded that the pitfalls of many social skills interventions are that they try to teach too many skills at once or teach one skill for too short a period of time, and they fail to individualize the program to meet each child's specific needs. The less effective interventions also failed to help children generalize skills to school, home, and the community because skills were not taught in the settings where the child would be expected to use them.

Social skills intervention should not only focus on helping the child to acquire social skills but also encourage him to actually use those skills so often that they become "fluent" or automatic. Like any other skill (such as driving or playing the piano), repeated and frequent practice will make the skill more natural. If the skill has become more natural and automatic, the child will be able to pay attention to the other children and their reactions rather than coaching himself through the behavior. And he will find it easier to apply it in new situations.

Do not assume that because your student can say a social script that he will automatically know when or how to use it or will attempt to use it at all. As social skills are taught, it is essential that prompted practice occur in all environments (the classroom, the playground, at home, with peers, and with adults, in both structured and unstructured situations). So, for example, if you know that the therapist has been working with your student on how to enter a game, watch him on the playground, and remind him that this would be a good time to apply these skills.

S.O.S.: An Integrated Approach to Social Skills Intervention in School

The S.O.S. Program—Social Skills in Our Schools (Michelle Dunn, 2005) is one model of a comprehensive approach to social skills intervention in school for verbal children with ASD. It is proactive rather than reactive and promotes acquisition, generalization, and fluency of social skills. It includes both therapist-mediated and peer-mediated approaches. In the rest of this chapter, we will describe some of the specific aims and techniques in this approach. (A complete description can be found in *SOS: Social Skills in Our Schools*.) Although ideally you will have the opportunity to be trained in this method and your whole school will adopt the entire package, involving the school administration and multiple staff, we hope that some of the specific techniques described here will be useful to you, even if this is not the case.

The program begins with staff training in autism spectrum disorders and social skills intervention by an autism intervention expert. School staff members then carry out this program with supervision and further training by the autism consultant, during the first two academic years, and independently thereafter. The idea of such an approach is to empower school staff through training and consistent supervision to address the needs of children with ASD.

In addition to staff training, this program has four other components. One is *social skills pull-out sessions* in small groups (of no more than six children) for the children with ASD. Children are grouped by social level within a three-year age range. These sessions provide direct instruction in social rules, strategies, and problem solving to the children with ASD. This is the therapist-mediated component.

The second component of the program is *general education of typical peers regarding fairness, tolerance, and individual differ-*

ences. You could carry out this part of the program with help from the staff member who delivers the social skills pull-out lessons.

The third component is a ***peer-mentoring component*** in which the social skills therapist trains and supervises same-age peers on a weekly basis, teaching them to provide incidental and direct instruction on social skills to children with ASD in natural contexts during the unstructured times of the day (lunch and recess). Each child with ASD has four to five mentors. This engenders flexibility in the child with ASD and ensures that mentors are not overtaxed.

The fourth component is ***parent education*** to help parents follow through with the social skills being taught in school, to promote the child's generalization of skills to all environments, and to help the parents troubleshoot difficult behaviors at home. Generalization is strongly supported by having school staff, parents, and peers teach all social skills in all environments. Educating all members of the child's social network encourages the child to maintain and generalize newly learned social skills.

A program like this actually has two purposes. One is to develop appropriate social skills in high functioning, verbal children with ASD. The other is to foster understanding of individual differences and a stronger sense of fairness in typically developing classmates, as well as the ability to act on it. Children learn about fairness and tolerance not only by hearing about it but also by doing. The idea is not to simply extinguish bullying but rather to teach students to be proactive. Just as the major goal of the SOS program for the children with ASD is to replace inappropriate behaviors with appropriate ones, so it is for the children with typical development. Consequently, this intervention program benefits both children with ASD and their typical peers.

The sections below present general concepts and some specific details of each component so you can adapt them to your particular situation.

Aims and Methods of SOS

SOS Component 1—Social Skills Pull-out Sessions

These groups are typically run by a speech-language pathologist, guidance counselor, or psychologist, but may be run by a teacher who is knowledgeable about autism spectrum disorders.

In SOS, social rules (see examples below) are taught through direct instruction. Each child writes out the rules in his or her social skills notebook. The adult therapist then demonstrates inappropriate social behavior (which usually makes the kids in the group laugh) and then models the appropriate alternative. The children then practice the rule through role-plays. It is best if you do not let the children demonstrate the inappropriate behaviors, as they can get carried away with them. Allowing them to role-play an inappropriate behavior is actually having them practice it. It is important that the child with ASD have lots of practice appropriately implementing the new social rules. There is homework so that the parents can reinforce the new social skills behavior at home.

The major aim of the S.O.S. pull-out sessions is to teach children with ASD to replace their inappropriate social behaviors with appropriate ones.

There are 5 objectives in the SOS program pull-outs:

- modulation of behavior and emotional responses;
- learning social rules;
- understanding and responding to the main idea in language and social situations;
- reducing repetitive behavior and preoccupations;
- developing insight.

In developing social skills and behavioral goals for your student with ASD it is important to keep these five objectives in mind. Here are some specific techniques you could use with your student with ASD.

Modulation of Behavior and Emotional Responses

Modulation of behavior and emotional responses is developed through:

A. directly teaching *a rule* in the form of a *script for self-calming/stopping* ("Take a deep breath. Count to 10. Say I can stop _____. I can do _____ instead).

B. *providing practice stopping* by helping the child, in a structured session, to feel what it is like to begin to lose control and regain control. Tell the child what you're going to do. ("We're going to play a silly game now to get you to feel silly. Then I'll give you your calming cue and you'll do your calming routine. Are you ready?") Then you can do a chase or pretend tickle game that will be clearly safe and permissible but will make the child feel silly or riled up. When the child starts to exhibit these emotions, give the child your agreed-on signal and model, if necessary, his calming techniques (deep breath, relaxation, self-calming phrase, etc.)

The feeling of regaining control can be practiced in any stop-and-go game such as freeze dance, freeze tag, red light-green light, or one favorite from the SOS program, "freeze and look when I talk." "Freeze and look when I talk" is played like freeze dance, except that the children run, jump, dance around, and talk to each other until they hear your voice. Then they freeze, put an index finger to their lips, and look at you.

It is very, very important for parents, teachers, and therapists to realize that the child will not be able to use these calming techniques in the heat of the moment if they are not well-practiced ahead of time. Once your student has practiced and can implement the strategy in structured sessions, practice can begin in real life.

Day to day, in real life, regaining control of emotions is practiced repeatedly when the child is only a little out of control in situations that elicit silliness, mild anxiety, anger, or engagement in preoccupations or repetitive behavior. Practice makes the scripts and strategies more automatic so that the child will have a better chance of using them when he really becomes upset.

C. *teaching the child to anticipate situations* that elicit strong emotions for him. As the child develops self-control, it is important to teach him about situations that consistently elicit strong emotions for him so that he can anticipate them. You must explicitly articulate the connections between situations and the strong emotions they arouse in the child. This not only involves teaching him about external stressors, but internal ones as well, such as hunger and the need for sleep. If he can anticipate his emotions, he has a better chance of regulating them.

It is important that teachers, parents, and the child understand that the child can only successfully use the self-calming script if he is not too far out of control. Once behavior has reached a critical point and stopping is beyond the child's ability, an adult must intervene to help the child stop. At that time it is important to get the child to a quiet place and the only demand at the moment should be for the child to stop. When he starts to become calmer, he can be helped to use the self-calming script.

The visual aid of a paper "control" thermometer where the "mercury" can be slid up and down is helpful in self calming. It gives the child a visual image of how out of control he is. He can draw a line on the thermometer to show the point at which he can no longer calm himself and needs help from an adult. He can learn a script such as "I am over the line" to say when he is seriously losing control to let others know he needs help. As the child gets better at self calming, the line on the thermometer signifying how out of control he can be and still calm himself will move up. One child said, "I used to only be able to be one-fourth out of control and then I needed help. Now I can be three-fourths out of control and get back in control by myself."

In addition to teaching self-calming rules and helping the child draw connections between his strong emotions and their causes, it is important to help him develop a sense of responsibility for himself, his belongings, and his own progress. Developing a sense of responsibility and experiencing success in achieving goals will increase your student's self-esteem and motivation as well as self-control.

Learning Social Rules

Many social behaviors are taught effectively in social skills group "pull-out" sessions. A list of important, specific, social behaviors is provided at the end of this chapter. Simple rules, at an age appropriate level, can be given for each. General categories of behaviors are body language, friendship, play, expressing and understanding feelings, conversational skills, and perspective taking.

Within each of these categories, there are a number of skills to teach, not all at once but in developmental succession. For example, lessons on conversational skills teach the four parts of conversation (greeting, small talk, main topic, closing) in turn and then how to continue topics by asking questions, making comments, and adding information. Emphasis is on talking about a range of topics of interest to others as well as of interest to oneself. Rules are taught for shifting topic appropriately. Children with ASD are also directly taught about humor, figurative language, idioms, irony, sarcasm, metaphor, and how to interpret cause and effect and make inferences.

Children with ASD will need a lot more practice in these skills than other children in your class. Practice is important for initial acquisition of skills and to make the newly acquired behaviors more potent than the old, inappropriate, automatic ones, especially in stressful situations. Stress often elicits old inappropriate behavior.

The program is flexible so that it is not necessary to rush through and teach each individual skill. For example, the student may master greetings and closings relatively quickly, but need many lessons, broken down into many rules, to learn how to make small talk and stay on a topic. Also, remember once again that just because a child can give back a rule perfectly does not mean he knows how or when to use it, without lots of practice.

Understanding and Responding to the Main Idea in Language and Social Situations

Children with ASD naturally attend to and remember details but have trouble seeing the forest for the trees. All details are given a similar weight. In fact, especially if part of a preoccupation, they may give details that are peripheral to the main idea even more importance than details that are central. For example, as one boy with ASD looked at a page in the picture book *Tuesday* by David Weisner, he focused on a barely visible cat in the shadows in the corner of the room instead of the main idea of the picture, which was quite striking. A large group of frogs were floating on lily pads in someone's living room and watching TV. One of the most relevant details was that a frog was changing the channel with the remote using his tongue, but the child with ASD did not even notice this funny detail!

Because of this tendency to focus on details and not the main idea, the SOS program teaches children to understand the main idea (topic) in language and social situations. In developing social skills in a child with ASD it is extremely important to emphasize identification of the main idea of language/conversation, pictures, and social situations. If a child cannot identify main ideas, it will be impossible for him to join in conversations on topic and stay on topic. To help the child begin to understand the main idea of social situations, show him pictures of social situations and ask "What is the main idea of what is going on here?" Help him identify relevant details and discriminate them from irrelevant details. The same can then be done with real social situations on the playground.

The next step is to help the child learn how to organize a response to the social situation. First, he is helped to determine whether he should initiate an interaction in the situation, and, if so, what he could do to initiate and sustain the interaction on topic.

Reducing Preoccupations and Repetitive Behaviors

If a student with ASD has preoccupations or repetitive behaviors, they can present significant challenges in the inclusive classroom and interfere with social interaction. There are several approaches to helping the child reduce these unwanted behaviors. First, you can teach the child a script for interrupting the behavior. For example, "it's not time to talk about Pokemon now. I can talk about that at 3:00. It is time to talk about math." This serves several purposes. First, it interrupts the obsessional thinking. Since these children often can't think about several things at once, you've given him something other than his obsessional topic to think about. Second, it tells him what to do (stop talking about the inappropriate topic and talk about math instead). Third, it reassures him that he will have a chance to fill this need at a later time. See Chapter 14 for more strategies for reducing obsessions and repetitive behaviors.

Developing Insight

It is important to help children with ASD develop insight into their own behavior as soon as possible. They need to understand the impact of their behavior on others and especially the consequences of their behavior on themselves. In the SOS program, insight is developed in two ways: through social skills lessons and through "personal story graphic organizers."

Social skills lessons are taught through books about fictional characters that behave in socially inappropriate ways. The link between the character's behavior and consequences, including social impact, is made explicit. The therapist also articulates the relationship between the child's inappropriate behaviors and the reactions he gets from others. The key to doing this in a positive, productive way is to make certain that the child understands that he can change the way people react to him for the better by ending inappropriate behaviors and developing appropriate replacement behaviors. It is helpful to teach the child the concept that it is great to be proud of what you are good at but you can be even prouder when you work on making your weaknesses better.

The other approach used in the SOS program, "personal story graphic organizers," was described above in the therapist-mediated interventions section of this chapter. These organizers are given as part of the child's homework from each social skills session every week. The parent and child then fill them in together.

SOS Component 2: Educating Classmates Regarding Fairness, Tolerance, and Individual Differences

In the SOS program, the student with ASD receives social skills pull-out training from a counselor, psychologist, speech-language pathologist, or special education teacher. The general education teacher's unique contribution is to help the child implement and practice in the classroom the skills he's being taught in his pull-out sessions. This job is much easier if your other students are supportive. Children with ASD over time often develop a reputation as being odd or difficult. Repetitive behaviors, preoccupations, meltdowns, failures to respond to others' social overtures, or inappropriate responses can be confusing to other children and are often seen as something to avoid. Children who make too many social overtures and are perseverative come across as pushy and intrusive, while children who hang back appear as if they are not interested in interaction. Both kinds of children will end up on the social periphery unless all the children in your classroom are given support and guidance.

Typical peers often do not interact with children with ASD because they are uncertain of or do not like the response they get from the child with ASD. Children with ASD may be teased or bullied about their unusual behaviors and social weaknesses. Even kind, well meaning children may avoid associating with the child with ASD because they are afraid to risk their social position. Poor responses from typical peers, especially when a child with ASD is trying out newly learned, appropriate social behaviors, can result in confusion for the child about which social behaviors work. The upshot may be that the child gives up.

Helping peers develop understanding and supportive behavior is a necessary component of an effective social skills program in school. In the SOS program, specific class lessons are given by the classroom teacher in the beginning of the school year and sporadically throughout the rest of the year. You can use the lessons from the SOS book, develop your own, or get such lessons from other sources, such as the

Internet. You can read books about children with differences and play games about fairness. The key is to gear the lessons toward developing an attitude of fairness and tolerance in the classroom.

SOS lessons cover the following topics: understanding that all people have strengths and weaknesses and deserve to be treated with respect, helping others, complimenting others, being fair, learning how others feel when they are not treated fairly or with respect, and being assertive (as opposed to being passive or aggressive). The class is taught that in a community, people use their strengths to support others' weaknesses. It helps to establish classroom rules about treatment of others, to discuss these with the children, and to post them permanently.

To help the other students understand the behavior of your student with ASD, you can talk about the idea that some children have weaknesses in math, some in sports, and some in social skills. All of your students, including the student with ASD, should be present during these lessons. You should not specifically point out children with weaknesses but talk about them in a general way. Do not talk to the children about diagnoses and certainly not in connection with any individual child (unless it is the explicit desire of the parent that you do so and you have written permission). Rather, talk about kids on the playground who do not play with others but rather just walk around by themselves. Suggest that maybe these kids don't really want to be by themselves but that it is hard for them to get into games and talk to others. Make certain that all of your students know that if they are confused about another child's behavior or what to do in interacting with another child, they can come to you to discuss it. In sum, establish the rules, help your students develop understanding of differences, and encourage interaction among all of your students.

SOS Component 3—Peer Mentoring

In order to develop peer interaction skills, children with ASD need to be accepted by their typical peers. Your student's attempts at appropriate social behaviors will lead to further attempts if he is reinforced by a good response from peers. However, acceptance alone is insufficient to encourage a child with ASD to try interaction skills in less structured settings such as the lunchroom and playground. Children with ASD require prompting in a given situation before they will spontaneously use a social skill in that situation.

The most difficult times of the day for a child with ASD are those unstructured times. Without social supports, the child with ASD may sit silently as he eats and then walk the periphery of the playground; or worse, he may alienate his peers by interrupting, chasing, even hitting or throwing food in an effort to interact with them.

Although there is adult supervision during lunch and recess and some children with ASD have an individual assistant or aide, the SOS program emphasizes prompting by the child's peers. In fact, for a number of reasons, other children are more efficient at encouraging social skills in their peers with ASD than adults are. Peers know best what games kids their age play and how they interact. In contrast, adults tend to be more invested in the child's physical health and safety rather than in peer interaction. In addition, children socialize quite differently when they are with each other than when there are adults watching.

A formal peer mentor program encourages children with ASD to generalize their social skills beyond the therapy room. In the SOS program, trained same-age peer mentors prompt and model (demonstrate) appropriate social skills for the child with ASD, bringing him into social interactions during lunch and recess. Direct prompting by peers produces immediate and significant increases in the social interactions of the child with ASD.

In the SOS program, mentors are first trained and later supervised in a once a week meeting. Peer mentors who are trained and have the opportunity to monitor their own interactions with the child with ASD are more effective and more likely to stick with the program. You may want to assist in training and supervision of peer mentors. Mentors are taught how to engage the student with ASD, to facilitate play interactions, and to coach him to use the skills he is learning in his pullout social skills sessions. They are taught to help the child interpret social actions and ultimately to initiate interactions on his own.

Mentors learn about the preoccupations of the child with ASD and about contingency plans, just in case there is a problem. For example, if the child with ASD becomes very upset on the playground and has trouble calming down, the mentor needs to know what to do. When the child is upset, the mentor will either remind the child of his self-calming script, or get an adult, depending on the age of the child and the degree of upset. If the child with ASD does not respond to the mentor's play initiations, he can engage the child with ASD on his own turf at first. For example, if the child being mentored is preoccupied with "Calvin and Hobbes" comics, then the mentor should read or draw "Calvin and Hobbes" with the student he is mentoring for a while until that student is used to him.

Mentors are also taught that although the child with ASD is motivated to interact with others, some days he may simply want to be alone and should not be forced to play. Mentors learn that they can bring all questions and concerns to their supervisor. Supervision is most effective if done by the staff member who runs the social skills pull-out sessions for the child with ASD, since this is the staff member who will understand the social skills issues of your student with ASD best.

At the start of a program like this it can be difficult to recruit peer mentors. The typical children are nervous about interacting with a child who is different and often afraid they will fail. However, in our experience, by the end of the first year, mentoring is usually seen as important and prestigious and recruitment becomes easier. Mentoring allows children to be social leaders for all the right reasons and other children often begin to emulate them.

Interestingly, generalization of skills to new situations is an issue for the peer mentors just as it is for the children with ASD. For example, typical children do not necessarily generalize their supportive behaviors to other children with social skills issues besides the students they are mentoring. This idea must be incorporated into training. That is, you specifically teach the children that *any* child who seems to be isolated or friendless is worthy of their support.

In the SOS program, peer mentoring is only offered in combination with the "pull-out sessions" since it is likely to be ineffective for the child with ASD in the absence of direct instruction in appropriate social behavior. If he does not have the benefit of instruction in social rules, the child with ASD is unlikely to have the skills to engage in or sustain an interaction with his typical peers, and the peers cannot prompt behaviors that have not been taught and practiced by the child with ASD in a more structured setting. This arrangement allows the child's social skills therapist to prepare him for interaction with his mentors. For example, the therapist can concentrate during "pull-out sessions" on teaching games that the mentors typically play and then encourage the child with ASD to play those games during recess with his mentors after he has had some practice.

SOS Component 4—Parent Education

Parents play an integral part in social skills intervention. With help from you, they can promote generalization and a sense of responsibility, and they can help their child build a social network.

To promote generalization beyond the school environment, it is important to involve parents in reinforcing the social skills taught in school. In SOS, social skills homework assignments each week acquaint the parent with the social skills lesson of the week and facilitate practice of it. Reinforcing the child's social skills at home and in the community will not only allow him to generalize those skills to these settings but will give the child opportunities to find out how the new social behavior functions for him in life.

In SOS, meetings are held throughout the school year to teach parents methods to further develop social competence at home and to respond to their questions. You or the social skills therapist could hold parent meetings to help parents understand their child's behavior, learning style, and social goals and to teach parents the methods for developing emotional modulation, for understanding main ideas (graphic organizers), for successful play dates, limit setting, and promoting a sense of responsibility and independence in their child. Regular meetings also allow parents to ask questions about individual issues that arise. For example, parents often question whether they should set limits for their child with ASD in a given situation or whether they should adjust the environment to avoid whatever promotes meltdowns. Childrearing decisions can be difficult since many assumptions based on understanding of typical development do not hold true in children with ASD. Parents may need support in promoting a sense of responsibility in their child. They should be encouraged to give their children responsibilities (chores) at home.

Group parent meetings are not only helpful for teaching social skills methods and providing counseling, but they also allow parents to see that they are not alone. They gain support from other parents who are dealing with similar issues. You may only have time to hold a couple of group parent meetings during the school year, but even this would be invaluable. Parents can also be referred for outside parent counseling and (or) parent support group meetings.

Parents need guidance in helping their child to build a social network outside of school. You may be able to help by letting parents know which classmates seem to like your student with ASD and about parents who might be particularly receptive to getting together with your student with ASD outside of school. You can also provide guidance about how to structure play dates. Play dates are the best way to foster closer friendships and more interaction with other children in school. However, the typical loosely structured play date can be overwhelming and unsettling for a child with ASD.

It is recommended that a plan for activities during the play date be established in advance. The child can participate in making the plan or at the very least be familiar with the plan in advance. The first play dates with a new child must be short, highly structured, and parent supported. Parents should help their child find out what kinds of snacks their playmate likes and what games he likes to play. This information gathering can happen over the phone or in person at school. If a game that the guest likes to play is unfamiliar to the child with ASD, parents might try to teach him to play the game before the play date.

The play date schedule could have time built in for snack, a play activity that the guest enjoys, one that the child with ASD enjoys, and a collaborative project. A simple arts and crafts activity where each child has an identical kit can work well. A nice way to develop interaction is to have both children work on one kit at a time. The child who is the helper (because the kit belongs to the other child) should ask the other child to make choices about how he wants the project done and how he can help. Let parents know that they should provide supervision, stick to the schedule, and not let the play date go on for too long. Play dates

---

Summary of Social Skills Objectives

Remember that the major social skills objectives for students with autism spectrum disorders should include:

1. self-control—learning to stop, and to know when they need to stop;
2. knowledge of social rules;
3. understanding the main idea or point in language and social situations and responding in an organized way with focus on the main idea;
4. reduction of odd-looking behaviors and preoccupations;
5. insight about how their own behavior contributes to their social difficulties and affects others.

should not stress conversational skills. For older children, a movie or bowling are good activity ideas, but it is best to avoid over-stimulating activities until the child with ASD has good ability to modulate his behavior and stop an activity when asked. With some preparation and supervision, play dates can go very smoothly.

Conclusion

In sum, social skills should be taught in school, which is where the child with ASD spends most of his time with his peers. Social skills must be reinforced through specific practice with peers in school, at home, and in other environments outside of school. A combination of therapist- and peer mediated interventions with parent training is effective in helping children with autism spectrum disorders to acquire and generalize social skills.

Optimally, your school will adopt a social skills education model such as the SOS program, not only to teach social skills to students with ASD, but to encourage interaction with peers and generalization of skills to all environments; a program that is proactive and developmentally ordered rather than an approach that is only reactive to problem behaviors. However, even if your school does not opt for a structured, proactive approach, you can use the concepts and some of the individual aspects of the methods described throughout this chapter to develop a systematic way of responding to social skills issues in your student with ASD.

Remember that simply telling the children in your class what *not* to do will result in a reduction in inappropriate behaviors but not an increase in appropriate ones. You must tell them what you expect them to do instead.

The main purpose of social skills intervention should be to help your student with ASD develop appropriate social behaviors to substitute for inappropriate ones. The cognitive style of most children with ASD dictates that, at least in the beginning, it is best to directly teach the child social rules and strategies for both behavioral modulation and learning new social skills. But remember that just teaching the children appropriate social behaviors is not enough. They must be given the opportunity to practice. So, if your student with ASD says untactful (if true) things about you or other students or does other things that he doesn't realize are rude, or if he ignores or rebuffs other children's attempts to talk to him or play with him, despite being socially motivated, you can make him aware of his behavior, the consequences of such behavior, and what he should do instead through the use of "personal stories." Then it is important to set up scenarios where, with advance warning (since preparation reduces anxiety), he can practice his skills. Give lots of positive reinforcement for appropriate behaviors.

Engaging all of your students in supporting the social interactions of your student with ASD builds a community where people use their strengths to support each other's weaknesses and where there is understanding that everyone deserves attention and respect. This type of environment will surely benefit all of your students.

Social Skills Goals

Pick and choose social skills goals for your student depending on his age and skill level:

- Interrupting appropriately
- Asking for help
- Offering help
- Initiating interactions
- Recess games (outdoor and indoor)
- Joining in and staying in play
- Body language including eye contact, body position, proximity, voice, gesture
- Compliments
- Listening
- Parts of conversations including greeting, small talk, main topic, closing
- Identifying the main topic in conversation
- Identifying the main topic in play
- Continuing talk about a main topic with questions, comments, and by adding information
- Initiating conversations on topics of interest to others
- Modulating emotional reactions
- Dealing with anger
- Dealing with anxiety
- Acknowledging mistakes and apologizing
- Responsible choices
- Building a good reputation
- Assertiveness
- Being a good sport
- Concept of friendship
- Making new friends
- Keeping friends
- Dealing with bullies
- Giving information
- Manners
- Dealing with the unexpected
- Understanding one's own strengths and weaknesses
- Physical perspective taking (understanding that what another person sees may not be the same as what I see)

(Continued on next page.)

- Emotional perspective taking (understanding the feelings of others and that what another person feels in a situation may not be the same as what I feel in that situation)
- Dealing with failure
- Friendly teasing versus bullying
- Thanking others
- Working in a group
- Empathy and giving emotional support
- Getting stuck and flexibility
- Reading nonverbal cues
- Hygiene
- Using self-control
- Asking permission
- Staying out of fights
- Problem solving
- Accepting consequences
- Dealing with an accusation
- Negotiating
- Dealing with boredom
- Deciding what caused a problem
- Making a complaint
- Answering a complaint
- Dealing with being left out
- Dealing with embarrassment
- Accepting no
- Saying no
- Dealing with group pressure
- Dealing with wanting something that isn't yours
- Making a decision
- Being honest

12 | Troubleshooting Behaviors in the Classroom

Most children with autism spectrum disorders will display at least a few challenging behaviors in the classroom. This chapter discusses how to address common behavior problems of children with ASD—problems that can interfere with the education of the child as well as that of the other children in your class. Problem behaviors not only interfere in the classroom but also make it harder for the child to make friends and feel like part of the class. These problems do not simply go away with maturation but require intervention. Research on the effectiveness of interventions for problem behaviors is very encouraging.

Sometimes a student with ASD will enter your class with a "behavior plan" incorporated into her IEP. It will list "positive behavioral supports" for the child; specifically, strategies for decreasing disruptive and "off-task" behaviors, while increasing appropriate, productive behaviors. The fact that a child comes to you with a "behavior plan" does not necessarily mean that she will pose many behavioral problems in your class. It simply means that behavioral issues have been formally identified and that there is a way to address them.

Functional Behavior Assessment

Functional behavior assessment (FBA) is a formal system of evaluating and analyzing problem behavior that is often used with children on the autism spectrum. This type of assessment doesn't simply examine the behavior, but seeks to identify the function served by the behavior. The FBA assumes that behavior is communication. Some people call it the ABC's:

1. What are the **A**ntecedents (what comes before the behavior)?
2. What is the **B**ehavior itself? and
3. What are the **C**onsequences (what comes after the behavior and may be serving to reinforce and maintain it)?

For example, a particular negative behavior (tantrum, silliness, fidgetiness) might be consistently preceded by the beginning of a language lesson, and followed by removing the child from the classroom, thus effectively rewarding her for this behavior by allowing her to escape from an activity she doesn't like.

This type of analysis requires a baseline period of a few days or even weeks, during which you're not trying to change anything, and data are taken frequently so that the antecedents and consequences can be figured out. This analysis is best done by, or with, someone who has training and experience.

Antecedents are analyzed for precipitating factors. For example, if a child begins to melt down every time she is given a writing task, it is important to determine which aspect of the task is frustrating or anxiety provoking. Does she have trouble formulating her language, or with handwriting, or is something else going on? Determining the cause of the behavior is critical to developing an effective intervention strategy. It allows you to develop appropriate modifications to task demands so that the child can better cope with them. It also gives you the chance to target specific areas of weakness for direct intervention. This will help the child be a more successful learner and will also help you predict other circumstances that may elicit the challenging behaviors.

Consequences must be carefully analyzed. Does the student get to leave the classroom when she has a meltdown? Do you walk over to her desk and give her your full attention? It is possible that the student enjoys these consequences more than she enjoys her writing tasks, so the consequences of her meltdowns are rewarding to her. It is vital to make sure that only appropriate behaviors are reinforced and the inappropriate behaviors are not. Once the FBA is complete, intervention can be planned and a "behavior plan" drafted.

Occasionally, other children in the class may instigate or exacerbate inappropriate and challenging behaviors on the part of your student with ASD. Some children may take advantage of the child's gullibility or desire to have friends and put her up to doing things that she doesn't realize are wrong, or they may make a point of annoying the student with ASD just to see her reaction. These are forms of bullying and should be addressed as such, making the bullies accountable for their behavior and teaching the student with ASD how to deal with bullying.

If your student does not have a behavior plan but is experiencing significant behavioral issues in your classroom, you can request that she have a functional behavior assessment. Most likely your school has a formal process for requesting that a child receive an FBA. Ask your principal, special education coordinator, or school psychologist how to set the process in motion. Also be sure to communicate with the child's parents that you think an FBA might be useful. No thorough FBA is complete without input from parents, siblings, and other people who may be familiar with the problem behavior. For more information on how and why an FBA is conducted, you may wish to read *Functional Behavior Assessment for People with Autism* by Beth Glasberg.

Types of Problem Behaviors

Problem behaviors of children with ASD in the classroom fall into a number of categories, including:

- verbal and physical aggression (toward self or others);
- repetitive and inflexible behaviors;
- socially inappropriate behaviors;
- inattentive, disorganized behavior;
- withdrawal or refusal to participate.

You can see from this list that interfering behaviors can either be overt, inappropriate behaviors or quiet detachment (e.g., the child becomes very shy/anxious when called upon in class). Although the latter does not usually interfere with the classmates' learning, it certainly interferes with the learning of your student with ASD. Both types of behaviors must be addressed.

Most problem behaviors in a young child with ASD, even aggressive behaviors, are not intended by the child to hurt others. Instead, they may be related to the child's limited ability to control her emotions, including silliness, anger, and anxiety. They should not be interpreted as malicious. *When stressed, children with ASD often have difficulty regulating their emotions.* It is part of who they are. This does not mean, "don't stress the child." It means that the child must be taught how to cope with stress and how to calm herself. Helping a child learn this is one of the greatest gifts you can give her.

What Stresses the Child with ASD?

Major stressors in the classroom are often one of three types:
1. language, social, or academic demands that are too high (or the child perceives them as being too high);
2. violations of the child's expectations, including rapid, unexpected transitions and changes in routine; and
3. an environment that is too noisy, bright, or chaotic (and what the other children find pleasant and cheerful may be too much for the child with ASD).

Difficulties with emotional regulation are made worse by hunger, illness, or lack of sleep, and by the child's limited ability to express herself verbally. (This is why it's so important to teach children words and phrases they can use to let you know they need help, they find the work too hard, they need a break, etc.) On the other hand, emotional regulation is supported by a trusting relationship with the teacher. The child will be easier to calm if she feels that you:

- are predictable,
- have clear rules and expectations,
- care about her, and
- can be counted on to help her control herself.

What Are the Major Types of Behavior Intervention?

Behavioral interventions to address problem behaviors can be either *preventive* or *reactive*. A reactive intervention is one in which you're reacting to a behavior that has already occurred, by changing the usual consequences, or controlling the child directly. Very commonly, paying attention to the child or letting her escape from unpleasant work unintentionally reinforces problem behaviors. However, once the behavior (such as a tantrum) is well under way, the child may not even notice the consequences. For example, if your student with ASD is screaming at you because you just gave the class a writing assignment and she feels it is too difficult, that child, at that moment, cannot process what you say to her. Therefore, exclusively reactive methods of intervention tend to be ineffective. Preventive or proactive interventions anticipate the child's possible reactions and provide supports to help the child react in an appropriate way.

Proactive (Preventive) Techniques

You can use two general methods to proactively address the problem behaviors of a child with ASD in your classroom. One is to *modify the environment* while the other is to *teach the child to cope with the environment*. We'll give you some details on both types of intervention in this chapter. The best intervention often involves a combination of the two approaches. The best balance between *environmental modifications* and *expectations for the child* is based on the child's level of functioning. Some level of demand for appropriate behavior should always be there, but the environment should be modified as necessary for the child to be successful (e.g., you wouldn't expect an eighteen-month-old not to stick a fork in an outlet—you keep forks away and outlets covered—but you do expect a four-year-old to exercise this self-control).

The approach selected also depends on expectations for the child's future. All children need to learn to follow rules and control their emotional reactions. However, many individuals with ASD will always require some level of environmental accommodation. For others, environmental accommodations could be minimal or unnecessary. They can learn to follow social conventions in a typical environment. The goal is always to help the child become as independent and responsible as his or her abilities allow.

Isn't It Best to Modify the Environment or the Demands on the Child?

Not necessarily. Modifying the environment too much, while placing minimal demands on the child, results in an individual who cannot comply with social conventions but rather depends on others to arrange the environment to prevent problems. Some parents and teachers of even high functioning children with ASD take complete responsibility for the child's problem behavior, blaming their own failure to take the child's state into account or to modify the environment. This may be appropriate for a very young child with ASD, but if it goes on too long, she may not learn responsibility for her own behavior as she matures.

For example, it is appropriate for a parent not to include her child with ASD in weekly food shopping trips if the supermarket stresses the child beyond her limits. However, the goal should be to help the child become accustomed to the supermarket, by visiting the market at relatively quiet times and with no shopping to do, and by starting with short trips and building up. During those times, the child can be taught rules for appropriate behavior in the supermarket. A program like this will eventually allow the child to go food shopping with her parent and to behave appropriately.

An approach that exclusively modifies the environment turns out to be a bad idea, especially for bright children with ASD. Not only do they learn to rely on others to make accommodations for them, but they ultimately blame others for their failures and cannot attribute their successes to themselves. There are many examples of parents and teachers making accommodations in the environment and in their own behavior that clearly do not help the child or may even be unsafe. For example:

- The family of one nine-year-old with ASD banned peas from their home because the child did not like the smell.
- A very bright ten-year-old boy with ASD was not allowed to line up with the other children at the end of recess because his individual assistant was afraid he would have a meltdown.
- A five-year-old with ASD was allowed to climb and walk on high furniture and window ledges, the parents explaining that she would have a meltdown if they stopped her and she had excellent balance anyway.
- Parents of an obese toddler with ASD insisted that they had to feed him fatty foods because he would not eat anything else.
- A very young child with ASD attended a nursery school class. He insisted that he take his shoes off at the beginning of each class and was allowed to do so to prevent a tantrum. Then the original teacher left and a new teacher took over. The new teacher felt strongly that all of the children should keep their shoes on to protect their feet, especially during gross motor activities. This little boy reacted by having a meltdown every time he was asked to keep his shoes on. His mother told the teacher that she could make a choice—to let him take his shoes off and keep him in the

class or to insist that he wear shoes and be removed from the class. The teacher allowed him to take his shoes off.

If a child's environment is needlessly modified as described in the examples, he will learn that he does not have to follow rules. Later on, as expected, the child who refused to take his shoes off did not attribute his behavior to himself but rather blamed others for his problem behavior ("You made me do that.") At thirteen, he now has an external locus of control. That is, he believes outside forces control his behavior. He reacts to frustration by sometimes throwing chairs, breaking others' property, or hitting others. He actually said that he hit his teacher one day when he was angry about his class work because she put her arm near him. It was not his fault that he hit her; it was her fault. Well, of course it wasn't, but this is how he now views the world.

When teachers tell us that the child's behavior is difficult and parents say they don't understand this because they have few problems at home, it almost always turns out that the parents place few or no demands on the child—no chores or responsibilities, no homework, no nonpreferred activities or foods. Clearly parents, individual assistants, playground supervisors, and other school staff must all be educated in behavioral intervention techniques and consistently implement the same behavioral intervention plan across settings to help the child learn to comply with rules and limits.

Choosing Effective Environmental Modifications, When Appropriate

Having warned you against too many environmental modifications, let's return to the first point: you want to help the child succeed, and you may need to modify the environment, especially in the beginning, to accomplish this. Think of it this way. You want your student to succeed 75 to 80 percent of the time so that you can reinforce appropriate behaviors and the child can feel successful. Reinforcing appropriate behaviors is very effective in modifying the way the child acts.

Reduce Demands. The first environmental modification is reducing demands on the child. Try backing off a bit, if a child is emotionally fragile, and you feel that she is under significant stress (rather than feeling that she is manipulating the situation with tantrums to get out of work), or it's the beginning of the year and she's adjusting to your class. Just the transition from being at home over a vacation back to school can cause significant stress. Give the child extra room for the first few days back.

During the year consider the academic, social, physical, and speech/language demands that are being placed on the child and think about which ones could be overwhelming her. Make academic assignments easier. Intersperse new material with material that the child is already comfortable with, so she can relax and experience success. Keep work sessions short, and gives lots of praise. Try to sense escalating frustration and deflect it with a distraction, such as an easier task demand, or an errand. However, do make certain you are not reinforcing inappropriate behaviors associated with escalating frustration. The child needs to know that she is expected to accomplish reasonable tasks but that you will help by breaking up or modifying the task if it is truly too difficult.

Change the Physical Environment. The other major environmental strategy is modifying the physical environment. Some children with ASD are very sensitive to sensory stimuli, and are distracted or distressed by sensations that other children may not even notice (smells, the hum of florescent lights, noise, movement). Most children with ASD have trouble articulating that they are overwhelmed by the sensory environment, but appear irritable, frustrated, and upset. Triggers are idiosyncratic—what bothers one child with ASD will not bother another.

Especially at the beginning of the year, when demands for adjustment are highest, you can try to keep the environment manageable for the child. Naturally, this is easier if parents, therapists, or the child herself can tell you what aspects of the environment are distressing to her. It may be necessary for the child to go with her one-on-one aide or a therapist to a quiet room to complete some of her work. If her attention is waning and work is getting hard for her, but she is still behaving appropriately, consider giving her a gross motor break by letting her do a classroom chore and thus avoid the problem behaviors. Similarly, some children will give you warning signs that a meltdown is impending (increased fidgeting, humming), but no actual negative behavior has begun. Take advantage of this information to change gears for the child, removing her from the situation and changing activities.

Environmental Modifications for Common Problems
Answering Questions Aloud. If the child's difficulty with answering questions in class provokes problem behaviors, give her a starter

phrase (e.g., "Columbus sailed to America in the year _____"), or, if necessary, model the whole response to the question for her and then let her copy you. Remember that some children with ASD have trouble understanding "wh" questions, and may need help understanding what information you're asking for. Remember that giving the child visual cues (e.g., write the question down or draw a picture) is helpful.

Problems Writing. If the child consistently becomes over-whelmed with anxiety every time she is asked to complete a writing assignment, assess the cause. If the issue is the graphomotor component (holding the pencil and forming letters), then someone should help the child write down or type her ideas. (She does a little, and then the teacher or another student does some.) Eventually, she should be taught to type instead. If the issue with writing is formulating her answer, then the method for completing this task should be modified. The child can be taught to use graphic organizers to outline her ideas prior to beginning to write (see Chapter 9). Note that in both of the examples, an accommodation is made but there is also a demand that the child learn a behavior that makes her responsible for the work and moves her toward independence.

Auditory Processing. To diminish the stress related to auditory processing and language comprehension issues, always provide visual cues in the form of written instructions, pictures, and demonstrations along with auditory information. In addition, make it clear to the child with ASD that the information is meant for her. For example, she may not understand that what is written on the blackboard refers to her. You can also write important instructions on paper and hand them to the child. Have her read them and then question her to make sure she has understood. It can also be helpful to provide a high functioning child with ASD with a graphic organizer outlining the information presented in a content area like science or social studies in advance of the lesson on that material (Chapter 9).

Transitions. Transitions and violations of expectations often are associated with problem behaviors in children with ASD. Tran-sitions can be eased in a number of ways. For example, attaching a visual schedule for each day to the top of the child's desk or inside a notebook can be helpful in making the day predictable. At first, you or the child's assistant should review the schedule at the start of each day. To ensure that the child is attending to the schedule throughout the day, she should check off activities as they are completed. For young children and nonreaders, the schedule can be comprised of photographs of the child doing the activities in her schedule. If you put Velcro on the backs of the photos, they can be stuck to a board in the order they will occur that day. Also, the order can easily be changed each day. As each activity is completed, the child removes the picture from the schedule. Older children who are reading can be provided a written checklist.

To increase the child's flexibility and ability to deal with the unexpected, include a "surprise" card that can be inserted into the schedule if there is to be a change of plan for the day or if something out of the ordinary will occur, such as an assembly. Teach the child that a "surprise" is a possibility each day. When the "surprise" card is inserted into the schedule, be sure to specify what the surprise activity will be.

The level of detail in a child's written schedule will vary depending on the level of direction necessary for the child to succeed. For example, a general schedule listing all activities may be enough for most of the day, but she may need a separate, more detailed schedule to complete each step of what is required during independent math work.

If the child has particular trouble transitioning from place to place within the school, she can be provided with visual cue cards to facilitate transitions to and from specials and pullout services. For example, the child is shown an index card with the next required classroom activity written on it prior to leaving her special or pullout. When she gets back to the classroom, before she enters, she should be asked what she will do when she enters the classroom. She should state what is on the card. Then she walks into the classroom and an adult should make sure she begins the required activity promptly. For younger or nonverbal children who don't yet read or understand how pictures can symbolize an upcoming activity, it may help to give or show them an actual object related to the coming activity to prepare them for the transition (e.g., if it is almost time for P.E., let the child carry the ball that she will use there; if it's almost time to go to the library/media center, give her her library card to hold).

It is helpful to remove visual distractors from the child's immediate environment and visual field. Reducing visual clutter as much as possible makes it easier for the child to identify relevant visual cues. For example, only visual information related to the lesson should be on the child's desk during the lesson. The child should not be seated next to the window or next to the class pet or fish tank.

The classroom environment should be supportive and a setting in which the child with ASD can trust that she will be able to obtain help when she needs it. It is very important that the child feels liked. One of the simplest things a classroom teacher can do is teach her students to compliment each other for effort or a job well done.

Teaching Appropriate Behaviors

Not all of a child's problem behaviors can be addressed at once, nor should they be. It is important to choose your battles. A good place to start is by addressing the emotional modulation issues that underlie or worsen many challenging behaviors.

Stopping Out-of-Control Behavior

The child should be taught a script for stopping and getting herself back in control when she starts to lose control either emotionally or with a perseverative or repetitive behavior. We have the child:

1. take a deep breath,
2. count to 10,
3. say "I can stop _____,"
4. then say "I can _____ instead."

Practicing this script a great deal "out of the heat of the moment" will facilitate the child's use of it when cued at the beginning of a meltdown. We use the term "script" here to refer to a sentence or phrase that a verbal child is taught to say in a specific situation to help her control her own behavior. These scripts are not to be confused with the recorded "scripts" that might be used with a nonverbal child to help him or her begin to talk.

A five-year-old boy who was not allowed to play with a toy with which he was obsessed became agitated and angrily yelled, "I won't play with anything." When prompted by an adult to use the stopping script he immediately took a deep breath, and counted to 10, then said, "I can stop being angry about the plastic food; I can play with the trains instead." He was able to do this because he had *rehearsed the strategy numerous times* when he was not experiencing any strong emotions. In addition, he had played lots of stop and go games such as musical chairs, freeze dance, etc., at home and in his social skills group sessions, and so he had learned to suspend his behavior and freeze, a very useful skill.

You cannot expect that a child will automatically implement any strategies or scripts in the heat of the moment just because she has been told what to do. Sometimes the child will be too far out of control to use a "stopping" strategy herself. If so, you or the assistant will need to remove the child from the classroom to a quiet place for a time-out until she is calm. You must make it clear to the child that she is expected to use the strategy and calm herself if she can, but if she cannot, an adult will then take over and help to get her calm. As she starts to regain composure she should be helped to use the "stopping strategy" to completely calm down and then she should receive lots of praise for pulling herself together. She needs *lots of practice* during calm times to gain the ability to use the "stopping strategy" herself. The stopping script should be affixed to the child's desk in case she needs reminding.

In addition to getting lots of practice with this stopping strategy (enlist the aid of the parents and the child's therapists), the child should practice relaxing her body through relaxation techniques. You can ask the school psychologist or OT, or an outside therapist, or parents, to practice having the child relax upon hearing a specific verbal command. Then, at the moment you need her to relax to her cue, it will be a well-practiced skill. Progressive muscle relaxation, slowed breathing, visualizing calming scenes, and self-talk are components of relaxation that can work well for children with ASD and are not difficult to do. Many books and websites give specific instructions. (See Resources.)

Asking for Help

The child with ASD should be directly taught rules and scripts for how to obtain help when she is becoming overwhelmed by frustration. The ability to ask for help or attention from others leads to reductions in problem behavior. Optimally, you will be able to teach the student to verbally indicate what she needs help with. However, if she has difficulty telling you verbally, she should be taught to ask for help, nonverbally, in an appropriate way (e.g., raising her hand and then pointing).

For verbal children, a script to use should be written down or drawn in a notebook and on an index card and affixed to the child's desk. (Older children might keep the card in a pocket.) An example of a script for requesting help verbally might be:

First think, do I need help or should I keep trying myself? If I really need help, I

■ *Interrupt appropriately*

- *Clearly say what I need help with*
- *Listen*
- *If I do not understand, I will ask questions*
- *Say thank you*

Verbally Expressing Feelings

It is important to help children with ASD to verbally express their feelings. Help the child to recognize when she is feeling overwhelmed or otherwise stressed (e.g., feeling tired) and needs help from an adult. Label what you think she is feeling. For example, "It looks like you might be getting frustrated with that worksheet. Do you want help?"

As your student develops skills in this area, she should be taught to anticipate how she will feel in a future situation. For example, you're planning a class trip to a farm. Meet with the child privately. Review the plan for the day, and stress that not all plans work out; remind her of her helpful mantra "Sometimes surprises happen. That's OK." Review what aspects of the activities are not optional (e.g., safety on the bus, staying with the group), as well as what activities will be optional (e.g., petting the animals). Discuss with her what aspects of the day she may not like (the bus ride, the smell, etc.). Discuss with her how she will ask for help should she feel uncomfortable.

Making Substitutions for Problem Behaviors

Teaching the child verbal rules to use can also be helpful in managing frequently occurring problem behaviors. For example, if she is inappropriately touching other people, teach her alternative ways to show affection in the form of a rule (e.g., give a high five, thumbs up, or OK sign; wink; say 'hi'; give compliments, etc.).

In choosing an alternate behavior, look for something the child can do easily so she won't revert to the problem behavior because it's simpler (or less aversive) for her to do. For example, if the child had been indicating that she wanted a break by throwing her books on the floor, don't expect her to substitute the behavior of saying "I need a break, please" if she is anxious about talking in class. Instead, it might work to give her a special card to hold up or put on the edge of her desk when she is ready for a break.

To motivate the child to continue to use the alternate behavior, adults and children must be sure to give the child what she is seeking through the appropriate behavior. For example, if she had been pulling classmates' hair to get their attention and learns to tap them on the shoulder instead, classmates should oblige by turning around, smiling, and saying "yes"?

Perseverative (Repetitive) Behaviors

Some perseverative and repetitive behaviors will only interfere with the learning of your student with ASD (e.g., whispering to herself about favorite topics). Other behaviors will interfere with learning in all of your students (e.g., repetitive talk to others about preoccupations). These behaviors clearly need to be limited.

If you have a student who is engaging in perseverative (repetitive) behaviors in the classroom, give her a rule about the appropriate time and place for those behaviors or preoccupations. For instance, make a rule that she may talk about her favorite topic at a specific time in school. Or the rule may be that she can do the behavior in her room after school. If necessary, use a visual sign or brief verbal remark to remind the child that now is not the time and to remind her when it will be the time and place.

In addition to setting a limit on repetitive behavior, you must also give the child a competing appropriate behavior to substitute for the repetitive behavior. For example, a child who was inappropriately and repetitively touching himself in class was prompted to hold a pencil and put his other hand on his paper or book. When there were no materials to hold, he was given a ball to squeeze instead. The rule to set the time and place for the inappropriate behavior and the rule for the replacement behavior were discussed with him and written in a notebook.

How you address a repetitive behavior will depend on how frequently it occurs. Important questions to ask are: "Is it really interfering with my student's learning or the learning of the other students in the class?"; "Is the behavior significantly impeding the child's social interaction with her peers because it makes her look very odd?" Stopping an occasional flap of the hands may take enormous energy for the child and draw her attention away from where her focus should be for optimal learning.

It is possible that a behavior you think indicates inattention does not. As a graduate student, psychologist Helen Garretson did a study of attention to a boring task and found that some children with ASD were on task *more* while doing their favorite repetitive behaviors (in contrast to typically developing children who tended to be off task while doing repetitive behaviors like jiggling or playing with pencils or hair). This observation is controversial among behavior therapists; many behavior therapists believe that *all* repetitive behaviors take the child's attention and prevent learning, and should be suppressed. If you are working with a behavior therapist or consultant, you should discuss these issues with him or her.

If, despite your best efforts, your student with ASD cannot stop a repetitive behavior when asked and that behavior is frequent and interferes with her learning, then enlist the aid of the school psychologist and the autism consultant. They can help you set up a reinforcement schedule in your classroom and can hold pull-out sessions with her to practice regulating the behavior one-on-one and stopping when prompted.

Addressing Rigid Behavior and Noncompliance

Setting limits on inappropriate behavior and reinforcing appropriate behavior is extremely important in reducing problem behavior in children with ASD in your classroom. Just because a child has ASD does not mean that she is incapable of defiant behavior or should not be held responsible for her actions. On the contrary, it is important to engender a sense of responsibility and accountability. Limits and consequences, especially for defiance or aggression, are just as important for children with ASD as for other children.

What if your student with ASD is completely capable of doing what you request and is not worried but she just digs in her heels and insists on doing something you don't want her to do? Or she insists on doing something in a way you don't want her to? Her behavior is not necessarily out of control, but she is being "noncompliant" and not doing as asked. She may be trying to manipulate the situation or she may simply be rigid and inflexible and need things to go the same way every time (e.g., like the child who insists on being first in line all the time and won't budge out of that position or the child who repeatedly pushes the desks back the way they were because they don't look right to her in the new way you have arranged them).

It is essential for children to learn to be flexible and do the work they are asked to do. Pick your battles. Do not try to address all behaviors at once. Choose behaviors that interfere in the classroom first. If a child needs to be first in line, that behavior may not interfere as much as refusal to do work or the need to move furniture during class. At a time when the child is not engaging in the behavior, give her the rule about the behavior (write it down, draw a picture, take photos of the child engaging in the desired behavior, write a Social Story about it). State the consequences of noncompliance with the rule. Be consistent in setting limits on the behavior and in giving positive consequences for appropriate behavior and negative consequences for negative behavior. Use "personal stories" (see next section) to discuss the behavior and consequences. Help her to think about the consequences in advance.

Teaching the Child to Monitor Her Own Behavior

Your student with ASD should be helped to evaluate her own behavior, its consequences, and possible alternatives to the problem behaviors. After a problematic situation occurs, you and the child can outline a "personal story" together using a graphic organizer. The main topic of the organizer can be "something that happened today." One subtopic of the organizer is "what happened." Another subtopic is "consequences," and the third subtopic is "what should I do next time?" The appropriate details are connected to each subtopic. It is very important to also outline stories of times when the child effectively inhibited an inappropriate behavior and did the right thing instead. This will make the good consequences of appropriate behavior explicit and she will see that the answer to the question as to what she should do differently next time is "Nothing. Do just the same."

All rules and personal stories should be written out in a notebook and the child should review them each day at home and in school. It will take time for her to learn new routines and appropriate social behaviors. Each day you will have the opportunity to help her implement the rules for appropriate behavior in a range of contexts. Only by using and understanding the rules in a range of contexts will the child generalize the appropriate behaviors. Old maladaptive strategies are the automatic ones and therefore are the ones that are immediately available to the child in times of stress. *New routines and behaviors must be practiced consistently to help make them automatic. These new behaviors must become automatic for them to compete with the old behaviors.* Make sure your student is rewarded for success in implementing the rules. It is important that rewards and consequences be consistent and relatively immediate. Let's discuss that next.

We Can't Overemphasize the Importance of Positive Reinforcement!

Positive reinforcement of appropriate behavior is more effective than punishment. It's very easy to ignore good behavior (with any child, in fact); be sure to notice and reinforce good behavior. Catch the child behaving appropriately and reward her.

Choosing Reinforcers

You must realize that what is reinforcing (rewarding) for most children may have no power for the child with ASD. Most typically developing children are reinforced and motivated by social approval in an environment of fair and clear expectations. For example, they enjoy being praised by the teacher, and will work for a smiley face sticker or a good grade on their class work. At least initially, the child with ASD may not be reinforced by social approval but rather by gaining time to engage in her preoccupations, by a preferred snack, or by a break away from interaction with other people. You could sometimes use the reinforcer of some alone time if the child has been working hard at interacting with the other kids.

It is important to discover the most potent reinforcers for a given child. You can find out by asking the parents or previous teachers and by watching what the child does when left to her own devices. Make sure you identify several things that are reinforcing for the child, because any given reward may lose its power over time. See *Incentives for Change* (Delmolino and Harris) for more information. For most children, success in itself is highly reinforcing and will result in increased compliance and higher self-esteem.

When selecting reinforcers and consequences for your student, it is also important to identify what is unintentionally reinforcing to her. For example, unlike their typically developing peers, some children with ASD might enjoy having to stay in from recess to complete their work or they may actually enjoy being put in time out, away from other people. For this reason time-outs should not be used to deter behavior but to help the child calm down when upset. In addition, an adult should be present during time-outs. You would not want to use consequences in an attempt to deter inappropriate behavior, when in fact they would reinforce it!

Initially, the most potent reinforcers may be concrete rewards and activities. The child's aide can provide these kind of rewards discretely. When possible it is important to gradually help the child work for naturally occurring reinforcers—praise, classmates' admiration, and grades—just like any other student.

Sometimes it is quite difficult to move a child from a tangible reinforcement system (toys, snacks) to social reinforcers (praise). One particular boy was highly motivated by having an adult stick stars to a Velcro board when he stayed on task. When I first met him he was unresponsive to any other type of reinforcer and had great difficulty participating in any task without the star system. Finally, I told him that I used secret, invisible stars and he would know he got one when I put my hand on his back and said, "You're doing a great job." This worked. After a while, I started to use a variety of socially reinforcing comments when I put my hand on his back. At first he would ask how many secret stars he got at the end of each session, but soon he was responding to many social reinforcers and did not even talk about stars.

Using Reinforcers in the Classroom

When establishing a child's schedule, be sure that the child has the ability to meet the demands placed on her. Following the completion of a task, she should be reinforced with a scheduled break, meaning that breaks are built into the schedule she is given at the beginning of the day. These breaks can involve talking about a favored topic or doing a favored activity. The child must fully meet the demand prior to receiving the reward. The reward should be accompanied by plenty of verbal praise (e.g., "great job doing _____. I am so proud of you"). Most children will like a loud, "Great job, Julie!" and a vigorous handshake, and so will some children with ASD. But if you see the child shrink or flinch, tone it down. A quiet "Great job, Julie" with only brief eye contact may be more pleasant to the child with sensory sensitivities. Pairing social reinforcers (praise, playtime with another child) with what is naturally reinforcing for the child, such as favorite activities, breaks, or snacks, actually makes the social reinforcers more pleasant to the child.

As soon as possible, you should begin gradually increasing the length of time the child must wait between rewards. Visual supports can be used to help the child learn to wait. Token reinforcement systems can also be used to lengthen the amount of time that passes before a child receives a reward. Children with ASD can be highly motivated by a token reinforcement system. This is a system where a tangible "token"—a penny, a ticket, anything you can get a lot of—is used as a kind of classroom money to buy special privileges. Depending on the age of the children, their awareness of the disability of the child with ASD, etc., you can use this system just for the child with ASD, or for the whole class.

We have found that a token reinforcement system with a new twist is particularly effective for children who need feedback on their behavioral errors and need to gain a sense that they can redeem themselves. A clear jar is kept on the teacher's desk or on a shelf nearby. Only the teacher and the child with ASD have discussed and are aware of the system to be used. Specific behaviors are identified as the inappropriate behaviors to be addressed. These are often such things as impulsively interrupting or grabbing other students' things. Each time the child behaves inappropriately, a token is dropped into the jar. If the child gets a specified number of tokens in one day, she will lose something, for example, computer or recess time. Tokens are removed from the jar for any pro-social behaviors, especially if the child starts the inappropriate behavior and then stops herself or she apologizes for it. The idea is that everyone makes mistakes but that each person can and should take responsibility for making things better after she has made a mistake. This method gives the child an immediate indication that she has done something inappropriate and positive reinforcement for both pro-social behaviors and the ability to stop an inappropriate behavior.

What to Do If the Child Loses Control

There may be times when your student with ASD loses control. The following procedure should be employed when a meltdown begins to happen.

- Tell her to use her "stopping strategy," as described in the section on "Stopping Out-of-Control Behavior," above.
- If the child cannot use this strategy because the behavior or emotional reaction escalates too much, an adult should immediately remove her from the room. (If you have a student who loses control, at times you may be the only adult in the room. Make a contingency plan. You need a specific adult you can call to the room to remove the child if she loses control when you are alone with your students. If the student loses control frequently, she must have a classroom aide.)

- The adult who leaves the room with the child should seat her in a chair and say, "Today you could not control yourself, so I need to help you get back in control."
- If the child is completely out of control and has to be removed from the situation, the only demand should be that she stop. The adult who is with her should continually reassure her that she can get back in control.
- Make sure that you use a calm, firm tone. Do not yell at the child. Do not physically restrain her (unless she becomes aggressive and there is a chance she will physically hurt herself or others). After the episode, it is important to let the child's parents know about the incident. It is, however, a bad idea to ask the parents to come to school and take the child home. This often powerfully reinforces the out-of-control behavior.
- Later, during a time when the child is not upset (out of the heat of the moment), remind her that when she starts to lose control, she will have a chance to control herself, but if she cannot get herself under control, an adult will take over and help her.

What If I Think a Child May Need Medication?

The behavioral interventions described in this chapter are often very effective in addressing problem behaviors. However, after giving the strategies suggested in this chapter a good try (several months at least), and deciding that the child is really not able to control her mood and behavior, it may become necessary to make a referral for a medication evaluation. It is unlikely that your school system will allow you, the child's teacher, to directly suggest to parents that they consider medication. Instead, try meeting with the parents to discuss the continuing behavioral problems the child is having, as well as what has been tried. You might then ask for an IEP team meeting where a child psychiatrist who understands children with autism may suggest a medication evaluation.

Some of the children in your classroom will already be taking medications to modify behavior, mood, or attention. It is important for a classroom teacher with a child with ASD in her class to learn about medications the child may be taking, so that she can provide informed feedback to the parents and doctor about its effectiveness or side effects observed in the classroom. If you're informed that a child is on a particular medication, ask the parents if they would like you to watch for any particular changes in the child's behavior (see discussion of commonly used medications in Chapter 6). Medication does not negate the need for the behavioral interventions discussed, but may help the child to become more available for, and benefit from, these interventions.

Conclusion

There are two major types of preventive intervention (modifying the environment and direct teaching) for addressing problem behaviors in children with ASD that interfere in the classroom. The most effective approach involves directly teaching a child appropriate behaviors to replace the inappropriate ones and then modifying the environment to the extent necessary for the child to be able to behave appropriately in the classroom. It is important that parents and school staff all understand and consistently implement behavioral interventions.

13 | The Balancing Act

Educating a child with autism in the regular classroom can be daunting at first. It will require modification of both your group and individual teaching methods to make it easier for your student with ASD to learn. It will require that you follow through with specific methods that the child has been taught in outside therapies. A good inclusion experience can benefit the child with ASD in a way unlike any other therapeutic experience. Luckily, the modifications you will need to make to group lessons will also enhance the learning of your other students.

Remember: inclusion means inclusion. It doesn't mean physically putting the child in the classroom but keeping him essentially separate. (See Chapter 14 for a rather depressing example of this.)

If this is your first experience with a child with ASD in your mainstream classroom, you will learn quickly at the beginning. You will need to spend some time modifying work, preparing special materials, planning with the child's team, addressing the child's behaviors, as well as educating the typically developing students in your class about their classmate with ASD. Allocating your time effectively will be a challenge. Your typically developing students will have many feelings about their classmate with ASD. They may feel nervous about interacting with him and uncertain of how he might behave or what he might do. Younger children may feel neglected when their classmate with ASD needs extra attention from you. Attending to the academic and emotional needs of all of the children in your class is a real balancing act. If the balance is right, all students benefit.

It is important to learn as much as you possibly can about ASD in general and your new student specifically, and to do this prior to the outset of the school year so that you can begin planning modifications. (You are already doing this by reading this book!) You may at times be uncertain of how to effectively teach this child. You will have access to the school team, and perhaps outside professionals to help you with this.

We have identified five basic issues in balancing the needs of the child with ASD and the needs of the other children. These will be discussed in turn in this chapter:

1. How do you *manage the behavior* of the child with ASD while attending to the entire class? We devote the most time to this issue, because it is often the most concerning to teachers.
2. How do you *deliver a modified curriculum*, when necessary, to the child with ASD, while teaching all the other children?
3. How do you find time to *reinforce social and language skills* in the child with ASD?
4. What is the *effect on the typical children* of having a child with ASD in the class?
5. How do *parents of typical children* react to having the child with ASD in the class?

Managing Behavior

The child with ASD may require your full attention if he is having a difficult time behaving appropriately. This is a legitimate concern. However, if the right modifications are in place, then your student with ASD should not require your complete attention very often. And, his demands on your attention should get lower as the school year progresses (unless circumstances in the child's life change).

It is very important to keep in mind that simply being reactive in your approach to the behavior and needs of your student with ASD is not nearly as effective as being proactive. It is essential that rules regarding behavioral expectations be made explicit and taught from the start. These issues are discussed in more detail in Chapter 12. *Please note, however, that if the child is often having tantrums, despite everyone's best efforts, or showing uncontrollable aggressive or destructive behavior, or is being educated in isolation within your classroom, then the child is not yet ready to be placed in a regular education classroom.*

Difficult behaviors in children with ASD include repetitive behaviors, preoccupations with objects or topics, and inflexibility. It may be difficult for the student to stop a repetitive behavior, once he begins. Inflexibility can make it difficult to transition from one activity to another as well as to cope with changes in schedule or location (especially unexpected changes). The child with ASD often has difficulty not only modulating his behavior but also his emotional reactions, including silliness, anger, and anxiety. Often the refusals of a child with ASD are not simply oppositional or defiant behavior but rather a reaction to being emotionally overwhelmed.

Verbal or physical aggression is a serious problem. You are unlikely to encounter very much physical aggression from your students with ASD. A child who is physically aggressive would not be appropriately placed in your general education classroom. However, you still need to understand the emotional modulation issues that many of these children have.

The child with ASD will likely feel anxious, overwhelmed, and confused and have some trouble transitioning into your classroom during at least the first few weeks of school. Know that difficult behaviors are likely to escalate during times of transition or uncertainty. Times of transition include not only the beginning of the school year but the days before and after any vacation or time out of school due to illness. These behaviors usually subside as soon as the environment becomes more predictable, when the student comes to know the classroom routines (keep this in mind if you're feeling frustrated!).

Other difficult and more persistent behaviors are inattention, disorganization, and lack of knowledge or ability to implement social rules. At first addressing these behaviors may require that you modify the environment, but the ultimate goal is to teach the student to cope with the demands of your typical classroom. Of course, the most important behaviors to target are those that violate the rights of the other students or adults in your class (e.g., inappropriate physical contact or disruptive behaviors). However, it will not be enough to simply extinguish these behaviors. As explained in Chapter 12, the child will need to be taught appropriate behaviors to substitute for the inappropriate ones.

Often the need for you to give exclusive attention to your student with ASD will be precipitated by the student's anxiety. Prevention is the best approach. This is done both through modifying the environment, making school predictable for the child, and through teaching the child strategies in advance of when he will need them.

Preparing the child and making school predictable is one of the major keys to success. Establishing a routine is very important. Pictorial prompts (i.e., picture schedules and cards to cue appropriate behaviors when making transitions between activities and classrooms) are very helpful. If you provide a schedule and pre-teach material, the child will be forewarned about what is to come, he will be less anxious, and he can transition more easily. If he knows the exact activities that will take place in gym, art, or music those classes can go more smoothly.

During a class lesson the child may "need" to talk about his preoccupations. In advance, you should set clear limits on talk about preoccupations and other repetitive behaviors, giving the child a specific, limited time and place in his schedule to do these things. See Chapter 12 for more advice on dealing with these behaviors.

Please note that the strategy of using a visual schedule should not be discontinued abruptly because the child is doing a lot better. These kinds of cues should be faded slowly and reintroduced at times of stress or transition, or you could all end up back at square one.

You can help your student with ASD become more independent by teaching him strategies for self-management. If you are successful, you will gain time to devote to instruction rather than behavioral management. With the rest of the child's team it is important to teach the child to understand the difference between appropriate and inappropriate behaviors, to teach appropriate behaviors to replace the inappropriate ones, to teach the child to anticipate the consequences of his behavior, and to provide reinforcement. Again, it is important to teach the child strategies and more appropriate behaviors in advance of when he will need them, not at the moment he is struggling. Remember that the child with ASD will not be able to process and learn new skills when in the middle of feeling overwhelmed.

The bottom line is that you will need contingency plans in case the child does start to melt down. You can help your student with ASD by watching for signs of escalating anxiety and try to address it before it goes too far. Work out cues with the child in advance to help get him back on track by using strategies he has learned when he is starting to have difficulty. If that does not work at that moment, try to deflect and defuse. If the child with ASD is getting too anxious or cannot complete his work without a great deal of help, you might give him some independent work that is well within his capability until the lesson is over and you have time to address his needs. You could also ask his aide to work with him.

There will be times, especially at the start, when your student with ASD may become overwhelmed during a full class lesson. He may have trouble modulating his anxiety and require all of your attention. These times may not be convenient. How do you deal with this when you are in the middle of teaching twenty other students? If he gets to the point of a full-blown tantrum, he will need to be removed from the room. The child's aide could remove him. If you feel you must be the one to help him regain control, you may need to give your class independent seatwork. Make a plan with school staff, in advance, that if a tantrum lasts too long or becomes too big for you to handle (involves physical aggression), the child's social skills therapist, the school psychologist, the principal, or assistant principal will be called to the room to help.

Modifying the Curriculum

This actually should not be a major issue in the balancing act. Modifying the curriculum, when necessary, must be done outside of regular classroom hours, either by you or by a special education or resource room teacher. You will initially teach the modified material to your student. Then, you should have support in teaching the modified curriculum, either from an aide or a resource room teacher. If the modification consists of shortening or simplifying assignments, you can probably do this with little assistance, but if the content of the lesson is substantially different, you will need assistance. It is not reasonable to expect you to teach two different lessons simultaneously!

The academic abilities of students with ASD varies. Many high functioning children with ASD have strong basic academic skills in the areas of decoding of written language, spelling, mathematical calculations, and memorization of content material. Others will have difficulty learning to read and with basic math skills. Nearly all have difficulty at some level with:

- reading comprehension (from more basic comprehension of vocabulary and grammar to ability to understand

main ideas and relationships, emotions, motives, and the
author's purpose),

- written language organization and formulation,
- relating newly learned content information to previously
  acquired knowledge,
- understanding cause and effect, and
- drawing inferences.

It will be important for you to become acquainted with the cognitive profile of your individual student with ASD so that you can appropriately modify your teaching materials and methods, in consultation with the special education or reading specialist.

Keep in mind that children with ASD often have difficulty following the complex language of a science or social studies lesson. If the aide or special education teacher pre-teaches (and then reviews) material, it will be easier for the child to understand and keep up with a lesson. It will often be useful to provide a graphic organizer representing the concepts of the lesson (see Chapter 11 for more details). You can help reduce your student's anxiety by meeting the child at his level when it comes to the curriculum, and by appropriately modifying his work.

Finding Time to Reinforce Social and Language Skills

Impaired social interaction is the hallmark of children with ASD. Peer relationships are weak. Children with ASD often approach and respond inappropriately to peers and adults in social situations. One reason is that they have trouble understanding others' body language. Their own body language often conveys messages that are not what they intend. Also, perspective taking, particularly their ability to understand other's emotions, is limited. In addition, understanding of language, particularly complex, rapidly presented language, is usually a problem.

Your student with ASD will benefit tremendously from your helping him with these problems. Specifics are discussed in Chapter 9 on language and Chapter 11 on social skills.

This may be the biggest challenge in managing your time. Therapists or other teachers working on language and social skills will, hopefully, have told you what specific skills are being addressed, and your own judgment and knowledge of the child may suggest others. What you are trying to do is keep an eye out for opportunities for the child to practice these skills, while going about your other teaching activities. Slip in prompts, praise, and suggestions:

- "Kyle looks upset. Maybe you can help him with his project."
- "Pablo asked you a question. He would probably like it if you could answer him."
- "You're doing a great job sharing the materials. You could tell Madison you like her picture."
- "Start by figuring out the main idea in the story."

This will definitely get easier with practice, and hopefully it will help you hone your sensitivity to the social and language issues that other children in the class may have.

Effects on Classmates

The other, typically developing, children in your classroom, no matter how young, will notice that there are differences in their classmate with ASD. It will help to explicitly tell the children that all children are the same in that they all have strengths and weakness but that not all children are good at the same things.

Your "neurotypical" students may feel confused and overwhelmed by socially inappropriate behaviors. It may be hard for them to predict how your student with ASD will behave in any given situation and that may worry them. They may find the student with ASD annoying if he has trouble modulating silliness and anger or limiting talk about his preoccupations. Younger children may feel neglected when you need to give your student with ASD more time and attention. The other students in your class could react by ignoring, avoiding, or bullying the child. Without your intervention, it can be difficult for your student with ASD to be integrated into your class. Integration requires that your student with ASD develop more appropriate behavior and that the typical students develop a better understanding of that student.

Educating your typical students and enlisting their aid can enrich everyone in the classroom community. It is important to establish an accepting school environment for all children, but this takes a special effort for the child with ASD. Set clear class rules about how you expect all students (including the child with ASD) to treat each other with respect, to be supportive and helpful. Define unacceptable behaviors (inappropriate touching, pushing, or other verbal or physical aggression) and help your students to assertively set limits on those behaviors when children behave inappropriately or bully others. Post the rules where all the children can see them, in a format that they can understand. For example, for children who can't read, take photos of unacceptable behavior or use symbols they can understand. Teach them to get help in setting limits when they need to.

It is particularly important to identify the strengths of a child who is having difficulties in your classroom, for the other students as well as for yourself. Highlight the child's strengths in front of the other children in the class. Establish the fact that all people have strengths and weaknesses and encourage all of your students to talk about theirs. If your student with ASD has academic strengths, such as reading, have him read aloud in class or help another child who is struggling with reading. You might make a deal that he will help the child who is having difficulty reading and that child will help him with social skills on the playground. Sometimes the strengths of a student with ASD are more evident outside your classroom; for example, in music or art. Use those strengths to enhance interaction with other children as well as the child's image.

At the start of a new school year, many teachers take the time to get to know a little about all their students' interests and outside activities. For example, in the younger grades, they have the students bring in five objects that are important to them and explain why to the class, or make a collage of pictures showing things they care about and feel they are good at. Older students might be asked to fill out a short form with questions about their favorite hobbies or sports or whatever they are best at. You might also send a short list of questions about the child's interests and abilities home for parents to answer. After you have gathered information in this way, you may be able to use it to find topics of discussion or activities your student with autism will excel in. Or you might use it to help him find common ground with classmates, perhaps seating him near some children who share some of the same interests.

As opportunities present themselves, discuss with your class the impact of weaknesses in academics, sports, and social skills and the frustration associated with having trouble with something and not being able to get help. Focus in particular on the impact of social skills issues during lunch and recess. For example, you might read (or have the students read) a story about a character who has trouble fitting in. Do not single out and talk only about your student with ASD, but rather talk about all of the students' strengths and weaknesses, about how everyone feels left out sometimes, and how hard it is if your specific weakness is in social skills. Support the idea that your classroom is a community where people are expected to use their strengths to help others with their weaknesses. Help your students to talk about and interpret the behavior of others in the class including the child with ASD. Again this discussion should be about all of your students.

Teaching the other children in your class about your student with ASD must be done with issues of confidentiality in mind and without exclusive focus on the child. (More detailed discussion can be found in Chapter 11.) Discussion of the child with school staff, including diagnosis, is appropriate. However, issues of confidentiality dictate that the child's diagnosis, school classification, and results of evaluations are privileged and not to be discussed with other children or their parents. It is the sole prerogative of the parents of your student with ASD to reveal this information to others at their discretion. You can discuss only those behaviors that are directly observable in order to help others understand the student with autism.

Parents of Typical Children

In our experience, the majority of parents of the typically developing children in your class will not have an issue with having their son or daughter in a class with a child with ASD. Occasionally, however, you will encounter parents who are concerned or even angry. Often, these parents just need reassurance that their own child will get the attention he or she needs. You can provide this reassurance by explaining how your time is allocated and that you have help in the classroom so that your time is not consumed by one child.

You should also go a step further. You can talk with parents about the benefits to their child of spending time with the child with ASD, again, without revealing the child's actual diagnosis, unless the parents of your student with ASD have okayed that. For example, you can discuss the child with ASD as a child who has some trouble knowing how to play or converse with his peers. Explain how interaction with your student with ASD can:

- broaden their child's perspective,
- increase their child's social skills and sense of fairness and tolerance,
- boost his problem solving ability, and
- even help him improve his academic skills as his problem solving improves.

In addition, if a child is able to help a classmate with ASD, it can boost that child's self-esteem and feelings of competence and worth.

Conclusion

Teaching a child with ASD requires a different perspective, flexibility and creativity, and constant learning on your part and the rest of the staff who see him. Within the school community you will have access to and support from the rest of the child's team. Each member can support your student's classroom learning by giving advice in his or her area of expertise. Talk to the child's art, music, and other "specials" teachers about how the child is doing outside your classroom to gain their perspective. In addition, you will need to help the specials teachers interpret behaviors and get the best from the child. They are balancing the needs of the child with ASD and their typical students, too. Ultimately, aside from the child's parents, *you* will spend the most time with him and know him best.

If the school staff is at a loss at any given time with the child, the school district can provide access to an outside consultant who is an expert in addressing the needs of children with ASD. If the child's optimal learning style is unclear, a detailed neuropsychological evaluation can be helpful. Outside of school, many children with ASD have a team of private therapists who often have known the child for years. Getting access to these professionals and their reports—of course, only with permission from the parents—can be highly enlightening.

It is important to engage in continuing professional development regarding children with ASD, as there are continual advances in basic research and research into the efficacy of interventions. It is also helpful to seek out resources available through the Internet and local and national organizations. A list of some helpful resources is provided at the back of the book.

The keys to balancing the needs of your student with ASD and the needs of the typically developing children in your class are:

1. organization and making your classroom predictable;
2. understanding the abilities, needs, and motives of your student with ASD;
3. establishing an accepting community environment in your class where the child with ASD is truly included.

It is important for you and the other students in the class to understand the perspective of the student with ASD. It is also helpful for you to understand the perspective of the child's parents. You will need to communicate your knowledge and recommendations to them. Often parents are only contacted about problems. They need to hear about successes too.

Having a child with ASD in your class will be an enriching experience, although it will require extra preparation time on your part. It will challenge your creativity and problem solving. It may make you think in ways you have not before and thereby make you a stronger teacher overall. For example, the fact that some children with ASD can speak better than they understand, or have limitations in reading comprehension in the face of superb decoding, challenges our notions of skill development. The level of task analysis required in teaching children with ASD will hone your abilities to pull apart a task and teach it to any child who is having difficulty.

Fortunately, general methods that support the learning of your student with ASD (such as graphic organizers) also support the learning of typically developing students. Methods relevant only to your student with ASD can be implemented by the child's classroom aide. In addition to developing your teaching skills, observing cognitive, behavioral, and emotional growth in a child with ASD and knowing that you have played an important part in that growth can be enormously gratifying. Clearly, time is limited and you may occasionally feel overwhelmed by the amount your students need. The addition of a child with ASD to your classroom *could* tip the balance, but it doesn't have to. In fact, with the support of training, other school staff, and the rest of your class, you have a remarkable opportunity to profoundly affect the lives of all of your students through this experience.

A final note: We have given you a lot of information and suggestions in this book and you may be feeling overwhelmed. Remember, not all of this information or these suggestions will apply to your student or your classroom. Don't feel pressured to use it all. Take what applies to your situation and seems useful *now*. As the year goes on and new situations arise, you can refer back to this book.

14 | Case Studies of Success and Failure

In this chapter, we will relate two stories about inclusion. The first is a cautionary tale. In this story, the general education classroom, as it was run, was not the appropriate place for the child with autism, and the year ended prematurely in failure. We will attempt to identify the main difficulties with this child's inclusion experience and offer some suggestions about what could have been done differently.

The second is a success story. For this child with ASD, the inclusion experience worked well. In this classroom, the general education teacher and the child's aide, together with the special education staff and other consultants, were able to accommodate the child's needs and integrate them with the needs of the other children in the class, resulting in a successful year for everyone.

Henry's Inclusion Experience

Henry was seven when he entered first grade. He had been diagnosed with autism when he was under two years old. His parents, both professionals, did a lot of research immediately after his diagnosis and rapidly mobilized a highly sophisticated and effective program, consisting mostly of Applied Behavior Analysis administered one-on-one for the first couple of years. Largely because of this programming, Henry made rapid cognitive gains and his language and nonverbal problem solving abilities progressed well.

For Henry's preschool and kindergarten years, the one-on-one teaching was combined with part-time integration into a typical classroom, with one of his therapists accompanying him. Henry had persistent language difficulties, however, including many of the problems discussed in Chapter 9. In particular, he had difficulty with rapidly presented language, or language coming from several people talking simultaneously or in rapid succession. He also took language very literally (even more so than the typical literal-minded first-grader). Henry had difficulty interpreting the unspoken messages carried in tones of voice or body language, unless they were made explicit for him. He was fundamentally uninterested in interacting with the other children and did not enjoy their company, although he had learned some social rules, which he could verbalize. Like many other children with ASD, Henry had pronounced sensory sensitivities. He had trouble tolerating loud or chaotic environments, being touched unexpectedly, or having his space intruded upon.

Henry's school system provided him with a behavior therapist as a classroom aide. Unfortunately, however, his general education teacher was not given any significant training about autism or about modifications to the environment or curriculum that Henry might need. Furthermore, the other children were not taught anything about individual differences, either in general or about Henry's needs in particular. Henry's desk was set away from the other children's, and he spent most of his day being instructed by the behavior therapist. The other children gradually stopped showing any interest in Henry and began to ignore him.

Henry's sensory sensitivities, which had not been discussed with the teacher, interfered with his ability to function in the classroom at every turn. He rode the bus to school; by the time he arrived, he was already distraught, upset, and unable to concentrate because of the constant noise and proximity of the other children on the bus. In circle time, other children sat too close to Henry and sometimes accidentally brushed against him. The classroom was bright and noisy, and he spent so much energy controlling his overstimulation that he had little energy left for focusing on lessons.

By the end of the day, Henry was an emotional train wreck. He could usually hold it together until he got home, but then he would have an emotional meltdown. Since Henry did not act out in school, the school staff naturally enough assumed that there must be a problem with how his parents handled him at home, rather than understanding that (as is often the case) stresses in school were being vented at home. (After all, first graders cannot resort to the after-work martini!)

Henry's emotional distress worsened as the months went on. He eventually began engaging in distressing and potentially dangerous self-injurious behavior, and his parents insisted that he be removed from the inclusive classroom.

Henry is now much older. When asked what he remembers about this class, he recalls two things: struggling to understand what was being said to him, and being scolded by the teacher for sitting on his legs in circle time, which was very upsetting and confusing to him.

What could have been done differently? Here are possible ways in which Henry's year might have gotten off to a better start, perhaps leading to a better year for all concerned:

- **Enlist the help of the other children:** With permission and assistance from Henry's parents, the teacher and therapist could have had a series of lessons on differences—how different children learn, what different children are uncomfortable with, what kinds of help different children need. It could have been a mark of honor to be selected to help Henry with some lessons, to help him learn some simple games on the playground, and to be his buddy at lunch on a regular basis. That way, the children would have come to regard him as a real member of the class, and to accept his differences as a part of the natural order of things. If Henry did anything that looked odd to the other children, the teacher or aide could have provided simple, but reassuring explanations. ("Henry is covering his ears because he has very sensitive ears, and they hurt when there's a lot of noise.")

- *Integrate the behavior therapist and Henry into the classroom:* The behavior therapist could have taught an occasional lesson (including perhaps lessons on differences among children) and occasionally could have left Henry's side to help other children or could have worked with small groups of children, including Henry. That way the children would not have seen the therapist and Henry as occupying a substantially separate classroom that just happened to be within the classroom walls.

■ *Appreciate the modifications necessary to accommodate Henry's sensory sensitivities:* Henry may well have needed to start the year by coming into the classroom for limited periods every day, and as he grew accustomed to the classroom environment and schedule, to gradually increase the time. Since his sensory sensitivities worsened as the day went on, these inclusion periods could have been timed for the morning. In addition, these times could have included the most structured periods of the day, so that he would not initially have been exposed to unpredictable and noisy periods. When Henry needed to be redirected, the teacher could have talked to him in a firm but quiet tone (including explaining that it's better for his knees if he does not sit on his legs) instead of showing anger or annoyance, which was very hard for him to tolerate. Henry could have been given more personal space when required to sit in circle time—perhaps by giving each of the students a carpet square to sit on.

■ *Appreciate the kinds of language difficulties children with ASD are likely to have.* Providing the teacher with language evaluations, or even with general information about language in autism spectrum disorders, might have enabled her to speak to Henry in a way that he could understand. She might have employed short, concrete sentences, repeated herself as necessary, avoided metaphor, sarcasm, and idioms (e.g., "you have a green light"), and explained concretely anything that the other children said that Henry did not understand (e.g., "Henry, "you have a green light" means "you can go now"). She might have helped Henry understand the emotional states of the adults and children around her. ("Look at Eddie's face. The way he's moving his face means he's mad.") A speech-language pathologist or an inclusion specialist could have consulted with her about these types of issues.

■ *Conduct a functional behavior assessment.* As discussed in Chapter 12, an FBA could have been done to pinpoint the reasons that Henry arrived at school so frazzled, was not able to concentrate in circle time, etc. If the teacher had understood the source of Henry's problem behaviors, she and the rest of the staff could have figured out ways to change the environment and interact with Henry so he was more available for learning.

- **Emphasize the child's strengths:** Henry's teachers could have explained some of his unusual skills to the other children, including his excellent memory and fine motor skills, so that they would get a picture of his difficulties balanced with her abilities. They could have arranged for activities that would allow Henry to shine publicly, such as by posting his artwork in a prominent place or calling on him for answers that they knew he was likely to remember. They could have asked the parents for information about Henry's favorite activities and interests and incorporated them into art, writing, and other assignments so he would be more motivated to participate in class and show other students his abilities.

The overarching problem with Henry's placement in this classroom was probably that Henry's teacher was not encouraged by the school to really take ownership or be invested in the inclusion process. She was satisfied to have Henry and his therapist perched in a corner of the room, not participating with classroom activities or the other children in any meaningful way, and she did not understand the importance of establishing a trusting relationship with Henry and his family (nor was this encouraged by the administration). In addition, the goals in Henry's IEP focused on academics alone, even though neglecting his emotional, social, and sensory needs prevented him from adjusting to the classroom and therefore from making academic progress.

Jasmine's Inclusion Experience

Jasmine is a seven-year-old girl with autism who is in first grade in a public school. She receives occupational therapy once a week to work on fine motor skills such as writing; speech and language therapy four times a week; and physical therapy once a week to work on gross motor skills. An inclusion specialist works full time with four children in the school, including Jasmine. This specialist helps the classroom teacher adapt class work and lesson plans, communicates frequently with parents, and supervises Jasmine's one-on-one aide.

Jasmine has the same classroom aide she had last year in kindergarten; this talented woman knows Jasmine very well. She can tell when Jasmine's mood is escalating, and can usually prevent her potential "meltdowns" by deflecting her to some other activity or by telling her how to express herself appropriately (say, "This is too hard"; "I can't wait"; "I'm getting mad"). As a result, Jasmine is learning to verbalize her feelings and to state her needs instead of whining, crying, or hitting.

Jasmine's aide is also very skilled at knowing what parts of the first grade curriculum Jasmine will be able to understand, and in simplifying the concepts or reducing the work load when she feels Jasmine will be too challenged. Under the inclusion specialist's direction, Jasmine's curriculum has been modified by decreasing language demands (e.g., by allowing her to use manipulatives for math problems and by limiting her need to participate in circle time and attend school assemblies), providing one-on-one instruction when needed (math and writing), and using small group instead of large group instruction.

Much of the time, Jasmine and her aide sit in the middle of the classroom and work along with the other children. Occasionally, the aide works separately with Jasmine in a corner of the classroom. Sometimes when Jasmine is working well on an assignment, the aide leaves her and circulates around the room to see if other children need help. Visual supports are used to prepare Jasmine for upcoming events and for coping with stressful moments. These supports include picture schedules, token boards, and Social Stories with pictures. Jasmine understands and is motivated by her token board. (She earns one token for each piece of work, and when she has 5 tokens, she gets to have a break for a preferred activity.)

About six weeks into the fall, Jasmine went through a bad period, melting down more frequently when confronted with academic or social challenges. As her parents described it, "the school was right on it." Teachers and specialists figured out that the work, especially math and writing, was getting too hard for Jasmine, and they modified the work more, substituting visual and manipulative material for language-based math lessons, and having Jasmine work on drawing simple lines and shapes instead of letters. They cut back her participation in instructional circle times from seven times per day to two, and they paired her with a child she liked to make reading time more fun. They also instituted a behavioral plan, where inappropriate behavior cost her tokens.

Jasmine does not have sensory issues that make the classroom environment difficult to handle, but she did have a hard time tolerating the gymnasium at first. The inclusion specialist worked with the male gym teacher to get him to lower his booming voice, especially when talking in Jasmine's direction, and worked with Jasmine to prepare her for each day's gym activities so that she would know what to expect. She now loves gym!

Jasmine's parents think that the classroom teaching and behavioral strategies, as well as the staff's sensitivity to Jasmine's learning and behavioral and emotional needs, have provided her with the support she needs to have a successful year. It is striking how warmly Jasmine's parents feel toward the school staff. They believe that staff members are personally invested in Jasmine's success, welcome her into the classroom, and are available for communication whenever necessary. They understand that Jasmine cannot handle all of the first grade material and that her problem behaviors are not 100 percent under control, but they see constant progress and are convinced that inclusion in the general education classroom was the right placement decision for their daughter.

15 | Myths and FAQs about Autism

In this chapter, we present and answer frequently asked questions about autism. Most of them were suggested to us by teachers.

Children with ASD have "refrigerator mothers" or "refrigerator parents."

During the 1950s, '60s, and well into the '70s, this was a common belief. Psychologists and physicians were taught that autism, which literally means turning inward, happened because the child retreated into him- or herself in response to cold and rejecting parents. Although most psychologists and physicians did not say this directly to parents, the fact that they held parents responsible was often conveyed subtly (and sometimes not so subtly), making distressed parents even more upset and adding guilt to their burden. The understanding that ASD is neurological began to gain ground in the 1970s and is now universally accepted in the U.S. The psychological view is still held by some European doctors. For a vivid description of what parents' experiences were like when the psychological view was prevalent, see Clara Park's beautifully written book *The Siege*.

Children with ASD are all like "Rain Man."

In the movie *Rain Man,* Dustin Hoffman does an excellent job of portraying a high functioning young man with ASD. The character, in fact, is based to some extent on Mark Rimland, an artist with autism and the son of Bernard Rimland, author of the 1964 classic work in which a neurological theory of autism was presented. However, this character is only one type of individual with autism. He has high intelligence in very specific ways, severe social disability, extreme need for sameness, striking repetitive motor behaviors, and a variety of special skills such as being able to instantly count numbers of objects (remember the spilled matches?), knowing the day of the week for any given date, and photographic memory.

In individuals with ASD, intelligence can vary from profound mental retardation to above average. Some people have isolated skills, and others have equal development of cognitive (but not social) skills. Likewise, the need for sameness and repetitive behaviors can vary from very mild to severe, etc. It is also unusual for an individual with ASD to have as many special skills as the Rain Man character. Therefore, although the portrayal is sensitive and accurate, the character is by no means a "typical" individual with ASD.

Children with ASD are not aware of their surroundings.

How much a child is aware of his or her surroundings varies a great deal in ASD, and depends partly on the degree (if any) of mental retardation. Individuals with ASD who have severe or profound mental retardation may indeed be unaware of many events occurring around them, or be able to interpret them only in a very simple way. Individuals with mild to moderate mental retardation or average intelligence show a much more complex picture. Depending on their level of social understanding, they may be very aware of the physical world but miss social cues. Often, children with ASD appear unaware of events or lessons because they are attending to their own repetitive behaviors or repetitive thoughts. Sometimes, however, when they are questioned, it turns out they were paying attention all along. It is up to the teacher or aide to check how much information the child actually absorbed. Some children with ASD may be overly aware of their surroundings, especially sensory aspects of the environment, such as smells or sounds.

Children with ASD will always be severely disabled.

There is an enormously wide range of outcomes for children with ASD. Some continue to have significant disabilities throughout their lives, restricted in their ability to have social relationships, manage their own affairs, or live independently. Others will be more mildly disabled, able to work and manage their own affairs, but limited in their social relationships and needing assistance with decisions requiring social judgment (should I buy the real estate package in Arizona that this nice man wants to sell me?). Still others will have essentially normal lives, with some remaining personality quirks. A child's ultimate level of functioning depends somewhat on cognitive and language ability, and somewhat on the degree of social disability and repetitive behaviors.

Children with ASD cannot learn to talk.

As with so much else, there is an enormously wide range of outcomes for children with ASD. A minority (and before good special education and speech therapy it was at least half) remain nonverbal, speaking and understanding very little. These children are less likely to be placed in a general education classroom, especially at older ages. Some children are quite verbal, but use somewhat simplified grammatical structure and vocabulary, like children of a younger age. Others are on a par with their peers in the formal aspects of language (such as grammar and vocabulary) but have trouble in the social use of language (such as knowing how to converse with other children, stay on topic, pick up on their listener's reactions, and maintain the proper physical distance).

Children with ASD are not attached to their parents.

In an earlier version of the official diagnostic manual, children with autism were described as having a "pervasive" lack of emotional relatedness to others. This has been changed in the current version of the manual, in recognition of the fact that children with ASD usually do differentiate among adults and are attached to their parents. They may not show all the usual signs of attachment that one would see in a typically developing child (coming for comfort, looking for mom's reaction when uncertain, playful emotional contact, joyful greeting, being upset when separating, etc.), but most children with ASD do seek out their mother or other caregiver for security, comfort, and familiarity. This is true even when cognitive disability is severe.

Are all children with ASD mentally retarded?

Children with ASD can be found at any level of mental ability, from profound mental retardation to well above average. Research studies have shown that as one goes down the IQ scale, the percent of children showing autistic features such as social isolation and repetitive behaviors goes up. One large-scale study of autism and mental retardation in which we were involved showed that about half of the children with ASD whom we studied had IQs of 65-70 and above—in other words, borderline mental retardation or normal IQ—while the other half showed mental retardation sufficient enough to cause significant disability.

Are parents of children with ASD more likely to have ASD themselves?

Autism is now regarded as very heritable (genetically transmitted), although the actual genes remain elusive. Therefore, one would expect parents of children with ASD to show some features in common with their children. Research has shown that a number of parents, but still a minority, have tendencies to be like their children in some way, either socially isolated or somewhat obsessive in their interests and abilities. These tendencies, however, have not prevented most of them from having successful relationships and jobs. Furthermore, in our clinical experience with thousands of children with ASD, the vast majority of these parents are like parents of all children with disabilities—doing the best they can to get information on how to help their children and grateful for professional help.

Is it possible to use ABA (Applied Behavior Analysis) in a public school setting?

Yes, in several ways. First, a child who still needs mostly one-on-one or discrete trial teaching can be taught in a separate space in the school, and have the benefit of occasional inclusion in a regular classroom (with one of his ABA teachers). When the child is able to control his behavior, attend to and understand a teacher, and learn in a group, the ABA therapist may accompany the child into the classroom for all or part of the day. At this point, the aide should work with the child to ensure attention, to prevent or manage behavioral issues, and to pull the child out for pre-teaching or review, or for special teaching in weak areas. Even when the child no longer needs regular ABA-style teaching, an ABA consultant can help the regular education teacher with behavioral issues, social skills training, or teaching subject matter that is proving too challenging.

Is autism a life-long disorder? Can it be cured?

Most autism experts reject the idea of a "cure" or of "recovery," preferring to talk about maximizing the child's potential. It is true that most individuals with ASD—even the minority who go on to achieve success in higher education, jobs, and life skills—remain somewhat "different," with a tendency to restricted relationships and interests. However, we have seen children (although definitely a small minority) who became truly indistinguishable from other children. In some cases, parents have moved the child to a different school or town, no one in the new setting is told about their history, and no one guesses. How much more "cured" can one be? Although no research data on this type of "recovery" exists, our guess is that if this is going to happen, it happens by the age of 10.

How common is autism?

Estimates vary a great deal, with the highest estimate being about 1 in every 100 children, and the lowest estimate being about 1 in 1000 children. Estimates are higher when autism is defined more broadly.

Is autism on the increase?

There has been an intense interest in this question in the last ten years, and especially since 2003. An increase in the prevalence of ASD has been reported in the US and in Europe. A recent study in California reported an increase of almost 600 percent in the last decade! Naturally, parents, teachers, and public health officials are all very concerned, and searching for possible causes, such as toxins in the environment.

But we also have to ask what could erroneously cause such an apparent increase. Some of the research has "ruled out" changes in diagnostic criteria because they are using the same official criteria for autism now as they were 10 years ago. However, we still think it possible that changes in diagnostic practice are contributing to the apparent increase. Here's an example: "poor peer relationships" are one of the diagnostic criteria and this has not changed. But what if in the past, a child had to be aloof and unsocial to meet this criterion, and now an aggressive, or socially clumsy, child is considered to meet it? You can see how, even though the criterion has not changed on paper, it would include more children.

Another cause is probably the very laws governing services to children with special needs. What if a psychologist or doctor were right on the fence about whether a child met criteria for ASD? Perhaps in the past the main motive in the decision was to avoid alarming parents or stigmatizing the child, and now the main motive is to allow the child to get services that are only available for children with ASD. Finally, some researchers have found that the increase in ASD seems to be offset by a decrease in diagnoses of mental retardation—suggesting that some children who used to be diagnosed with mental retardation are now diagnosed with autism. This is not to say that ASD is *not* on the increase—only that, for us, it hasn't been proved.

Can you tell that a child has ASD just by looking at him?

A colleague of ours, Doris Allen, used to show us pictures of children in her therapeutic nursery and ask us to pick out the children with ASD. Sometimes you could do it, based on a dreamy, far-away expression, or overly broad and odd looking smile, but more often than not, you couldn't. It's when you put the facial expression in a social context that it begins to look out of place. Children with ASD sometimes have fixed facial expressions that look stereotyped and unnatural, a smile that looks more like a grimace, or a frown of unusual concentration, and their expressions might seem too extreme for the social situation. Odd movements also don't show up in static pictures or glances. But if you watch the child moving, especially in a free situation, like on a playground, his movements may seem clumsy or immature, or you may notice repetitive movements or odd postures, especially of the arms and fingers. Of course, not all clumsy children have ASD, and many children with ASD are graceful and adept, especially with fine motor skills. Even facial expression can seem normal, especially in young children.

Are children with Asperger's disorder the result of a high IQ couple?

As discussed in more detail in the text, Asperger's disorder is a label given to a wide variety of children. But the "classic" child with Asperger's has a high IQ and obsessive interests. Since children with very high IQs do tend to come from parents with high IQs, the parents of these Asperger's children are often very bright and may be gifted in specific ways, such as mathematics. But remember that this "classic" picture is not the only type of child who gets the Asperger's diagnosis, and many other children diagnosed with Asperger's have parents who run the gamut of intelligence. By the way, the opposite is not true: children with very low IQs do not tend to have parents with low IQs.

If you have one child with ASD, what's the risk of having another?

Studies have estimated "recurrence rates"—the risk of having a child with ASD following a first child with ASD—as anywhere from 2 to 10 percent. That means that although the risk is still relatively low, it's much higher than in the general population. Some studies of younger siblings of children with ASD suggest that an even higher percent may have more minor problems, such as delayed language development (that may catch up) or a tendency to show repetitive behaviors, but not full blown ASD.

Why is one sibling autistic and not the other?

No one knows. Presumably, the genetic reshuffling that takes place in the formation of each egg and sperm dealt one child a different hand than the other. Several large studies going on in the U.S. and Canada are examining sibling pairs where the children are differently affected, to examine suspected genes and to see what features in a child with ASD might predict high risk for younger siblings. As yet, no results have been published.

Can the child with ASD understand what I'm saying even though he appears not to?

It's definitely true that children with ASD sometimes appear to be inattentive, but that if you give them extra response time, they can answer questions you wouldn't think they could. However, the opposite is probably more often true: the child appears to be listening to you, and you're explaining concepts that you think are simple, but if you probe his understanding, it turns out that: (a) he wasn't really listening; or (b) he was trying, but the language was going by too fast for his processing speed; or (c) the apparently simple concepts were too abstract; or (d) despite his good comprehension of the specific parts of what you were saying, he didn't get the "point" or the way the parts hang together. The only way to know is to test his comprehension—by asking probing questions, such as "why" questions, or "what would come next" questions, or by asking the child to explain the material back to you.

Why don't children with ASD understand social rules?

For many children with ASD, social rules are a foreign language with which they will never feel truly at home. They often are very socially motivated and really want to have friends and fit in, especially as they get older. Therefore, they try to master social rules. But imagine trying to teach a child all the social rules he needs to know to seem natural and fluid in social situations! A colleague of ours, Dot Lucci, once took a high functioning young man with ASD to a concert. He sat on the aisle and she sat next to him. Just as the hall was hushed and the conductor raised his baton, this young man stood up and announced loudly, "No! The woman sits on the aisle because they have to go to the bathroom more." He had learned one rule, but, obviously, not a more important one!

Not only are social situations and social rules immeasurably complex, but they go by at a very rapid pace, so that if the child has to think about the rule that applies to that situation, it's already too late. One of us came to empathize with this problem on a trip to Japan. I had memorized a few of the social rules that were specific to that culture, but it quickly became obvious to me that the nonverbal communication was flowing about me with a subtlety and at a rate that I would not be able to master even at a simple level if I lived there the rest of my life. I imagine that children with ASD often feel like that.

Why do children with ASD repeat what I say?

When this tendency is pronounced, it's called "echolalia." Immediate echolalia is when the child repeats back the last few words or phrases right after you say them. Delayed echolalia is when the child repeats phrases or longer bits at a later time; often these are phrases they've been taught to use in certain situations, things they've heard adults say, or dialogue from favorite videos or TV shows. Echolalia is very common in ASD and can serve several purposes. Typically developing toddlers often echo words or grammatical forms as they are learning them—it can be a stage in the learning process. So the child with ASD may tend to echo kinds of language that he or she is trying to master.

Secondly, it can buy time—sometimes the child needs the extra processing time to understand what you said and to formulate an answer. Echolalia can actually help the child focus on what you said and better understand and respond. Often, the child really doesn't understand what's being asked or what kind of answer is wanted, so he searches his memory for something relevant, and out comes a piece of delayed echolalia that has something (at least in his mind) to do with your question. Sometimes the "script" that he's saying has a highly personal meaning to him that may be impossible to figure out.

For the younger or more cognitively delayed child, the echolalia may not serve a communicative function at all, except that he knows you want him to say something. There are neurological patients (such as people with advanced dementia) who have no language left except echoing; in these cases, echolalia is an automatic response that comes out when there is no real language processing going on.

So, you can see that echolalia is extremely complex and can represent anything from a normal part of the language learning process to evidence of a severe language impairment. It will be up to you to figure out for your particular child whether the echolalia is part of a real attempt to learn and respond appropriately, or an uncommunicative (maybe even avoidant) response strategy that needs to be discouraged.

Are any of the social skills teachable?

Even though it is almost impossible to formulate and teach all the social skills that typical children pick up without even being aware of them, many specific social skills can be formulated and taught. For example, you can teach a child the proper physical distance to stand from other children in different situations, how and when it's allowable to change a topic in a conversation, etc. (See Chapter 11 for specifics on teaching social rules.) And even though *all* the social rules can never be taught, there's a positive feedback that can develop: if a child masters some basics that make him more acceptable as a playmate, this will give him more opportunities for social interaction. The more he plays with other children, the more he's likely to pick up the subtle rules that are needed for true social success. It's like learning a foreign language: you'll never become fluent without lots of exposure in natural settings.

Why do children with ASD like routines so much?

As with so many aspects of these complex disorders, no one really knows, but there are several ideas. First, it's not always true. Even though resistance to change in routine is actually a diagnostic feature of ASD, we found that in a large sample of preschoolers with ASD, only about a third of them showed this behavior. It is, however, more common in school-aged children than in preschoolers. The fact that insistence on routine tends to appear later than some other core features suggests that it may develop as a reaction to experience. Imagine that you live in a terribly complex world where you are expected to "get" things you don't get. Because different things are important to you, or because you can't really tell what's important, changes that seem trivial to other people loom large to you. Furthermore, because you don't really "get" what other people are thinking, you have no way to anticipate changes in their behavior. So, the only way to feel in control is to insist that things stay the same, both in the physical environment, and in the way things are done. Another idea is that the repetitive behavior is a biological part of the syndrome, rather than a reaction to a poorly understood environment. This would mean that it results from specific chemical or anatomical features of the brain.

Why do children with ASD like to line things up?

Children with ASD often have strange visual fascinations. Straight lines seem to be one of them. Some children line up toys or other objects and then look along them, apparently because they get pleasure (no one knows why) out of looking at straight lines. Some like to look along table edges or other straight lines in the environment. This should be discouraged (not punitively), both because it makes the child look odd to others, and because it encourages the child to be preoccupied. We suggest distracting the child and providing other activities. One creative mother made a bowling game out of her child's obsession with lining up Coke bottles, changed the arrangement of the bottles, involved other siblings, and made it into a constructive game instead of an isolating obsession.

If a child in your class shows this lining up behavior, talk to the special education teacher, school psychologist, behavior consultant, or parent, to see how it's being handled. If no specific program is in place to handle it, try to gently discourage the behavior by distracting the child from it and giving him other interesting activities or objects in its place.

Do vaccinations cause autism?

ASD often becomes apparent during the child's second year, and sometimes shortly after the second-year vaccinations. This has naturally led some parents and professionals to examine the relationship between vaccination and the onset of ASD. Some have questioned the safety of giving combined vaccinations (measles-mumps-rubella) and its effect on the child's immune system; some have questioned the effect of the measles antigen itself; and some have questioned the mercury-containing solution in which the vaccination used to be given. Most authorities, however, including the Centers for Disease Control, have concluded that there is no relationship between vaccination and ASD, and stress the dangers of *not* vaccinating children. A recent large scale epidemiological study in the Netherlands found no difference in rates of ASD between vaccinated and unvaccinated children.

Do people with autism ever marry and have children?

Sometimes, but not often. For children with normal or near-normal cognitive ability and somewhat odd, socially isolated, or rigid personalities (many of whom would be diagnosed with Asperger's), marriage is certainly a possibility. For people who are more affected, friendships based around specific interests, as well as emotionally rewarding relationships with other family members, are quite likely, but successful marriage is less of a possibility. There are so few documented cases of truly autistic people marrying and having children that the expected outcomes for their children are not known.

Are children with ASD deaf?

This is such a common suspicion among parents of children with ASD that it is often part of a standard diagnostic interview: "Did you ever wonder if your child was deaf?" As with any child where hearing problems are suspected, this should be medically ruled out. It usually turns out that hearing is fine, but the child shows "selective hearing" to a striking degree. Parents sometimes report that the child will not respond to their name or even a loud noise in the house, but then immediately notices a candy wrapper being opened several rooms away! So, this is a matter of paying attention, of what's important to the child, not of hearing itself.

Are children with ASD dangerous to me or others?

This is covered in more detail in the chapter on behavioral issues in the classroom. In brief: children with ASD are not usually more aggressive than other children; in fact, they may be less so. But a particular child with ASD may "melt down" under specific circumstances: when sensory stimulation is really overloading him, when he was really looking forward to something and is disappointed with no warning, or if he's previously been reinforced for tantrums by escaping from classroom demands. You have the right to know whether a child in your class has a history of any aggressive or destructive behavior and under what circumstances, and to have a plan in place for any recurrence. These "triggers" are usually quite avoidable but only if you have the facts! You should ask the principal or special education director for information on the child's behavior in his previous classrooms, making it clear that you need this information to determine what plans or behavioral consultation you will need.

What is the relationship between ASD, PDD, Asperger's, and autism?

In brief: "Pervasive Developmental Disorders" (PDD) is the official term for all the disorders with autistic features. Unofficially, this set of conditions is often called "Autism Spectrum Disorders" because it's really more accurate than "PDD." In this book, we've chosen to use this more descriptively accurate term. "Autism" is one of these disorders that has all three of the defining features (social impairment, communication and play impairment, repetitive behaviors). PDD is also given as a specific diagnosis (officially called Pervasive Developmental Disorder- Not Otherwise Specified) for cases of mild autism or where some, but not all three, of the defining features are present. Asperger's is a disorder on the autism spectrum defined by social impairment and repetitive behaviors but good language and cognition. See the text discussion of diagnosis in Chapter 1 for more details.

How commonly is ASD paired with other conditions such as AD/HD?

It's very common for ASD to coexist with other conditions. Diagnosing a child who has ASD with ADHD is not officially "allowed" because it's considered that the ASD "explains" the attention difficulties. But, if you applied AD/HD criteria to a group of ASD children, the number who would meet criteria for an AD/HD diagnosis would be quite high. Some of the children are dreamy and inattentive, and some are hyperactive and impulsive. Even though (according to DSM-IV, the diagnostic manual of the American Psychiatric Association) children with autism are not supposed to be diagnosed with AD/HD, you might find a child who was, in fact, given both diagnoses by a psychologist or doctor, or a child who was given one diagnosis by one clinician, and the other diagnosis by a different clinician. Other conditions that are found in children with ASD include obsessions, anxiety, and depression (see Chapter 2 for more details).

Why are children with ASD often sensitive to loud noise, bright lights, etc.?

No one knows, although there are theories about differences in brain organization that leave the children feeling as though sensory input of normal intensity (to us) feels "as loud as a dentist's drill." See Temple Grandin's books for moving descriptions about how agonizing the normal sensory environment can be to a child with ASD. The most common channel for over-sensitivity is auditory. Many children with ASD cover their ears to "normal sounds" and are even disturbed by the hum of fluorescent lights. They may also hate being touched, especially with a light touch, although they may enjoy deep pressure, such as massage of the shoulders, neck, and back. They may also seem oversensitive to slight smells, although this is less common. See Chapters 2 and 12 for more discussion of these sensitivities and how to handle them in the classroom.

When are autism spectrum disorders typically diagnosed?

The average age of diagnosis for ASD is around age 4, but there's a lot of variation. Some parents notice social, language, or behavioral oddities or delays in their children in the second, or even the first, year of life, although a formal diagnosis may take months or years to obtain. Children with Asperger's syndrome, or very mild autism, may not get diagnosed until well into the school years or even adolescence or adulthood. Research shows that an ASD diagnosis is reliable by age 3. A diagnosis made at age 2 or younger is usually confirmed at age 3. The youngest child we've felt confident diagnosing was 13 months old!

What is the difference between ABA and Floortime?

ABA and Floortime represent extremes of a spectrum of treatment approaches for ASD. ABA is adult-directed, highly structured, with a specific curriculum of skills to be taught. Floortime is child-directed, relatively unstructured, with a goal of developing the child's capacity to engage in reciprocal relationships and communication. See the Chapter 5 for more detail.

How do you begin behavioral intervention?

There are two basic kinds of behavioral interventions—those designed to teach new skills, and those designed to eliminate undesirable behaviors. (Of course, they work best when instituted together.)

To teach a new skill, it should be broken down into components small enough for the child to learn. To work on an undesirable behavior, you first need a functional analysis—careful observation of the circumstances that precede and follow the behavior, so you can figure out what purpose the behavior is serving for the child, and why he is persisting with it. To do both of these kinds of behavioral intervention, you should have expert help (e.g., a behavioral psychologist or appropriately trained school psychologist). See Chapter 12 for more detail on behavioral intervention.

What is semantic-pragmatic disorder?

This is a term primarily used by speech-language pathologists. It refers to a type of language impairment, discussed originally by Isabelle Rapin and Doris Allen, and more recently by Dorothy Bishop. The term refers to the fact that some children have relatively good language structure (speech sounds and grammar) but relatively poor content and social use (semantics and pragmatics). Children with semantic-pragmatic disorder have social impairments, but may or may not have restricted interests, and therefore may or may not meet criteria for Asperger's disorder or another ASD. In reality, many or most children with "semantic-pragmatic" disorder are on the autism spectrum.

References

Allen, D.A. & Rapin, I. (1992). Children with autism spectrum disorders are also dysphasic. In *Neurobiology of Infantile Autism*. Eds. H. Naruse and E. M. Ornitz. Amsterdam; Excerpta Medica.

Attwood, T. (1998). *Asperger's Syndrome: A Guide for Parents and Professionals.* London: Jessica Kingsley.

Bieber, J. (Producer). (1994). *Learning Disabilities and Social Skills with Richard Lavoie: Last One Picked...First One Picked On*. Washington, DC: Public Broadcasting Service.

Belchic, J. K. & Harris, S. L. (1994). The use of multiple peer exemplars to enhance the generalization of play skills to the siblings of children with autism. *Child and Family Behavior Therapy, 16(2):* 1-25.

Bishop, D. V. M. & Adams, C. (1989). Conversational characteristics of children with semantic-pragmatic disorder. I. What features lead to a judgement of inappropriacy? *British Journal of Disorders of Communication 24:* 241-63.

Bloomberg, K., Karlan, G.R. & Lloyd, L. L. (1990). The comparative translucency of initial lexical items represented in five graphic symbol systems and sets. *Journal of Speech & Hearing Research 33(4):* 717-25.

Bonvillian, J. D., Nelson, K. E. & Rhyne, J. M. (1981). Sign language and autism. *Journal of Autism and Developmental Disorders 11:*125-37

Buggey, T. (1999). Videotaped self-modeling: Allowing children to be their own models. *Teaching Exceptional Children 4:* 27-31.

Burroughs, J. A., Albritton, E.G., Eaton, B. B. & Montague, J. (1990). A comparative study of language delayed preschool children's ability to recall symbols from two symbol systems. *AAC: Augmentative & Alternative Communication 6(3):* 202-206.

Carbone, V. et al. (2006). A comparison of two approaches for teaching Verbal Behavior Functions: Total communication vs. vocal-alone. *Journal of Speech-Language Pathology and Applied Behavior Analysis 1(3):* 181-91.

Charlop-Christy, M. H. & Daneshvar, S. (2003). Using video modeling to teach perspective taking to children with autism. *Journal of Positive Behavior Interventions 5:* 12-21.

Charlop-Christy, M. H., Le, L. & Freeman, K. A. (2000). A comparison of video modeling with in-vivo modeling for teaching children with autism. *Journal of Autism and Developmental Disorders 30:* 537-52.

Charlop, M. H. & Milstein, J. P. (1989). Teaching autistic children conversational speech using video modeling. *Journal of Applied Behavior Analysis 22: 275-85.*

Delmolino, L. & Harris, S. (2004). *Incentives for Change: Motivating People with Autism Spectrum Disorders to Learn and Gain Independence.* Bethesda, MD: Woodbine House.

DeLong, G. R. (1992). Autism, amnesia, hippocampus and learning. *Neuroscience and Behavioral Reviews 16:*63-70

Dowrick, P. W. (1999). A review of self modeling and related interventions. *Applied & Preventive Psychology 8: 23-39.*

Duke, M. P., Nowicki, S. & Martin, E. A. (1996). *Teaching your Child the Language of Social Success.* Atlanta, GA: Peachtree.

Dunn, M. & Rapin, I. (1997). Communication in children with ASD. In *Behavior Belongs in the Brain.* Eds. P.J. Accardo, B.K. Shapiro & A.J. Capute. Baltimore: York Press.

Dunn, M., Gomes, H. & Sebastian, M. (1996). Prototypicality of responses in autistic, language disordered and normal children in a verbal fluency task. *Child Neuropsychology.*

Dunn, M., Vaughan, H.G. Jr, Kreuzer, J. & Kurtzberg, D. (1999). Electrophysiologic correlates of semantic classification in autistic and normal children. *Developmental Neuropsychology 16(1):* 79-99.

Dunn, M. (2005). *S.O.S.—Social Skills in Our Schools: A Social Skills Program for Children with Pervasive Developmental Disorders, Including High-Functioning Autism and Asperger Syndrome, and Their Typical Peers.* Shawnee Mission, KS: Autism Asperger Publishing Company.

Fay, W. & Schuler, A.L. (1980). *Emerging Language in Children with ASD.* Baltimore: University Park Press.

Fein, D., Dixon, P., Paul, J. & Levin, H. (2005). Brief report: Pervasive Developmental Disorder can evolve into ADHD: Case illustrations. *Journal of Autism and Developmental Disorders 35 (4):* 525-34.

Fein, D., Dunn, M., Allen, D., Hall, N., Morris, R. & Wilson, B. (1996). Neuropsychological and language findings. In *Preschool Children with Inadequate Communication: Developmental Language Disorder, Autism, Low IQ.* Ed. I. Rapin. London: MacKeith Press.

Friedman, P. & Friedman, K. (1980). Accounting for individual differences when comparing effectiveness of remedial language teaching methods. *Applied Psycholinguistics 1:* 151-70.

Glasberg, B. (2005). *Functional Behavior Assessment for People with Autism: Making Sense of Seemingly Senseless Behavior.* Bethesda, MD: Woodbine House.

Gray, C. (1994a). *Comic Strip Conversations.* Arlington, TX: Future Horizons.

Gray, C. (1994b). *The New Social Story Book.* Arlington, TX: Future Horizons.

Gray, C. A. (1998). Social stories and comic strip conversations with students with Asperger syndrome and high-functioning autism. Eds. E. Schopler, G. B. Mesibov, & L. J. Kunce. *Asperger syndrome or high functioning autism?* New York, NY: Plenum Press.

Gresham, F. M., Sugai, G. & Horner, R. H. (2001). Interpreting outcomes of social skills training for students with high-incidence disabilities. *Exceptional Children 67:* 331-44.

Harrower, J. K. & Dunlap, G. (2001). Including children with autism in general education classrooms: A review of effective strategies. *Behavior Modification 25(5):* 762-84.

Hermelin, B. & O'Connor, N. (1970). *Psychological Experiments with Autistic Children.* Oxford: Peragamon Press.

Hodgdon, L.A. (1995). *Visual Strategies for Improving Communication: Practical Supports for School and Home.* Troy, Michigan: Quirk Roberts Publishing.

Howlin, P., Baron-Cohen, S. & Hadwin, J. (1999). *Teaching Children with Autism to Mind-read: A Practical Guide.* New York, NY: John Wiley & Sons.

Hunt, P., Farron-Davis, F., Wrenn, M., Hirose-Hatae, A. & Goetz, L. (1997). Promoting interactive partnerships in inclusive educational settings. *Journal of the Association for Persons with Severe Handicaps 22:* 127-37.

Kanner, L. (1946). Irrelevant and metaphorical language in early infantile autism. *American Journal of Psychiatry 103:* 242-46.

Kelley, E., Fein, D. & Naigles, L. (2006). Residual language deficits in optimal outcome children with a history of autism. *Journal of Autism and Developmental Disorders: 36:* 807-28.

Kennedy, D. (2002). *The AD/HD-Autism Connection: A Step toward More Accurate Diagnoses and Effective Treatments.* Colorado Springs, CO: WaterBrook Press.

Klin, A. & Volkmar, F.R. (June 1995). *Asperger's Syndrome Guidelines for Treatment and Intervention.* Learning Disabilities Association of America.

Kozleski, E. B. (1991). Visual symbol acquisition by students with autism. *Exceptionality 2(4):* 173-94.

Lincoln, A.J., Courchesne, E., Kilman, B., Elmasian, R. & Allen, M. (1988). A study of intellectual abilities in high functioning people with autism. *Journal of Autism and Developmental Disorders 18:* 505-24.

Loveland, K., McEvoy, R., Tunali, B. & Kelley, M.L. (1990). Narrative story-telling in autism and Down's syndrome. *British Journal of Developmental Psychiatry 8:* 9-23.

Marriage, K. J., Gordon, V. & Brand, L. (1995). A social skills group for boys with Asperger's syndrome. *Australian and New Zealand Journal of Psychiatry 29:* 58-62.

McClannahan, L. E. & Krantz, P. J. (1999). *Activity Schedules for Children with Autism: Teaching Independent Behavior.* Bethesda, MD: Woodbine House.

Mesibov, G. B. (1984). Social skills training with verbal autistic adolescents and adults: A program model. *Journal of Autism and Other Developmental Disabilities 14:* 395-404.

Minshew, N.J., Goldstein, G., Meunz, L.R. & Payton, J.B. (1992). Neuropsychological functioning in nonmentally retarded autistic individuals. *Journal of Clinical and Experimental Neuropsychology 14:* 749-61.

Minshew, N.J., Goldstein, G. & Siegel, D.J. (1997). Neuropsychologic functioning in autism: Profile of a complex information processing disorder. *Journal of the International Neuropsychology Society 3(4):* 303-16.

Ozonoff, S. & Miller, J. N. (1995). Teaching theory of mind: A new approach to social skills training for individuals with autism. *Journal of Autism and Developmental Disorders 25:* 415-33.

Parks, S. & Black, H. (1990). *Organizing Thinking* (Book 1). Pacific Grove, CA: Critical Thinking Press and Software.

Parks, S. & Black, H. (1992). *Organizing Thinking* (Book 2). Pacific Grove, CA: Critical Thinking Press and Software.

Partington, J. W. & Sundberg, M. L. (1998). *The Assessment of Basic Language and Learning Skills (ABLLS).* Pleasant Hill, CA: Behavior Analysts.

Pehrsson, R.S. & Robinson, H.A. (1985). *The Semantic Organizer Approach to Reading and Writing Instruction.* Rockville, MD: Aspen.

Pehrsson, R.S. & Robinson, II.A. (1988). Semantic organizers. *Topics in Language Disorders 8(3):* 24-37.

Pierce, K. & Schreibman, L. (1997). Multiple peer use of pivotal response training to increase social behaviors of classmates with autism: Results from trained and untrained peers. *Journal of Applied Behavior Analysis 30:* 157-60.

Prior, M. (1979). Cognitive abilities and disabilities in infantile autism: A review. *Journal of Abnormal Child Psychology 7(4):* 357-80.

Prizant, B. M. (1983). Language acquisition and communicative behavior in autism: Toward an understanding of the "whole" of it. *Journal of Speech and Hearing Disorders 48:* 296-307.

Rapin, I. & Dunn, M. (1997). Language disorders in autistic children. *Seminars in Pediatric Neurology.* Ed. J. B. Bodensteiner. Philadelphia, PA: W. B. Saunders Company.

Rapin, I., Allen, D. A. & Dunn M.A. (1992). Developmental language disorders. In *Handbook of Neuropsychology, Vol. 7, Child Neuropsychology.* Eds. S. J. Segalowitz & I. Rapin. Amsterdam: Elsevier Science.

Rapin, I. & Allen, D. A. (1983). Developmental language disorders: Neurologic considerations. In *Neuropsychology of Language, Reading, and Spelling.* Ed. U. Kirk. New York, NY: Academic Press.

Rimland, B. (1964). *Infantile Autism: The Syndrome and Its Implications for a Neural Theory of Behavior.* New York, NY: Appleton-Century-Crofts.

Rogers, S. J. (2000). Interventions that facilitate socialization in children with autism. *Journal of Autism and Developmental Disorders 30:* 399-409.

Schuler, A. L. & Prizant, B. M. (1985). Echolalia. In *Communication Problems in Autism.* Eds. E. Schopler & G. Mesibov. New York, NY: Plenum.

Smalley, S. & Asarnow, R. (1990). Cognitive subclinical markers in autism. *Journal of Autism and Developmental Disorders 20:* 271-78.

Strain, P. S. (1997). An experimental analysis of peer social initiations on the behavior of withdrawn preschool children: Some training and generalization effects. *Journal of Abnormal Child Psychology 5:* 445-55.

Sundberg, M. L. & Partington, J. W. *Teaching Language to Children with Autism or Other Developmental Disabilities.* Pleasant Hill, CA: Behavior Analysts.

Szatmari, P., Bartollucci, R., Bremner, R., Bond, S. & Rich, S. (1989). A follow-up study of high functioning children with ASD. *Journal of Autism and Developmental Disorders 19(2):* 213-25.

Tager-Flusberg, H. (1981). On the nature of linguistic functioning in early infantile autism. *Journal of Autism and Developmental Disorders 11(1):* 45-56.

Tager-Flusberg, H. (1982). Pragmatic development and its implication for social interaction in autistic children. In *Proceedings of the International Symposium for Research in Autism.* Ed. D. Park. Washington, DC: National Society for Children with Autism.

Tager-Flusberg, H. (1989). A psycholinguistic perspective on language development in the autistic child. In *Autism: Nature, Diagnosis, and Treatment.* Ed. G. Dawson. New York, NY: Guilford Press.

Tager-Flusberg, H. (1991). Semantic processing in the free recall of autistic children with autism: Further evidence for a cognitive deficit. *British Journal of Developmental Psychology 9:* 417-30.

Tager-Flusberg, H. (1994). Dissociation in form and function in the acquisition of language by autistic children. In *Constraints on Language Acquisition: Studies of Atypical Children.* Ed. H. Tager-Flusberg. Hillsdale, NJ: Lawrence Erlbaum Associates.

Tager-Flusberg, H. (1995). "Once upon a ribbit": Stories narrated by autistic children. *British Journal of Developmental Psychology 13(1):* 45-59.

Volkmar, F. R. & Klin, A. (2001). Asperger's disorder and higher functioning autism: Same or different? In *International Review of Research in Mental Retardation: Autism (vol. 23).* Ed. L. M. Glidden. San Diego: Academic Press.

Walker, H. M. et al. (1983). *The Walker Social Skills Curriculum: The ACCEPTS (A Curriculum for Children's Effective Peer and Teacher Skills) Program.* Austin, TX: Pro-Ed.

Waltz, M. (1999). *Pervasive Developmental Disorders: Finding a Diagnosis and Getting Help.* Sebastopol, CA: O'Reilly & Associates.

Weisner, D. (1991). *Tuesday.* New York, NY: Clarion Books.

Resources

Suggested Reading

Autism Spectrum Disorders

Attwood, T. (1998). *Asperger's Syndrome: A Guide for Parents and Professionals.* London: Jessica Kingsley.

Blastland, M. (2006). *The Only Boy in the World: A Father Explores the Mysteries of Autism.* New York, NY: Marlowe & Co.

Bruey, C. T. (2004). *Demystifying Autism Spectrum Disorders: A Guide to Diagnosis for Parents and Professionals.* Bethesda, MD: Woodbine House.

Grandin, T. *Thinking in Pictures: My Life with Autism.* New York, NY: Vintage, 2006.

Kephart, B. (1999). *A Slant of Sun: One Child's Courage.* New York, NY: Harper.

Newport, J. & Newport, M. (2007). *Mozart and the Whale: An Asperger's Love Story.* New York, NY: Touchstone.

Park, C. (1983). *The Siege: The First Eight Years of an Autistic Child: With an Epilogue 15 Years After.* New York, NY: Arrow.

Stewart, K. *Helping a Child with Non Verbal Learning Disorder or Asperger's Syndrome.* (2002). Oakland, CA: New Harbinger.

Social Skills & Behavior

Bieber, J. (Producer). (1994). *Learning Disabilities and Social Skills with Richard Lavoie: Last One Picked...First One Picked On.* Washington, DC: Public Broadcasting Service.

Delmolino, L. & Harris, S. *Incentives for Change: Motivating People with Autism Spectrum Disorders to Learn and Gain Independence*. Bethesda, MD: Woodbine House, 2004.

Dunn, M. (2005). *S.O.S.—Social Skills in Our Schools: A Social Skills Program for Children with Pervasive Developmental Disorders, Including High-Functioning Autism and Asperger Syndrome, and Their Typical Peers*. Shawnee Mission, KS: Autism Asperger Publishing Company.

Glasberg, B. (2005). *Functional Behavior Assessment for People with Autism: Making Sense of Seemingly Senseless Behavior*. Bethesda, MD: Woodbine House.

Goldstein, A. & McGinnis, E. (1997). *Skillstreaming the Adolescent: New Strategies and Perspectives for Teaching Prosocial Skills*. Champaign, IL: Research Press.

Gray, C. (1994). *Comic Strip Conversations*. Arlington, TX: Future Horizons.

Gray, C. (1994). *The New Social Story Book*. Arlington, TX: Future Horizons.

Kranowitz, C. S. (2005). *The Out-of-Sync Child: Recognizing and Coping with Sensory Processing Disorder*. Rev. ed. New York, NY: Penguin.

Leaf, R. & McEachin, J., eds. (1999). *A Work in Progress: Behavior Management Strategies and a Curriculum for Intensive Behavioral Treatment of Autism*. New York, NY: DRL Books.

McClannahan, L. E. & Krantz, P. J. (1999). *Activity Schedules for Children with Autism: Teaching Independent Behavior*. Bethesda, MD: Woodbine House.

McGinnis, E. & Goldstein, A. (1997). *Skillstreaming the Elementary School Child: New Strategies and Perspectives for Teaching Prosocial Skills*. Champaign, IL: Research Press.

Walker-Hirsch, L. *Circles: Intimacy and Relationships*. [video]. Santa Barbara: James Stanfield.

Weiss, M. J. & Harris, S. (2001). *Reaching Out, Joining In: Teaching Social Skills to Young Children with Autism*. Bethesda, MD: Woodbine House.

Teaching Strategies & Supports

Algozzine, R. & Ysseldike, J. (2006). *Teaching Students with Mental Retardation: A Practical Guide for Every Teacher*. Thousand Oaks, CA: Corwin Press.

Barbera, M. & Rasmussen. T. (2007) *The Verbal Behavior Approach: How to Teach Children with Autism and Related Disorders*. London: Jessica Kingsley.

Bondy, A. & Frost, L. (2001). *A Picture's Worth: PECS and Other Visual Communication Strategies in Autism.* Bethesda, MD: Woodbine House.

Cohen, M. J. & Sloan, D. L. (2007). *Visual Supports for People with Autism: A Guide for Parents & Professionals.* Bethesda, MD: Woodbine House.

Harris, S. & Weiss, M. J. *Right from the Start: Behavioral Intervention for Young Children with Autism.* (2007). Bethesda, MD: Woodbine House.

Hodgdon, L.A. (1995). *Visual Strategies for Improving Communication: Practical Supports for School and Home.* Troy, Michigan: Quirk Roberts Publishing.

Horstmeier, D. *Teaching Math to People with Down Syndrome and Other Hands-on Learners.* (2004). Bethesda, MD: Woodbine House.

McClannahan, L. E. & Krantz, P. J. *Activity Schedules for Children with Autism: Teaching Independent Behavior.* (1999). Bethesda, MD: Woodbine House.

Oelwein, P. L. (1995). *Teaching Reading to Children with Down Syndrome.* Bethesda, MD: Woodbine House.

Sands, D. J. et al., eds. (2001). *Teaching Students with Mental Retardation: Providing Access to the General Curriculum.* Baltimore: Paul Brookes.

Semple, J. (various dates). *Semple Math* (series). Victoria, BC: Trafford.

Tanguay, P. *Nonverbal Learning Disabilities at School: Educating Students with NLD, Asperger Syndrome, and Related Conditions.* (2002). London: Jessica Kingsley.

Voss, K. S. *Teaching by Design: Using Your Computer to Create Materials for Students with Learning Differences.* (2005). Bethesda, MD: Woodbine House.

Inclusion

Giangreco, M. F. & Doyle, M. B., eds. (2007). *Quick-Guides to Inclusion: Ideas for Educating Students with Disabilities.* Baltimore: Paul Brookes.

Hammeken, P. (2000). *Inclusion: 450 Strategies for Success: A Practical Guide for All Educators Who Teach Students with Disabilities.* Minnetonka, MN: Peytral Publications.

Hammeken, P. (2003). *Inclusion: An Essential Guide for the Paraprofessional.* Minnetonka, MN: Peytral Publications.

Janney, R. & Snell, M. E. (2004). *Modifying Schoolwork: Teachers' Guides to Inclusive Practices.* Baltimore: Paul Brookes.

Rief, S. & Heimburge, J. (1996). *How to Reach and Teach All Children in the Inclusive Classroom: Ready-to-Use Strategies, Lessons, and Activities for Teaching Students with Diverse Learning Needs.* San Francisco: Jossey-Bass.

Relaxation Techniques

Cautela, J. & Groden, J. (1978). *Relaxation: A Comprehensive Manual for Adults, Children, and Children with Special Needs.* Champaign, IL: Research Press.

Children's Hospital of Michigan. *Relaxation Station* [DVD]. Available for purchase at www.therelaxationstation.com.

Groden, J. et al. (2001). *Coping with Stress through Picture Rehearsal: A How-To Manual for Working with Individuals with Autism and Developmental Disabilities.* Providence, RI: The Groden Center [www.grodencenter.org].

Lite, L. (2006). *Indigo Dreams: Relaxation and Stress Management Bedtime Stories for Children* [CD]. Marietta, GA: Indigo Dreams.

Reznick, C. *Imagery for Kids: Discovering Your Special Place* [audio tape or CD]. Available at www.imageryforkids.com.

Vicker, B. (1999). "A Young Adult's Guide to Deep Breathing as a Relaxation Technique." Bloomington, IN: Indiana Resource Center for Autism. www.iidc.indiana.edu/irca/education/young.html.

Organizations & Websites

All Kinds of Minds Website
www.allkindsofminds.org

The Arc of the U.S.
1010 Wayne Ave., Ste. 650
Silver Spring, MD 20910
301-565-3842
www.thearc.org/welcome.html

Asperger's Disorder Homepage
www.aspergers.com

Autism and PDD Support Network
www.autism-pdd.net

Autism Resources
www.autism-resources.com

Autism Society Canada
Box 22017, 1670 Heron Rd.
Ottawa, ON K1V 0C2
613-789-8943; 866-476-8440
www.autismsocietycanada.ca

Autism Society of America
7910 Woodmont Ave., Ste. 300
Bethesda, MD 20814
800-328-8476; 301-657-0881
www.autism-society.org

Canadian Association for Community Living
Kinsmen Building, York University
4700 Keele Street Toronto, ON M3J 1P3
CANADA 416-661-9611
www.cacl.ca

Council for Exceptional Children
1110 North Glebe Rd., Ste. 300
Arlington, VA 22201
888-232-7733; 703-264-9446 (TDD)
www.cec.sped.org

Family Village
www.familyvillage.wisc.edu

Learning Disabilities Online
www.ldonline.org

National Dissemination Center for Children with Disabilities (NICHCY)
P.O. Box 1492
Washington, DC 20013
800-695-0285; 202-884-8200 (voice/TDD)
www.nichcy.org

Nonverbal Learning Disabilities Association (NLDA)
2446 Albany Ave.
West Hartford, CT 06117
860-570-0217; 860-570-0218 (fax)
www.nlda.org

Online Asperger Syndrome Information and Support (O.A.S.I.S.)
www.udel.edu/bkirby/asperger

Special Education Resources on the Internet (SERI)
http://seriweb.com

U.S. Department of Education
Clearinghouse on Disability Information
400 Maryland Ave., SW
Washington, DC 20202
800-USA-LEARN; 202-205-8245
202-401-0689 (fax)
www.ed.gov/index/html

Index

About the Authors

Deborah Fein, Ph.D., is a clinical and research neuropsychologist, and is currently a Board of Trustees Distinguished Professor of Psychology at the University of Connecticut. She has 35 years of clinical and research experience with children on the autism spectrum, and currently conducts NIH-funded research on early detection and recovery from autism.

Michelle Dunn, Ph.D., is an Associate Professor in Neurology at the Albert Einstein College of Medicine and pediatric neuropsychologist and neurophysiologist who has worked with children on the autism spectrum for the past 25 years and trained staff in many New York area school districts.